IN THE HANDS
OF A HAPPY GOD

IN THE HANDS OF A

HAPPY GOD

THE "NO-HELLERS" OF CENTRAL APPALACHIA

HOWARD DORGAN

The University of Tennessee Press / Knoxville

The paper in this book meets the minimum requirements of the American National Standard for Permanence of Paper for Printed Library Materials.
⊛ The binding materials have been chosen for strength and durability.
⊛ Printed on recycled paper.

All photographs are by the author.

Library of Congress Cataloging-in-Publication Data

Dorgan, Howard.
    In the hands of a happy god : the "no-hellers" of central
    Appalachia / Howard Dorgan.—1st ed.
          p.   cm.
    Includes bibliographical references and index.
    ISBN 0-87049-961-0 (cloth: alk. paper).
    ISBN 0-87049-962-9 (pbk. : alk. paper)
    1. Primitive Baptists—Appalachian region. 2. Universalism.
    3. Appalachian region—Church history.
    I. Title.
BX6383.D67 1997
286'.5—dc20   96-25214
                                               CIP

To Elder Roy McGlothlin, who did not see the conclusion of this effort,
and To Elder Wallace Cooper, who I hope will

CONTENTS

Recognitions xi

1. Primitives, Primitives, and More Primitives 1

2. "They Call Us the No-Hellers" 31

3. The Split between "Hellers" and "No-Hellers" 50

4. "Salvation for All" 73

5. The "Happifying" of God 100

6. "Carried Out" 122

7. "Keeping Them Near" 145

8. Migration of the Faith 157

9. Pilgrims in the Hands of a Happy God 180

Notes 191

Index 203

ILLUSTRATIONS

Holston Primitive Baptist Church near Riverview, Tennessee   2

Headstone for Elder Morgan T. Lipps, at Holston Primitive Baptist Church   3

Association Building, South Kentucky Association of Separate Baptists, Russell Springs, Kentucky   14

Ashworth Memorial Regular Baptist Church, near Princeton, West Virginia   16

Elder Wallace Cooper "in the Stand" at Washington Association's Annual Session, 1995   33

Preaching Arbor, Pilgrim's Rest Church, during Elkhorn Association's Annual Session, 1995   36

Elkhorn Association's Annual Session, 1994, at Pilgrim's Rest Church   37

Elder Roy McGlothlin "in the Stand" during Washington Association's Annual Session, 1994   42

Hale Creek Meetinghouse, Buchanan County, Virginia   52

The Old Log Hale Creek Meetinghouse, Buchanan County, Virginia 53

The Protest of Elmer Matney, Hale Creek Community, Buchanan County, Virginia 55

Salem Church Meetinghouse, Tazewell County, Virginia 59

Stoney Creek Church Meetinghouse, Carter County, Tennessee 74

Headstone for Charles F. Nickels and His Wife, Loula V. Nickels, at Point Truth Cemetery, near Nickelsville, Virginia 82

Footwashing at Oak Grove Church, Keokee, Virginia 103

Marker at Site of Consolation Church, between Hopkinsville and Macedonia, Kentucky 113

Old Universalist Church, near Croften, Kentucky 114

Hopkinsville Unitarian Universalist Church, Hopkinsville, Kentucky 115

Home of Dr. William Hale, Free Hill, Tennessee 119

Headstone for Dr. William Hale and His Wife, Lucy Hale, Free Hill, Tennessee 120

New Garden Regular Primitive Baptist Church Meetinghouse, near Honaker in Russell County, Virginia 125

Washington Association's Annual Session, 1994, at New Garden Church, Russell County, Virginia 126

Preaching Shed, New Garden Church, Russell County, Virginia 127

Elder Willard Owens "in the Stand" at Harrison-Beavers Family Reunion and Memorial, Thompson Valley, Virginia 130

Baptism by Elder Unice Davis, Moderator of the Elkhorn Association, in Dismal River, near Hale Creek Church, Buchanan County, Virginia 149

Under the Preaching Arbor, Harrison-Beavers Family Reunion and Memorial, Thompson Valley, Virginia 152

Members of the Harrison-Beavers Family, at the Harrison-Beavers Family Reunion and Memorial, Thompson Valley, Virginia 155

Rich Hill Primitive Baptist Church Meetinghouse, Rich Hill, Ohio 161

Brother McGennis Adair, Sr., and Sister Phyllis Adair 169

Elder Jennings Shortt Moderates the Three Forks of Powell's River Regular Primitive Baptist Association's Annual Session, 1994 174

RECOGNITIONS

With appreciation, I recognize the support of the Cratis D. Williams Graduate School and the Faculty Research Committee at Appalachian State University, both responsible for three travel grants I received during the course of the research for this book. I am especially indebted to Margaret Kilgore, whose dedicated work in connection with the appropriation of, and accounting for, these funds made my labors far easier than they otherwise would have been.

Several Appalachian State University administrators have been fully supportive of the research embodied in this volume, as they have been of my scholarly endeavors in the past: Harvey Durham, provost and vice-chancellor for academic affairs; Ming Land, dean of the College of Fine and Applied Arts; and Terry Cole, chair of the Department of Communication. Support also has come from a wonderful group of departmental colleagues. It is always comforting to work under the umbrella of such encouragement.

My warmest expressions of gratitude, however, always are reserved for the subjects of my field studies, in this case the Primitive Baptist Universalists (PBU) of Central Appalachia. I am particularly appreciative of the open spirit of three men—moderators, respectively, of the Regular Primitive Baptist Washington District Association, the Elkhorn

Primitive Baptist Association, and the Three Forks of Powell's River Regular Primitive Baptist Association—Elders Landon Colley, Unice Davis, and Jennings Shortt. By their gracious acceptance of me and my work, these men paved a path for my travels that seldom, if ever, included any obstacles.

In addition, a special group of PBU elders and laypersons has served as readers of all or significant parts of the drafts of this work, checking my reporting of PBU history, doctrine, and worship practices, and of various persons, places, and things. These readers have saved me from many potential embarrassments.

Foremost among these readers has been Elder Farley "Ronnie" Beavers, moderator of the Salem and Mt. Pleasant churches in Washington District, a retired Air Force communications technician and the proprietor of Zion's Clippers Barber Shop in Tazewell, Virginia. Elder Beavers devoted himself not only to careful scrutiny of my chapter manuscripts, but also to lengthy discussions with me concerning PBU doctrine, history, and practice. Moreover, he and his wife Sandra always opened their house to me when I was in Tazewell.

The list of other readers includes Elders Keith Bowers, Danny Davis, Ezra Davis, Jr., Unice Davis, Roy Flanary, Lewis Hill, Jack Horne, Reece Maggard, Willard Owens, Robert Whitt, and Aaron Williams; Brothers McGennis Adair, Sr., Millard Cooper, Bill Davis, Pat Flanary, Phil Flanary, Kelly McGuire, and Arnie Williams; and Sisters Phyllis Adair, Gail Asbury, Sandra Beavers, Adeleah Davis, Cathy Flanary, Anna Ruth McGuire, and Peggy Mickler.

Furthermore, I must express my appreciation to the memberships of twenty-three Primitive Baptist Universalist churches which I visited during the last three years, some of them three and four times. These congregations were always gracious in their hospitality, invariably making me feel completely welcome.

Darvin Marshall and Ganell Marshall, frequently my traveling companions during my fieldwork with the Old Regular Baptists, continued to assist me in this project. Darvin made the original connection for me with the PBU faith, and Ganell accomplished a monumental amount of work involved in transcribing to computer disks the handwritten minutes (1866–1995) of Point Truth Church. It was through those transcriptions, and other materials supplied by Ganell, that I learned much of what I was able to discover about Brother Charles F. Nickels, who contributed the only exposition of PBU doctrine published prior to this book.

My initial manuscript for this volume was submitted to two superb critical readers, Bill Leonard and Deborah McCauley. Since neither maintained anonymity in the evaluation process, I was able to work closely with each of them in achieving a revision that I am confident has strengthened the work. I gratefully salute these two exceptional scholars.

I also salute the University of Tennessee Press and the thoroughly professional crew of managers, editors, designers, and marketers with whom I have worked during the preparation of this and earlier volumes. It has been especially satisfying to work again with Acquisitions Editor Meredith Morris-Babb.

Finally, my love and gratitude goes out to my family—to Kathy, my wife; Shawn, my son; Kelly, my daughter; and Matt, my new son-in-law. Kelly and Matt married during the final work on this volume, and I hope that my long hours of writing never made me appear to participate less than fully in their joy.

1
PRIMITIVES, PRIMITIVES, AND MORE PRIMITIVES

On August 26, 1941, the Chattanooga office of the Tennessee Valley Authority recorded that 230 graves at Holston Primitive Baptist Cemetery, Grainger County, Tennessee, had been moved to higher ground, preparatory for the 1942 completion of Cherokee Dam. Since 179 reinterments were labeled in the TVA records as "unknown," it seems that, for the vast majority of these graves, no readable headstone existed, nor had it been possible to find anyone who could make an identification of the individual there buried.[1] For half a century, this burial site, as the large number of graves suggests, had been the repository of deceased Baptists from this particular area of the Holston River Valley. Indeed, among the fifty-one marker-identified graves were the entombments of Elder Morgan T. Lipps (1815–1894) and his wife Elizabeth (1812–1895). Elder Lipps is viewed by Primitive Baptists of Central Appalachia, at least in eastern Tennessee and southwestern Virginia, as one of the early patriarchs of their faith.

When the gates of Cherokee Dam were closed, that action eventually backed up water for thirty miles along the Holston River, creating a reservoir that now stretches from Jefferson City on the southwest end to near Rogersville on the northeast end. In the process, parts of four Tennessee counties—Grainger, Hamblen, Hawkins, and Jefferson—were inundated. TVA records relative to the site preparations for this expansive Cherokee

Reservoir indicate that Holston Primitive Baptist meetinghouse, along with the cemetery, had occupied a 2.2-acre plot of land that was to be flooded. Thus it was necessary to relocate to higher ground the 230 graves and the accompanying church.[2]

Today that same wood-framed, high-roofed, clapboard-sided structure, over forty years old at the time of the move, stands on the west side of Cherokee Lake, near the small community of Riverview. The reinterred monument-identified graves are arranged—on the lake side of the church—in lines neater than those graves probably created at the earlier site. These graves are well cared for today; but the area where the "unknown" reburials were made now has become overgrown with a thick network of small trees and bushes, between which one can see at least a score of native rocks that were placed as headstones for otherwise unmarked resting places.

At the time of the 1941 relocation, Holston Church had only fifteen members,[3] but now the number is much smaller. Only one name remains

Holston Primitive Baptist Church, near Riverview, Tennessee, summer 1993.

Headstone for grave of Elder Morgan T. Lipps (1815–1894), now located at Holston Primitive Baptist Church, near Riverview, Tennessee, summer 1993.

on the congregational roll, that of Sister Arminda Gann,[4] an elderly woman who recently has battled cancer and so has been spending most of her time in a hospital, unable to attend this or any other church. Nevertheless, services still are conducted once a month at the Holston meetinghouse. What keeps the facility viable as a place of worship is the fact that it is affiliated with Three Forks of Powell's River Regular Primitive Baptist Association, an organization composed of ten fellowships somewhat widely dispersed across northeastern Tennessee, southwestern Virginia, and one small area of eastern Kentucky.

Because each of these congregations meets only one weekend a month, members are free on the remaining weekends to visit each other's churches, sometimes driving long distances to do so. Thus, on the fourth Saturday and Sunday of each month, this meetinghouse, built partly of logs, provides an environment for all the sights and sounds of "Old-Time Baptist" worship: plaintively elongated lined singing, preaching that is emotionally charged and wailed or rhythmically chanted, and spirited and joyful congregational shouting.

As indicated above, on these occasions Sister Arminda Gann, Holston Church's one formal member, often will not be present; but through the attendance of the association's moderator, other elders, and numerous regular members, this century-old meetinghouse is kept alive as a place of worship. Furthermore, by the dogged determination of this group to preserve Holston Church, the Three Forks Association has established the structure in my mind as a very potent symbol, not only of devotion to this facility but also of commitment to the larger denominational group to which these worshipers belong. That denomination is a uniquely Appalachian institution, the Primitive Baptist Universalists (PBUs) of Central Appalachia, believers aptly described as "pilgrims in the hands of a happy god."

One of the central themes of this book is that PBUs view their god as "happy," simply because he found a way—they believe—to redeem all his children from the curse of Adamic sin. Like the eighteenth- and nineteenth-century Universalists, who flourished in New England and the old middle-colony region of America and who still exist in merger with the Unitarians (Unitarian Universalists),[5] this unique subdivision of the Primitive Baptist faith expounds an inclusive theology of universal atonement, claiming that, at the close of the temporal world, all humankind (past and present) will be redeemed from "sin, punishment, and death"; restored to that purified state that existed prior to Adam's fall; and thus prepared for an eternal and joyous communion with God. Known in Central Appalachia as the "No-Hellers"—a title which is a misnomer, simply because they view hell as a reality of earthy life—this unusual subdenomination of Baptists practices an extremely celebratory form of worship. This jubilant expression is motivated by a conviction that the eternity that is to follow the temporal world will sweep all of humankind—the full lineage, from Adam until the last birth before "Resurrection"—into a condition of inclusive, egalitarian, spiritual, and physical communion with an all-loving and gladsome godhead. Succinctly, PBU theology can be expressed by the following ten tenets:

1. Because of Adam's sin, all humankind is inherently sinful; therefore, "sinfulness" is the given characteristic of "natural man."
2. Indeed, Satan is nothing more than "natural man," warring against "spiritual man," and thus will have no existence beyond the temporal world.
3. In addition to the creation of "sinfulness" (the given nature of natural man), this Adamic transgression also instituted "punishment" (the "general judgment" hell of the temporal world; the absence-from-God's-blessing torment that sin generates) and "death" (humankind's ultimate punishment for Adamic sin).
4. Humankind cannot extricate itself from this natural sin-state and so requires Christ's atonement.
5. That atonement, nevertheless, is for all humankind and at "Resurrection" irrevocably will come to pass for all humankind, just as irrevocably Adam's transgression earlier condemned all humankind to that sinful state of "natural man."
6. However, there is the "elect," Christ's church (the established Primitive Baptist Universalists, and perhaps other individuals not known to the movement) that has been "separated from the rest of God's people here in time," chosen to be the earthly witness for Christ and the earthly preserver of his righteousness, "kept by the power of God through faith," and destined never finally to fall away.
7. Still, these elected individuals can sin, and in doing so suffer the hell on earth that a separation from God's blessing institutes, probably feeling that hell more intensely than the nonelect, simply because the elect have a sharply contrasting experience as a basis for comparison.
8. At "Resurrection," however, all temporal existence will terminate, both for the dead and for those still living, bringing an end to all "sin," "punishment," and "death."
9. Finally, at Resurrection, all humankind will go to a wholly egalitarian heaven, the culmination of Christ's universal atonement.
10. Since punishment is a factor solely of the temporal world, there will be no hell after Resurrection.

Chapter 4 of this volume examines these tenets in detail, and explains the primarily oral nature of this doctrine. Then chapter 5 advances a possible explanation of how one of the strains of early nineteenth-century American Universalist thinking may have reached the mountains of

Appalachia and there fused with traditional Primitive Baptist theology to create a small Baptist subdenomination that is largely unique to the region, having only four fellowships outside of northeastern Tennessee, southwestern Virginia, southeastern Kentucky, and southern West Virginia. Indeed, a limited area of Central Appalachia, where the majority of these PBU fellowships are found, can be identified as "No-Heller Country."

The western edge of this "No-Heller Country" starts on that northwest side of Cherokee Lake where Holston Primitive Baptist Church is located, then moves northeastward through the Johnson City–Kingsport–Bristol corridor of East Tennessee, including especially Carter, Sullivan, and Washington counties, from which two PBU churches, Hope and Stoney Creek, draw their congregations. All but two chapters of this volume begin with a description of one PBU meetinghouse; the Stoney Creek facility is featured in chapter 4.

When the boundaries of the PBU region cross the state line into southwestern Virginia, the map of "No-Heller Country" must be drawn to include significant parts of Buchanan, Dickenson, Lee, Russell, Scott, Tazewell, and Wise counties, with individual families also being pulled in from Bland, Smyth, and Washington counties. It is in these southwestern regions of Virginia that the largest collection of PBU fellowships is found, making this particular area of Central Appalachia the heartland of this Baptist subdenomination.

This midsection of "No-Heller Country" extends into two areas of Kentucky. The first is a small region of the Clover Fork of the Cumberland River (in Harlan County, Kentucky), from whence at least one family is drawn across to the east side of the Cumberland Divide, to attend services at Oak Grove Church in Keokee, Lee County, Virginia (featured in chapter 5). The second is the Colly Creek area of Letcher County, Kentucky, where one of the ten affiliates of the Three Forks of Powell's River Association is located.[6]

The westernmost and easternmost boundary points of West Virginia's PBU country are set by two churches resting several counties apart: Bee Branch Church, beside Highway 83 in Paynesville, McDowell County; and Mount Pleasant Church, located north of Lewisburg in Greenbrier County, near the small community of Trout. The main cluster of the West Virginia Primitive Baptist Universalists, however, is found in McDowell County, in and around the Paynesville, Jolo, and Bradshaw communities.

In addition to the ten churches of the Three Forks of Powell's River Regular Primitive Baptist Association, there are twenty-two other PBU fellowships scattered across this PBU heartland in Central Appalachia, plus four small congregations that have been established considerably north of this region—one in Pennsylvania and three in Ohio. The Regular Primitive Baptist Washington District Association has fourteen churches, located in Tennessee, Virginia, West Virginia, Ohio, and Pennsylvania; and the Elkhorn Association contains four churches—two in Virginia, one in West Virginia, and one in Ohio.

A second Elkhorn Association, not recognized by the other three PBU clusters, ties together eight West Virginia fellowships. Although I have had contact with this second Elkhorn Association, I chose, early in my PBU fieldwork, to exclude this alliance from my study. The two Elkhorn groups split from each other in the 1980s, and the emotions precipitated by that division are still active within the three PBU associations who correspond—so strongly, in fact, that I was advised by one Washington Association elder to avoid the negative dynamics that might ensue from the inclusion of this second Elkhorn cluster of fellowships.[7] I have been told, however, that the Elkhorn split was over practices rather than doctrine; therefore the ten tenets outlined above also would fairly represent the beliefs of that second Elkhorn Association.[8]

Membership totals in these PBU associations are extremely small. By 1994 statistics, the latest available at the time of this writing, there are only 571 formal members of the three associations dealt with in this study: 374 in the Washington Association, 146 in the Three Forks Association, and 51 in the Elkhorn Association.[9] However, these tallies may be misleading, in the sense that Primitive Baptist Universalists, like the Old Regulars, tend to be baptized later in life than is the norm for more Arminian Baptist groups, such as the Missionary Baptists, Separate Baptists, and Freewill Baptists. Therefore, it is not unusual for an individual to be found attending a PBU church for years before he or she actually joins the fellowship. Short of a long-term study in which average church attendance is compared with actual membership growth, there appears to be no way to fix the relationship between these two factors; nevertheless, these nonmember attendees must be mentioned.

Still, even if we doubled the total provided above, we would have only 1,142 Primitive Baptist Universalists, spread over roughly twenty counties of Central Appalachia, not counting the limited regions in Ohio and

Pennsylvania where PBU migrations have created outposts of the denomination. Why write a book about a religious group that is so small? My answer is simply that this "small group" constitutes one of the most fascinating phenomena to which I have been exposed in this region of the upland South. Theologically and behaviorally, these believers appear to have no parallel in Appalachia, except, to some degree, with the German Baptist Brethren (the "Dunkers"), who apparently espouse some Universalist thinking,[10] and with those Appalachian remnants of the Universalist denomination discussed in chapter 5.

Where and how, then, did these Primitive Baptist Universalists originate? Chapter 3 details the history of the 1924 Washington Association split that produced the initial formal "No-Heller" association. For now, however, suffice it to say that Universalist doctrine evidently first began to find acceptance within some Central Appalachian Primitive Baptist fellowships near the close of the nineteenth century. Again, chapter 5 traces a route that may have been followed in the introduction of this theology to Appalachia. Here, however, it must be stated clearly that current PBU elders believe that their doctrine has a lineage that goes all the way back to Christ and the church his disciples instituted.[11]

Nevertheless, like the Universalist denomination itself, which by 1961 had become so small in number that it sought a merger with the Unitarians, the Primitive Baptist Universalists of Central Appalachia seem poised on the edge of extinction; their memberships seem insignificant when compared with the numbers affiliated with mainline Christian denominations. While this book is not intended as the "swan song" of this theological movement, it is aimed at capturing the phenomenon as it currently exists, in part out of a concern that this group may not long survive. For the moment, that is enough to say about the Primitive Baptist Universalists. The remainder of this chapter is devoted to placing this subdenomination within a historical perspective, through an overview of the Old-Time Baptists of Central Appalachia.

HISTORICAL BACKGROUND: THE OLD-TIME BAPTISTS OF CENTRAL APPALACHIA

For persons unfamiliar with Baptist diversity, it is confusing enough just to encounter the titles of what might be called the mainline divisions of the denomination—American Baptists, National Baptists, Southern Baptists, and The General Association of Regular Baptist Churches (not to be confused with the Regulars of Appalachia). It becomes increasingly perplexing, however, when titles such as the following are added to the list: Primitive Baptists, Missionary Baptists, Regular Baptists (the Appalachian associations), Old Regular Baptists, Separate Baptists, United Baptists, Union Baptists, Free Will (or Freewill) Baptists, German Baptists, Seventh-Day Baptists, Duck River Baptists, Six-Principle Baptists, Two-Seed-in-the-Spirit Predestinarian Baptists, and Truevine Baptists. The mix becomes even more baffling when one of the divisions mentioned above is further splintered, into Old School Primitives, Original Old Line Primitives, Regular Primitives, United Baptist Primitives, Predestinarian Primitives, and Primitive Baptist Universalists. This list is by no means exhaustive. The frustration of grappling with such a diversity of titles perhaps was best expressed by an audience member who, after a lecture on this range of Baptist subdenominations, asked, "Why can't a Baptist just stay a Baptist?"

Avoiding the mainline groups—and several of the region's divisions that are not mainline, such as the German Baptists and the Free Will Baptists—the following discussion examines the Central Appalachian Baptist subdenominations which fall loosely under the title "Old-Time Baptists." For purposes of this introductory review, this term "Old-Time Baptists" will encompass the direct descendants of either the Regular or Separate traditions and will refer to those individual subdenominations characterized by the following:

1. Observance of such old-time-way practices as lined *a cappella* singing, rhythmically chanted impromptu preaching, congregational shouting, and warmly tactile worship behavior.
2. Strict adherence to what are understood, within these fellowships, to be biblical ordinances, specifically footwashing and "natural water" (or "living water") baptism.
3. The practice of such church/association governance rules as Paulinian gender mandates, early-church rules for elders and deacons, and articles of decorum that date from the earliest history of colonial Baptists.
4. Support of restrictions on divorce and "double marriage" (remarriage after divorce, while the original spouse still lives).
5. A common liturgical format that makes the typical Appalachian Primitive Baptist service appear remarkably similar to those service patterns followed by Regular, Old Regular, and United Baptists.

This worship format includes—among other liturgical elements—at least three sermons, and as many as seven or eight, depending upon the nature of the service.

Most of the region's Missionary Baptists, and some United and Separate Baptists, have moved away from several of these old-time practices; but a majority of the subdenominations mentioned in this introductory essay still hold to all or a significant portion of these traditional ways. The precise restrictions on divorce are becoming one possible exception. So uniform, however, is the adherence to these Old-Time Baptist practices that a traveler, uninitiated to the region, who visited churches representing the subdenominations soon to be examined, would experience no difficulty imagining the history shared by these groups. "Old-Time" is capitalized because the similarities among the various subdenominations placed under this title are so strong that the group warrants its own proper-name heading. When speaking of each other, these groups frequently employ the shortened term "Old Baptists."

This introductory essay does not examine Free Will Baptists, simply because that subdenomination did not emerge as a splinter group from either Separate Baptists or Regular Baptists (soon to be discussed) or from one of the various divisions from these two early subgroups. Free Will Baptists (frequently spelled "Freewill") trace their origins to a movement that was antecedent to, and largely disparate from, the Great-Awakening Baptists who split to form the Separates and the Regulars.[12] The same separate-origins rationale has warranted exclusion of the German Baptists, frequently referred to as the "Dunkers."[13]

In an effort to ascertain the present numerical status of some of these Old-Time Baptist subdenominations, this book draws heavily upon statistics supplied by Clifford A. Grammich, Jr., who served as a special researcher for the Glenmary Research Center, Atlanta, Georgia, during that agency's most recent church-affiliation census.[14] Grammich's specific charge was to gather data on the nonmainline religious groups of Appalachia, especially these Old-Time Baptists. Glenmary's 1980 census had indicated that the residents of many counties in Central Appalachia were substantially unchurched—a result reflecting the simple fact that a multitude of small groups were not reached by the 1980 canvass. (This problem was only partially corrected in the 1990 effort.[15])

At the close of his research for the 1990 census, Grammich shared with me hard copy of his computerized working notes, including 1989 or 1990 data on a large number of Old-Time Baptist associations.[16] Grammich has also produced, for the Commission on Religion in Appalachia, his *Appalachian Atlas,* a collection of statistical tables and maps, showing the presence in Appalachia of most of the region's formally constituted religious denominations and subdenominations.[17]

THE BEGINNINGS OF BAPTIST DIVERSITY IN APPALACHIA

Any answer to that audience member's question—"Why can't a Baptist stay just a Baptist?"—must go back at least as far as the "Great Awakening," a time (roughly 1726 to 1756) during which the American colonies were swept by successive waves of intense revivalism. The movement was led by a mixed lot of esteemed and not-so-highly-esteemed exhorters, such as Theodorus Frelinghuysen, a Dutch Reformed minister whose pietistic preaching in the Raritan River Valley of New Jersey in the 1720s may have begun the revival; George Whitefield, a Wesleyan-movement Methodist turned Calvinist, whose evangelistic tours throughout the colonies excited great religious enthusiasm wherever he went; Jonathan Edwards, that highly respected yet perpetually controversial Congregational theologian and philosopher who perhaps is best known for his 1741 sermon, "Sinners in the Hands of an Angry God"; James Davenport, a Presbyterian cleric whose intensely personal and highly intemperate attacks upon "Old Light" clergy almost wrecked the revival; William Tennent, Sr., and his three sons, John, Gilbert, and William, Jr., Presbyterians who became well known and historically significant for their involvement in the "log college" movement; and Shubal Stearns and Daniel Marshall, Baptists who were lesser lights in the movement but who are important to this study because they were largely responsible for the beginning of the Separate Baptists.[18]

This great revival was known for its high-pitched emotionalism (which repeatedly centered on fear of eternal torment); its sometimes confrontational methods; its itinerant clergy, who often preached in fields; its orientation largely outside the mainstream; and the fact that its following frequently consisted of working-class individuals. The fervor led to splits within three denominations: the Presbyterians (into the "Old Side" and the "New Side"), the Congregationalists (into the "Old Light" and the "New Light"), and the Baptists (into the "Regulars" and the "Separates").[19] In the case of the Baptist divisions, the Separates fell into line with the tone, temperament, and theology of the Great Awakening; while the Regulars defended the established Baptist churches and creeds, especially the Philadelphia Association, established in 1707, and the Philadelphia Confession, adopted in 1742 as a revision of the London Confession.[20]

THE SEPARATES

During the last half of the eighteenth century, when Baptist families—and sometimes entire church congregations—began their migrations toward what was then the western frontier (the Appalachian Mountains), they brought with them this division between Separates and Regulars. Shubal Stearns and his brother-in-law, Daniel Marshall, are credited with starting the Separates on their particular westward movement. By 1755, in what is now Randolph County, North Carolina, Stearns and Marshall had established the Sandy Creek Church, from which Separate Baptists would later expand into southwestern Virginia, move deeper into the Carolinas, travel farther south into Georgia, cross the Blue Ridge into eastern Tennessee, and eventually establish a number of churches along the forks of the Cumberland River in both Tennessee and Kentucky.[21] By 1785, 1787, or 1788 (the exact date is in dispute), the South Kentucky Association of Separate Baptists was formed, thus instituting the one Separate Baptist alliance still in existence that can claim the most direct tie to Shubal Stearns's initial movement.[22]

Stearns, a native Bostonian, apparently began preaching sometime in the late 1740s, operating under the strongly Calvinistic influence of George Whitefield. It was not until 1751, however, that he specifically embraced the Baptist faith, becoming ordained that same year by a Connecticut church of that persuasion. Four years later, he led sixteen Separate Baptists, including himself and his wife, to the North Carolina spot where he and Marshall founded the Sandy Creek church.[23]

Shubal Stearns and his followers had not labeled themselves as "Separates" initially. Indeed, on his way to North Carolina, he had, for a brief time, labored among those Regular Baptists of northern Virginia who were, in 1766, to found the Ketocton Association, a group of churches highly influential in the Regular tradition.[24] However, the Baptist congregations within the Stearns-Marshall movement quickly distinguished themselves by their "New Light" leanings, and particularly by their impassioned worship services.[25]

Because of the influence of such Great Awakening personae as George Whitefield and Jonathan Edwards, Separate Baptists at first were more staunchly Calvinistic than the Regulars, holding to a highly limited atonement doctrine: Christ died only for the "elect," that body of persons, known from the beginning of time, who were blessed by a selection that was particular, eternal, and unconditional. However, these Separates at that time lacked a creedal base, possessing no document similar to the Philadelphia Confession and apparently no precise articles of faith. The absence of such doctrinal anchorage allowed them to slide gradually toward the more Arminian general atonement theology advocated today by their heirs, the South Kentucky Association of Separate Baptists and the other affiliates of the General Association of Separate Baptists in Christ.[26]

Under Stearns's influence, the Separates also moved in another direction that clearly differed, then and now, from the Regular tradition: they allowed women to assume formal roles in worship, particularly in leading prayer, but also even in preaching.[27] That greater acceptance of female participation in both worship activities and church governance today remains one of the major differences between the Separate and Regular environments, although neither will ordain a woman. During the 1991 annual session of the General Association of Separate Baptists in Christ, held that year in Russell Springs, Kentucky, I observed considerable female involvement in the activities of the association, and a number of testimonies were delivered by women. That level of female participation, whether in church governance or in congregational worship, is uncharacteristic of most Old-Time Baptist subdenominations.

In 1991, there were five associations of Separate Baptists having churches squarely in, or on the periphery of, Central Appalachia: South Kentucky Association, thirty-seven fellowships in Kentucky and Ohio; Nolynn Association, nineteen churches in Kentucky; Christian Unity, six congregations in North Carolina and Virginia; Mount Olive, three churches in Tennessee; and Southwest West Virginia Association, only one fellowship, located in that state.[28] Although a strong similarity exists between the worship practices of these Separate fellowships and those of their cousins, the Regulars, there is a clear theological division between the two subdenominations. As mentioned above, Separates long ago moved away from their earlier Calvinistic doctrines and since have become one of the most Arminian of the Old-Time Baptist groups, practicing open communion and advocating a liberal atonement doctrine. At one point in its history, some leaders of the South Kentucky Association allegedly preached Universalism.[29] That South Kentucky Association form of Universalism— labeled by J. H. Spencer as "Hell Redemption" or "Restoration from Hell" doctrine—apparently was of the Elhanan Winchester (1751–1797) variety.

Association Building, South Kentucky Association of Separate Baptists, Russell Springs, Kentucky, fall 1991.

This theology suggested that sinners, after the end of the world, would spend a period in a purgatory state, suffering for all their temporal transgressions, before eventually being reunited with Christ and all their brothers and sisters who, in the temporal life, were purer.[30] We shall return to Winchester in chapter 5, which explores Central Appalachia's initial encounters with Universalism. Today, Universalist theology finds no place in Separate Baptist doctrines. Indeed, its influence on early-nineteenth-century Separates appears to have been minimal and short-lived.

THE REGULARS

In his *History of the Baptists in Virginia*, Robert Baylor Semple notes that the Regular Baptists began their movement into northern Virginia in 1743, coming first from congregations in and around Baltimore, Maryland, and then from fellowships in Pennsylvania. Both groups brought with them a connection with the Philadelphia Association and the Philadelphia Confession.[31] By 1766, Regular Baptist congregations in northern Virginia had reached such a number that they were able to "arm off" from the Philadelphia Association and form the Ketocton Association. During the remaining thirty-four years of the eighteenth century, these Regulars moved steadily down the Shenandoah corridor—among other paths—and found their way into frontier regions that now constitute southwestern Virginia, northwestern North Carolina, eastern Tennessee, and eastern Kentucky. In 1785, the Elkhorn Association was founded, the first alliance of Regular Baptist fellowships to be established west of the Alleghenies.[32] The following year, the Holston Valley Baptist Association was instituted; and, although these Holston churches contained many Separates who migrated across the Blue Ridge from North Carolina, the delegates to the first annual session of this alliance adopted the Philadelphia Confession and a constitution modeled after that of the Philadelphia Association.[33] Indeed, one of the ways of observing Regular Baptist influence upon any of the Old-Time Baptist associations of Southern and Central Appalachia, be they Regular, Old Regular, Primitive, United, or otherwise, is to examine the language of these alliances' constitutions, articles of faith, and rules of decorum. Clauses still appear that were lifted verbatim from the organizational documents of the Philadelphia Association or the Ketocton Association.

Although the nature of the two earliest Appalachian Regular Baptist associations has changed radically over the last two centuries—with the Holston Association having settled comfortably into the Southern Baptist tradition, and the Elkhorn alliance having moved primarily into the Primitive Baptist camp, including the two Primitive Universalist fellowship clusters mentioned earlier—there exist churches and associations which have retained their original "Regular" character. This is particularly true in Allegheny, Ashe, Avery, Wilkes, and Yadkin counties, North Carolina, and in Grayson and Smyth counties, Virginia, where a number of Old-Time Baptist fellowships are affiliated with such associations as the Little River Association of Regular Baptists (three churches in North Carolina, one in Virginia, and one in Maryland), the Primitive Association of Regular Baptists (fifteen churches in North Carolina), the Mountain Union Association of Regular Baptists (two churches in North Carolina, two in Maryland, and one in Pennsylvania), and the Original Mountain Union Association of Regular Baptists (nine churches in North Carolina and one in Virginia).[34]

The last two Regular associations just mentioned—the latter having split from the former in 1961—are frequently called "Union Baptists," a name that came into being because the churches that instituted the initial 1867 alliance had been pro-Union during the Civil War.[35] Nevertheless, the articles of faith and the practices of these two associations clearly place them within the Regular camp. *Giving Glory to God in Appalachia* treats the Union Baptists as a discrete subdenomination. Now, however, I no longer am willing to separate them from the rest of the Regular camp.

Two additional Regular Baptist associations have churches in the Appalachian region. Indeed, one of these, Enterprise, is the largest of the present Regular Baptist clusters. Enterprise Association of Regular Baptists has thirty-five congregations in Kentucky, thirty-four in Ohio, and one in Indiana. The second, in contrast, is the smallest: Mud River Regular Baptist Association has only three churches, all in West Virginia.[36]

Although there is considerable variety within this Regular Baptist family of fellowships, the general tendency is for these churches to be less old-time-traditional than their more Calvinistic cousins, the Old Regular Baptists and the Appalachian region's Primitive Baptists. For example, except

Ashworth Memorial Regular Baptist Church, near Princeton, West Virginia, summer 1989.

for special occasions, these Regular Baptist churches seldom practice lined singing, and they slide farther from the more rigid traditionalism of Old-Time Baptists by including musical instruments in some of their services, particularly the midweek or Saturday night sings. In addition, they allow "Sabbath Schools," a practice that the more staunchly Calvinistic Baptist subdenominations firmly reject, believing that any attempt to educate a child in the faith becomes a violation of the "God calls, not man" principle. Elder Earl Sexton, at the time of this writing the moderator of the Original Mountain Union Regular Baptist Association, for years even had a radio program on WKSK, West Jefferson, North Carolina,[37] a practice that Old Regulars and Primitives of the region would not condone. A final difference from their Old Regular Baptist cousins—and from most Primitive Baptists—is that Regular Baptists, especially in North Carolina, are more open and accepting in their interactions with other religious factions, as indicated by their ministers' willingness to "share the stand" (the pulpit) with preachers from divergent Baptist subdenominations.[38]

When one reviews the Regular Baptists' articles of faith, one invariably finds the same "election by grace" atonement clause that is present in the doctrine of most Old Regular Baptist associations. Nevertheless, the Regulars generally interpret "election" far less Calvinistically, sliding their theology toward general atonement.

THE GREAT WESTERN REVIVAL AND THE EMERGENCE OF UNITED BAPTISTS

At the beginning of the nineteenth century, a second general revival—called the "Second Great Awakening" or the "Great Western Revival"—swept the settled areas of the Appalachian frontier, culminating in extended and highly emotional camp meetings attended by Presbyterians, Methodists, Baptists, and others.[39] The three most pronounced effects of this revival on the Baptists were that it broke down some of the denomination's Calvinistic opposition to evangelism, it increased the denomination's numbers, and it nudged a few divergent associations toward unification. Beginning in Virginia and then extending into Kentucky, some Separate and Regular associations either consolidated or agreed to "correspond." In terms of the history of Appalachian Baptists, the most significant of these unifying actions occurred in 1801 between the South Kentucky Association (Separates) and the Elkhorn Association (then Regulars).[40] Although this particular union did not endure—in the sense that several of the South Kentucky churches later returned to their Separate affiliation, while the main body of Elkhorn fellowships ultimately became Primitive Baptists[41]—the initial coming together constituted the beginning of the Appalachian region's United Baptist subdenomination.

By 1801, the Separates of the South Kentucky alliance already had abandoned their earlier Calvinistic mooring and had adopted a more general-atonement position. The Elkhorn churches, on the other hand, were particular-election Baptists. Thus the union could be achieved only by agreeing to disagree on the issue of atonement: "We the committees of the Elkhorn and South Kentucky, do agree to unite on the following plan . . . , that . . . preaching Christ tasted death for every man shall be no bar to communion."[42] This 1801 action was not a full merger, in the sense that the two associations did not assume the same name, but they did establish correspondence, and the individual fellowships apparently began to refer to themselves as "united Baptists," perhaps with the "u" remaining for a while in the lower case. However, Spencer credited the 1801 agreement with going much farther and achieving both a general harmony among all Baptists in Kentucky and a statewide use of the title "United Baptists."[43]

Although this harmony did not last, as it became disrupted by more than two decades of debate between missionary and antimissionary stances, the nineteenth century did see a steady proliferation of Uniteds, with most of this movement occurring in Kentucky, and with a majority of the United Baptist churches adopting a theology of general atonement. "We believe," declare the present fellowships of Mount Zion Association of United Baptists, "in the free atonement of Jesus Christ, and that he tasted death for every man and that salvation is offered to all men and women upon the terms of the Gospel."[44]

In 1990, Clifford Grammich identified 176 United Baptist churches in the Appalachian Regional Commission areas of Kentucky, Tennessee, and West Virginia, with these fellowships containing a total of 20,147 members. Kentucky housed by far the largest number of these churches, 130 congregations, with a total of 13,193 members, distributed over a region bounded by Greenup County in the north, Pike County in the east, Whitley County in the south, and Rockcastle County in the west. In Campbell and Scott counties, Tennessee, Grammich identified twenty-seven United churches, containing 4,528 members; while in Cabell, Lincoln, Logan, Mingo, and Wayne counties, West Virginia, he located nineteen churches, representing 2,426 members. Grammich found some associations which still called themselves "United" but had aligned themselves with the American Baptists or the Southern Baptists. Such churches are not included in the count provided above.[45]

Most United Baptist churches in Appalachia would be called Old-Time Baptists by virtue of the fact that they have preserved so many of those traditions earlier identified as common to the other Old-Time Baptist subdenominations: footwashing, lined singing, chanted or sung impromptu preaching, Paulinian gender regulations, restrictions against divorce (particularly for elders), and the standard Old-Time Baptist liturgical format. However, these associations tend to be a diverse group in terms of precise doctrines and in terms of the other alliances with whom they correspond. Mount Zion Association of United Baptists, for example, has the very liberal atonement theology mentioned above, but disavows the practice of Sunday schools and corresponds with one of the Old Regular Baptist associations, Thornton Union.[46]

THE OLD REGULAR BAPTISTS

The Old Regular Baptists are treated so extensively in *The Old Regular Baptists of Central Appalachia* that nothing but the barest essentials of that discussion will be repeated here. The reader should bear in mind, however, that the Old Regulars are—at least in terms of worship practices, rules of governance, and Paulinian behavioral codes—probably the most traditional of the Central Appalachian Old-Time Baptist groups, preserving, as they do, the nineteenth-century absolutes relative to not only such customs as lined singing, natural water baptism, impromptu preaching, male-controlled church hierarchies, and a host of other liturgical or governmental issues, but also dress and hair codes that are especially confining for women. Indeed, it has been my experience that Old Regulars are more absolute in their defense of many of these traditions, particularly hairstyle regulations, than are most Primitive Baptists.

Old Regulars began as an offshoot of the Uniteds, when New Salem Association organized in 1825 under that denominational title and then gradually evolved into what became the mother association of Old Regulars. In terms of atonement doctrine, Old Regular theology stands roughly midway between the totally deterministic double-predestination doctrine (explained later in this chapter) of some Primitive Baptist groups and the freewill atonement tenet of the more Arminian groups, such as the Missionary Baptists (shortly to be examined).

Since *The Old Regular Baptists of Central Appalachia* appeared in 1989, the total number of associations in the subdenomination has increased from sixteen to seventeen, with the addition of the Little Dove Association (two churches in Kentucky), in correspondence with the Original Mountain Liberty Association of Old Regular Baptists;[47] but there appears to have been no significant increase or decrease in the total number of formal members—approximately 15,000, with as many as another 10,000 to 15,000 regularly attending nonmembers.

Traditionally the formal members sit in what is called the "stand area," those pews immediately to the right, left, or rear of the pulpit (the stand). This section of the church usually is elevated one or two steps, and within it men and women sit in clearly separated sections; in contrast, the section in front of the pulpit, where nonmembers sit, often shows no gender division. This seating arrangement reflects the idea that the nonmembers are awaiting their "calls," recognizable moments of religious exhilaration when the individual celebrant becomes aware that he or she personally is being summoned to redemption. Imbued with a strong streak of Anabaptist concern about early baptism, Old Regulars do not anticipate this "call" until at least young adulthood and find more assurance of its validity when it comes even much later. As a result, Old Regulars frequently "go down to the water" when they are in their mid-thirties or older, after having spent several years sitting in the nonmember section of the meetinghouse.

Old Regulars tend to be clustered in some two dozen counties of eastern Kentucky, southwestern Virginia, and southern West Virginia, with a small number of "outmigration" fellowships located in Arizona, Florida, Illinois, Indiana, Michigan, North Carolina, Ohio, Tennessee, and even Washington State. The annual late-summer or early-fall "Association Times," however, all are held in Central Appalachia and regularly draw hundreds—probably thousands—of these outmigrants back to "Old Regular country" for these three-day events. Two of these association meetings usually are quite large: the annual session of the Union Association of Old Regular Baptists of Jesus Christ, held the third weekend in September at the Union Association Building, Ash Camp, Pike County, Kentucky, which draws up to three thousand people; and the annual session of the New Salem Association of Old Regular Baptists of Jesus Christ, held the fourth weekend in September at the New Salem Association building, Minnie, Floyd County, Kentucky, which attracts up to four thousand people. Each of these events owes its large crowds to the fact that so many

Old Regulars belonging to one of the other fifteen associations try to attend one or both of these more heavily populated gatherings—for the singing, preaching, association business debates, and general socializing.

After 1989, some radical realignments occurred in the relationships between the associations. Indian Bottom Association and Old Indian Bottom Association essentially changed positions in the networks of "corresponding" Old Regular groups. Those two large Old Regular associations, New Salem and Union, until recently did not recognize the legitimacy of the Old Indian Bottom alliance of churches. Now New Salem and Union, in conjunction with several other smaller Old Regular fellowship clusters, reject Indian Bottom and correspond only with Old Indian Bottom.[48] Such shifts have occurred frequently in Old-Time Baptist circles, making it difficult to remain current in the intricate, ever-changing web of association alliances.

The Missionary-Antimissionary Split and the Missionary Baptists

During the first quarter of the nineteenth century, there was an intense growth in Protestant missionary activity, as Baptists, Methodists, Presbyterians, and the like took up what they believed to be their share of the "white man's burden." Eager evangelists and Christian teachers were sent to such faraway places as India, Burma, and the South Pacific, as well as such "home mission" spots as the American Indian territories and the Appalachian Mountains.[49] When this zealous missionary effort touched the frontier Baptist communities of Central and Southern Appalachia, whether to raise money for foreign missions or to establish home missions aimed at bringing religion to the mountaineers, two responses highly hostile to the mission movement arose. If the effort were home-mission-oriented, the Old-Time Baptists were incensed at the idea that their own religious institutions and practices were perceived as insufficient. And whether efforts were linked to home or foreign missions, the more Calvinistic subdenominations scorned the idea that man's work could increase the number of God's chosen. "God calls; not man," declared these Calvinists; in his own due time, he wins "the chosen" to repentance and redemption.[50]

Beginning in the 1820s and continuing to some degree throughout the remainder of the nineteenth century, many Baptist associations of Southern and Central Appalachia distanced themselves from missionary organizations, tract societies, Sunday school boards, Bible distribution groups, and all other bodies having mission work as either a primary or secondary purpose. Thus a major split developed within Baptist ranks of Appalachia and elsewhere, cleaving churches and associations into two sides, "missionary" or "antimissionary," and in the process creating new subdenominations of Baptists.

As their name suggests, Missionary Baptists sided with the practices and theologies of missionary endeavors, both at home and abroad. Since these churches held that new converts could be "won to Christ," their faith and practices placed them at odds with all limited-atonement (or "Particular") Baptists. Revivals, missionary work, and other forms of evangelism were sanctioned, making man a part of the process in "winning souls"; Sunday schools were accepted, as a method of nurturing the young in the faith; the doctrine of free will was avowed, as the individual's power to accept or reject the faith; and "backsliding" usually was recognized as a free-will corollary, since he/she who chooses can also reject and then eventually even choose again.

At the beginning of the controversy between missionary and anti-missionary partisans, the relevant Baptist churches were designated "missionary" purely as a generic classification: they believed in missionary efforts. Indeed, the period saw great confusion concerning which titles would be assumed by which groups. As will be seen shortly, initially there even was a controversy between the two sides of the emerging split as to which camp should inherit the term "Primitive," then being used in some quarters of the Baptist faith to signify that strain of the denomination most legitimately derived from the Paulinian church. However, *Missionary* gradually came to be viewed as a denominational label.

A large number of the original lowercased "missionary" Baptist fellowships eventually affiliated with those general-atonement Baptists who (after 1845) became either the Southern Baptists or the Northern Baptists (today the American Baptists); but quite a few fellowships kept their "missionary" designator, converting it to the capital *M* status mentioned above.

Presently Missionary Baptists of Southern and Central Appalachia fall roughly into three categories: those churches affiliated with one of the larger Missionary Baptist associations; those purely independent fellowships which label themselves "Missionary"; and those more "old-fashioned" Missionary Baptists—some in associations and some not—who, in addition to being "missionary," have preserved most of those Old-Time Baptist ways mentioned at the beginning of this chapter. Illustrative of the first category, Grammich found 9,749 Appalachian Baptists belonging to the Baptist Missionary Association of America, a subdenomination claiming 290,000 adherents nationwide.[51] Examples of the third category would include both the Enon Missionary Baptist Association and the Old Missionary Baptist Associations, each with churches well within the Appalachian region.[52] The second category includes hundreds of small independent Missionary Baptist churches found throughout Southern and Central Appalachia. One such fellowship is Mount Paran Missionary Baptist Church, Deep Gap, North Carolina, described extensively in *Giving Glory to God in Appalachia*.[53]

Grammich was unable to report the memberships of these "second category" Missionary fellowships, simply because they are independent and do not show up in statistical charts found in published minutes of annual association meetings. Nevertheless, these small congregations play a significant role in the religious life of Appalachia, while remaining largely uncounted in church affiliation canvasses.

The Primitive Baptists

It would be incorrect to view the missionary-antimissionary split of the 1820s through the 1840s as the sole cause of the Primitive Baptist movement. Divisions between the "Particular" and "General" Baptists had predated the controversy by well over a century, and the term "Primitive"—along with other terms, such as "Old School" and "Old Line"—also had been employed earlier as a designator for Baptists holding to more deterministic theology or to a church governance and practice structure based on a New Testament (Paulinian) model. However, after the missionary-antimissionary split began, titles became more important, in part because they both designated theology and laid claim to lineage. One of the most interesting of the formal debates staged between spokespersons for the two sides of the split took place in Fulton, Kentucky, over a four-day period in July 1887. Elder Lemuel Potter, from Cynthiana, Indiana, had been invited to represent the "Regular Old School Baptists"; and Elder W. P. Throgmorton, of Mount Vernon, Illinois, had been asked to speak for the "Missionary Baptists." The formal question for debate was "Who are the Primitive Baptists?" Each spokesperson argued that the faction he represented should be given that title, with such an assignment signifying legitimacy based upon both doctrine and lineage.[54]

Some of the opening arguments advanced by Throgmorton illustrate the Missionary Baptist interpretation of the line then drawn between the two camps. By reverse statements, his claims also indicate the positions being assumed by the "Regular Old School Baptists," who ultimately would inherit the "Primitive" mantle:

Let me define a Missionary Baptist Church . . . , as to policy and as to constitution: 1st. It holds that the gospel should be preached to every creature, and that every sinner should be exhorted to repentance and faith; that repentance and faith are duties as well as graces; and that the reading, and especially the preaching of the word, is a means of conviction and conversion of sinners. 2d. It holds (or may hold) that it is right to pay a minister a salary, but does not make such payment a test of denominational fellowship. 3rd. It holds (or may hold) that missionary associations, conventions, societies, boards and committees are warranted by the word of God; but it does not make co-operation with such things in the way of paying money into their treasuries a test of denominational fellowship. 4th. It holds (or may hold) that the Sunday-school is authorized by the word of God; but it does not make participation in Sunday-school work a test of denominational fellowship. 5th. It holds (or may hold) that it is right to have denominational institutions of learning; but it does not require patronage in the way of contributions, or otherwise, to such schools, as a test of denominational fellowship. 6th. It holds (or may hold) to the doctrines taught in the old Philadelphia confession of faith; but it does not make strict Calvinism a test of denominational fellowship.

A Missionary Baptist Church, then, is a local congregation of Baptists which holds the Gospel as its faith, and which keeps the ordinances according to the order in which they were delivered; which holds that the Gospel should be preached to every creature, and which does, or does not, pay its pastor a salary; which does, or does not, contribute money to the work of Mission Boards, etc.; which does, or does not, run a Sunday-school; which does, or does not, contribute to the work of denominational schools; which does, or does not, hold to a strict construction of what are known as Calvinistic doctrines; but which does hold denominational fellowship with churches which do all these things, or which entertain principles, which allow all these things.[55]

It should be noted that the only doctrine or practice concerning which Throgmorton drew an absolute line was the one he pronounced first, the argument that preaching the gospel to all humankind was a Christian mandate. Sinners and unbelievers should be "exhorted to repentance and faith," and "repentance and faith"—the order here appears crucial—"are duties as well as graces." (Apparently this meant that it is the obligation of the sinner to repent; but it is the love of God—given freely even though humans do not merit it—to forgive.) Moreover, the written word (the Bible) and the preached word (the sermon) are "means of conviction and conversion of sinners." For Throgmorton, therefore, evangelism had a causative role to play in humankind's freely chosen redemption. When responding to these "first principle" statements, Elder Potter essentially granted all but the last:

> We claim it is the duty of all people to repent of doing wrong, of sin, and that it is a right for them to believe the truth, and accept it, wherever they find it.
>
> But we do not think that the salvation of sinners is on condition of their hearing the Gospel. That is what makes the issue between us. We deny that repentance is a condition of salvation. My friend [Throgmorton] believes that heaven depends on the sinner voluntarily repenting and believing. We deny that.[56]

With this statement, Elder Potter drew the distinction that old-line Primitives traditionally have drawn. Whether the condition in question is identified as "salvation," "redemption," "election," or all three, it is a product solely of God's doing, not man's. The spoken word and the written word may become the particular instruments of God's will that result in a man's or woman's being "redeemed," but there will be no human volition involved. Potter believed that his deterministic theology was the pure gospel that was pronounced by Christ and the disciples, especially Paul, and so his side was "the Primitives." Throgmorton proclaimed his side to be following the mandate found in Mark 16:15–16: "Go into all the world and preach the gospel to every creature. He who believes and is baptized shall be saved; but he who does not believe shall be condemned." With this scripture in mind, he claimed the label "Primitive" for the Missionary Baptists, reasoning that, by following of Christ's command, the Missionaries earned true legitimacy.

The missionary-antimissionary battle for this title, however, was short-lived. In their later rhetoric, general-atonement Baptists let the term slide into a pejorative mode, along with "Hardshell," "Old School," "Old Line," and other phrases less widely used, such as "Backwater Baptists," which I heard used in an area of the Deep South. Readers today may be prone to associate the word with yet more negative imagery, with "Primitive" conjuring up a state akin to the characteristics of early man, even barbarism. Such connotations are decidedly unfair to the groups employing this title.

But let us return to the general struggle over missions. It is commonly understood that this controversy—augmented by aspects of the Campbellite movement, with its disdain for all extra-gospel creeds and ecclesiastical structures, and its emphasis upon restoration of the Paulinian church[57]—became the single most influential factor in the division of nineteenth-century Old-Time Baptists into two camps. One is now composed of various Primitive groups and the other of the considerably less deterministic Regulars, Old Regulars, Uniteds, and Separates. This does not mean that the latter groups cast aside all of their Calvinistic influences, but it does mean that they decided to expound a slightly less deterministic doctrine. Nineteenth-century annual minutes of the various Old-Time Baptist subdenominations are replete with records of the theological battles waged by warring sides, as association after association tried to determine its position on the issues of atonement, predestination, evangelism, extra-gospel organizational structures, the various gender-related mandates of the Paulinian church, and the general questions of traditionalism in worship styles and congregational behaviors. In chapter 4, we see this battle waged in the shifting relationship between the Washington Association (the organization from which Primitive Baptist Universalism would formally spring) and Washington's mother association, Holston.

One of the best examples of such a struggle over doctrinal and titular placement, however, can be seen in the history of the New Salem Association, which started off as "United" and has ended up as "Old Regular," with one brief stop along the way as a "Regular Primitive."[58] Indeed, almost every Appalachian Old-Time Baptist association has experienced some shift in its title and doctrine.

Consider a handful of associations that over the years corresponded, at one time or other, with the Old Regular New Salem Association. Burning Spring started off as United but later turned Primitive. Paint Union began as United, moved toward the Primitives, but finally remained United. Washington District had its roots in both the Regular and Separate movements but later became Primitive, before splitting (as we shall later) into two very divergent forms of that faith. And Elkhorn, one two parent associations of the Kentucky United Baptist movement, later splintered into several smaller units bearing that name, including two alliances currently within the Primitive Baptist Universalist camp.

During the nineteenth-century doctrinal struggles, association titles shifted about considerably; today one cannot always be certain of the precise theological affiliation simply by reading an association's title. In North Carolina, the Primitive Association of Regular Baptists is Regular; while in eastern Kentucky and southwestern Virginia, the Sand-Lick Association of Regular Primitive Baptists is Primitive.[59] And in eastern Tennessee and in southwestern Virginia, the Regular Primitive Baptist Washington District Association is Primitive Baptist Universalist, a subdenomination which this opening essay will introduce shortly.

By 1900, so much doctrinal diversity had developed among Primitive Baptists—both inside Appalachia and outside the region—that an effort was made by representatives from Alabama, Arkansas, Georgia, Indiana, Illinois, Kentucky, Mississippi, Missouri, Tennessee, and Washington State Primitives to write a confession of faith with which they all would agree. Thus was born the Fulton Confession, adopted November 18, 1900, in the same Kentucky town where the Throgmorton-Potter debate had occurred.[60] This document essentially is a reprinting of the 1669 expanded version of the London Confession, first adopted in 1644. What is added, however, is an accompanying Primitive Baptist interpretation of that original particular-election body of doctrine. Included are clarifications of Primitive Baptist positions on such troublesome questions as the sovereignty of God, the infallibility of Scripture, the nature of humankind's fall and sinfulness, the relationship of God to both righteousness and sinfulness, the particularity of election, the certainty of salvation for the elect, the finality of justification, the practice of baptism by immersion, the policy of closed communion, and the acceptability of divorce and remarriage.

There is no evidence that this document ever had a significant effect upon the Primitives of Appalachia, however. Indeed, to date I have encountered no Central Appalachian Primitive elder who was aware of the confession prior to my mentioning it. Furthermore, I have seen no indication of ratification of the document's positions by Primitive churches elsewhere in the nation. Therefore, it seems valid to conclude that the drafters of the Fulton Confession fell far short of their goal of unifying Primitive Baptist thought. Nevertheless, when we consider the Primitive Baptists as a generic group, we generally discover three key doctrines that are shared by members of this faith: (1) some version of the elect doctrine, which proclaims that this "elect" (the Church) is composed of individuals who were identified before the beginning of time to be the true followers and beneficiaries of Christ; (2) some version of the predestination doctrine; and (3) and some version of the "never finally fall away" doctrine, which proclaims an eternal justification for all the elect, meaning, among other things, that these individuals (if truly elected) never will finally fall from grace. Few Missionary and Free Will Baptist doctrines disturb Primitives more than the idea that a cycle of backsliding, regeneration, backsliding, and perhaps a culminating end-of-life return to the fold could have any relevance to true redemption.

Readers who interpret election and predestination as the same doctrine—or at least as "opposite sides of the same doctrinal coin"—should be aware that this is not the way some Appalachian Primitives view the issue. An individual may say that he or she believes in election but not in predestination, and what is usually meant by that declaration is this: the elect were chosen before the beginning of time, but they were not predestined in all acts that they perform. Since that argument introduces some "free will" into the picture, the individual may then assert that "the Church" was elected but not necessarily the individual; thus the "never finally fall away" doctrine is protected. It is "the Church," therefore, that never finally falls away.

Indeed, within Central Appalachia, the predestination/election category of doctrines encompasses great variation, and in my field interviews I occasionally avoided probing too closely in this area of theological thought, for fear of revealing to two or more elders that they are not of the same mind. My rationale has been that it is better not to highlight a doctrinal split, when perhaps no awareness of the split exists.

The introductory essay of *Giving Glory to God in Appalachia* is titled "Baptists, Baptists, and More Baptists." Reflecting the many divisions within the Primitive camp, this present chapter became "Primitives, Primitives, and More Primitives." The title does not convey disrespect; it simply recognizes another facet of the wonderful diversity that characterizes Appalachian religion.

Four Major Subdivisions of Primitive Baptists

Elder Robert Webb, founder and director of the Primitive Baptist Library of Carthage, Illinois, has classified Primitive Baptist churches and associations in three categories. Group I includes those Primitives who believe in the predestination of election, while rejecting the idea that God has predestined all things. Group II encompasses those churches and associations who pronounce a doctrine of eternal, absolute, and unconditional predestination of all things, including the selection and function of the elect. Group III comprises those Primitives who, although they have an anchoring in the faith, have moved their practices (and sometimes their doctrine) toward more Arminian postures, accepting one or more of the following: Sunday schools, paid ministers, evangelism, instrumental church music, youth organizations, radio ministries, or other elements of a nondeterministic religious expression.[61] A fourth category will be added, of which Elder Webb was unaware until engaging in some correspondence with me in 1993–94, followed by my visit to his collection in August 1994.

When Grammich made his 1989–90 canvass of Baptist affiliations, he adopted Webb's classifications, finding that the vast majority of Appalachia's Primitives belong to either Group I or Group II, with the former possessing a strong lead over the latter. The Webb-Grammich list of the Appalachian Group I Primitive Baptist associations includes such fellowship clusters as Burning Spring Association (nine churches in eastern Kentucky), New River Association (five churches in southwestern Virginia), Original Mates Creek Association (twelve churches in eastern Kentucky and two churches in southwestern Virginia), Mount Zion Association (ten churches in West Virginia), Sand-Lick Association (ten churches in southwestern Virginia), Saint Clair's Bottom Association (one church in northwestern North Carolina and two churches in southwestern Virginia), and Senter Association (six churches in northwestern North Carolina). The Webb-Grammich classifications include the following Group II Primitive associations with churches in Appalachia: Mates Creek Association (one church in eastern Kentucky and one in West Virginia), not to be confused with Original Mates Creek; New River Association, the total-predestination side (two churches in southwestern Virginia); and Smith River Association (seven churches in southwestern Virginia).[62]

Webb and Grammich list no Group III associations in Appalachia, but they do include a handful of independent Primitive Baptist churches in this category, three found on the western edge of Tennessee's Appalachian counties (one each in Coffee, Franklin, and Hamilton counties) and four found in northern Alabama counties (two in DeKalb, one in Elmore, and one in Madison).[63] Neither Webb nor Grammich classified the Eastern District Association of Primitive Baptists (eight churches in eastern Kentucky, six churches in eastern Tennessee, and twenty-six churches in southwestern Virginia). My observations of this Primitive alliance would place it either squarely in Group III or on the cusp of it, simply because of the Eastern District's liberal attitude toward associations of non-

Primitive Old-Time Baptists, particularly the Mountain Liberty Association of Old Regular Baptists and the Thornton Union Association of Old Regular Baptists, both belonging to a progressive faction of their subdenomination.[64]

As previously observed, at the time of the 1989–90 Grammich canvass, neither he nor Webb was aware of a fourth group of Appalachian Primitives, the small Primitive Baptist Universalist associations introduced briefly at the beginning of this chapter. The remainder of this volume is devoted exclusively to this highly unusual group of Primitives. Chapter 2— in addition to providing a glimpse of the Appalachian environment in which these churches have their presence—introduces these joyous people to the reader in much the same way they were first revealed to me. Then chapters 3, 4, and 5 move on in pursuit of the goals announced previously: to examine the 1924 split that formally initiated the movement, to probe PBU theology, and briefly to explore eighteenth- and nineteenth-century Universalist thinking, as well as to suggest how one branch of that Universalist theology may have reached Central Appalachia and fused with elements of traditional Primitive Baptist doctrine. Chapters 6 and 7 focus more closely on specific areas of PBU worship practice, while chapter 8 considers the outmigration of the faith to limited areas of Ohio and Pennsylvania. Chapter 9 closes the volume with a few of my personal responses to these "pilgrims in the hands of a happy god." Since these structures figure so keenly in my own mental pictures of this movement, every chapter but the last begins with an examination of one PBU meetinghouse. This book attempts, too, to convey a sense of the natural environment that surrounds this uniquely Appalachian religious phenomenon.

2 "THEY CALL US THE NO-HELLERS"

Pilgrim's Rest meetinghouse sits at a picturesque point on State Line Ridge, roughly halfway between Whitewood, Virginia, and Jolo, West Virginia. This traditional Old-Time Baptist structure literally straddles one of the southernmost segments of the Virginia–West Virginia state line, with the result that some of the Pilgrim's Rest members who worship in the church's right-hand benches do so in West Virginia, while those who sing, shout, and pray on the left side do so in Virginia. Indeed, during the course of one of the fellowship's monthly meetings, an elder often will end up having preached in both states, as a result of his vigorous surging from one side of the stand to the other.

The phrase "traditional Old-Time Baptist structure" is employed to compare this facility to a prototype that exists for churches in the Appalachian Old-Time Baptist subdenominations surveyed in chapter 1. This prototype is unlike that elaborately steepled, Gothic-windowed structure one sees on Christmas cards depicting rural settings. It is, rather, a structure much simpler and less ornate. Uncomplicated in its basic rectangular floor plan, it usually is devoid of such churchly symbols as stained glass, a cross-crowned spire, or a cruciform roof; is starkly functional in form; has no boldly promotional marquee or other roadside testaments to itself; is unpretentious in size or internal decor; and in general is largely anonymous in its nonverbal imagery. Most mainline churches, synagogues, mosques, and temples have external features that make them recognizable, even to the relatively untrained eye, as a particular place of worship. That is not always the case with these Old-Time Baptist structures, however. A majority of people would recognize them as religious facilities, but, beyond that very basic level of recognition, the communication would be limited.

The Pilgrim's Rest meetinghouse fits well that Old-Time Baptist church model—nothing elaborate, nothing wasted. It is a serviceable structure that is kept clean, painted, and in repair, but it is not treated as an icon in and of itself. Appalachian Old-Time Baptists traditionally do not worship their churches; they worship *in* their churches.

"It's not much to look at—just a church," pronounced Elder Wallace Cooper, ordained by the Pilgrim's Rest membership in 1934 and now very much the patriarch of the Elkhorn Association, with which Pilgrim's Rest is affiliated. "But it makes us all comfortable," Cooper continued. "We don't need more than that. I once lived up there on the rise," pointing to a house that sits perhaps two hundred yards east of the church. "I have memories of all the folks coming in year after year for the association meetings. We had them sleeping all over the place. We could always find a spot for one more. Fed those folks, too, when they wasn't eating here at the church."[1]

Elder Cooper, one of the individuals to whom this volume is dedicated, came to me when I first visited Pilgrim's Rest and informed me that, at the moment, I was standing in West Virginia. His statement confused me for a second. If I wanted to revisit Virginia, he quickly added, I should move about a foot to my right, which I promptly did. "That make you feel any different?" he asked.

"Not that I notice," I responded.

"Good. 'Cause the air's the same," he chuckled.

Of the people who frequent Pilgrim's Rest Church, Elder Cooper is only one of the individuals whom I have grown to cherish. He probably is in his eighties—exactly how old I never determined—but he still occasionally "takes the stand," and when he does, the moment becomes a very special one for the particular PBU congregation. Given his advanced age, his preaching is slow and disjointed, but he usually cries as he exhorts, and his emotions inevitably engender a comparable response in his audience. When he listens to the preaching of other elders, Brother Wallace occasionally is a shouter, somewhat atypical for a PBU male. Such responses usually are left to the women of these churches, but Brother Wallace does

Elder Wallace Cooper "in the stand" at the Regular Primitive Baptist Washington District Association's Annual Session, 1995, Hale Creek Church, Buchanan County, Virginia.

not follow all such codes. When he becomes happy, he is apt to express that joy in any of a number of ways—shouting, perhaps some hand-clapping, and even some jumps, all of them suggesting a physical style that must have been extremely vigorous when he was younger.

The structural core of Pilgrim's Rest Church probably is older than Brother Wallace, but the facility has been remodeled several times. The old clapboard outer walls now are hidden under vinyl siding, and modern paneling plays a similar role on the interior. At some point in the recent past, the original rear wall was removed, and another twelve or fifteen feet were added at that end, providing space in the stand area for the twenty or so elders who might be present on any of the three days of an association meeting. This renovation also lengthened the congregational area, permitting seating for approximately two hundred worshipers, with more persons than that being accommodated during the most heavily attended events of the church's year. On those occasions, folding chairs are placed in the center aisle and in a space between the front pew and the raised stand area. If these attendance figures seem large compared to the Elkhorn Association's actual membership, only fifty-one, remember that, in addition to nonmember attendance, all the visitors from the other two associations must be accommodated. Aside from the gatherings for the three days of an annual association meeting, the largest attendance usually is recorded for the yearly communion and footwashing service.

This elongation of Pilgrim's Rest's interior also allowed approximately ten feet of space between the pews and the raised stand area to be left free of furniture or other objects. It is in this open expanse that the most emotional episodes of congregational worship traditionally occur: the churning confusion of crying, shouting, and embracing or handshaking worshipers, who rush to this area at the close of a round of impassioned preaching; the footwashing celebrations that traditionally lift both women and men to peaks of stirring, cathartic interpersonal expression; and the climactic communications of joy unleashed when an individual feels a summons to redemption and rushes forward to proclaim that call.

That rear addition also made room for a small kitchen that juts out from the northwestern corner of the building. From here the women of the church serve hot coffee, sweet rolls, and ham or sausage biscuits during those early September "Association Time" mornings, as the crowd, beginning to arrive as early as 8 or 9 A.M., feels in the brisk State Line Ridge air a chilly suggestion of Appalachian autumn. Extending east from this kitchen is a covered porch that runs the length of the church's north wall and provides a sheltered area in which to serve the huge spreads of food required for dinners on the grounds. In this area, a long waist-high counter has been secured to the outer wall of the church. During a dinner-on-the-grounds, this space is occupied by a five-gallon electric coffee urn; the necessary Styrofoam cups; numerous two-liter bottles of soft drinks; several plastic milk jugs filled with tea, lemonade, and fruit drinks resembling Kool-Aid; and a variety of pies, cakes, and cobblers. Meat and vegetable main-course dishes are arranged on a table twenty-four feet long that runs just inside the outer support posts of this porch. The arrangement is an efficient one, allowing diners to pass between the two serving surfaces, filling plates before moving out to other places around the grounds. For Old-Time Baptists, these traditional midday dinners on the grounds—along with footwashings, union meetings, creek baptisms, association meetings, and a multitude of other shared experiences—are factors essential in maintaining the level of cohesiveness and community spirit found in these small churches and associations, qualities often sorely lacking in larger, more sophisticated religious congregations.

The covered porch and a narrow strip of grass on its northern edge also provide the social space that men in the church seem to need. More often than not, the women cluster inside the meetinghouse, particularly in the front left-side pews; but the men gather outside—to smoke, to chew tobacco, to talk of important church-related matters, and to consume that hot coffee and those sausage biscuits.

At the front of the church, there's another relatively new extension to the building, providing room for two modern restrooms that flank the entrance foyer. Nevertheless, the outhouses at the west end of the building have been preserved. The one for the women stands closer to the church, as is traditional; and the one for the men rests some twenty-five yards or so to the rear, near the entrance to the Pilgrim's Rest cemetery and outdoor preaching arbor. Beyond that men's facility lies a space where a half-dozen vehicles can be parked for funerals or other occasions. West of that spot, a short path leads to a tight cove encircled by woods, where are located the small cemetery, a covered but open-sided preaching arbor, and rows of rustic benches. These latter, along with the arbor, form a kind of outdoor amphitheater. For association business meetings—held in this area during good weather—the seating provided by these rough benches is augmented by metal folding chairs and several less rustic portable benches. This arbor also provides an environment appropriate for graveside funerals and for those annual memorial services that are so much a part of the Old-Time Baptist tradition.[2]

As of 1995, Elder Unice Davis of Paynesville, West Virginia, is the moderator of both the Pilgrim's Rest fellowship and the Elkhorn Association; during the business meetings of these two organizations, he or his assistant moderator, Elder Jack Horne of Jolo, West Virginia, presides from this arbor, usually surrounded by several other elders or deacons representing the three corresponding associations. Outdoor environments—utilized not only for association sessions, but also for numerous memorial services—seem to inspire special heights of homiletic passion. Some of the most "carried out" preaching that I have heard while witnessing PBU events has taken place under the rustic Pilgrim's Rest arbor.

During heavily attended special occasions—union or communion meetings, memorial services, annual association sessions[3]—the Pilgrim's Rest meetinghouse literally will be surrounded by cars, probably with a line of twenty or more vehicles stretched along the asphalt road that runs at the south side of the church. License plates most frequently will show a

Preaching arbor at Pilgrim's Rest Church, on State Line Ridge between Whitewood, Virginia, and Jolo, West Virginia, during the Elkhorn Primitive Baptist Association's Annual Session, 1995.

Virginia or West Virginia registration, but it is not unusual for Kentucky, Tennessee, North Carolina, and even Indiana, Ohio, Maryland, Pennsylvania, or Florida to be represented.

THE PILGRIM'S REST GEOGRAPHICAL ENVIRONMENT

Pilgrim's Rest Church was not selected to begin this chapter because it was the first or even the second PBU meetinghouse I visited. The first happened to be Point Truth Church, about which I'll say more shortly. Rather, I chose Pilgrim's Rest for two reasons. First, I have been very strongly attracted to the church's specific environment, perched as it is atop State Line Ridge. Second, its selection gives me an opportunity to describe a particular section of "No-Heller Country" that is especially rich in PBU tradition. The area in question covers parts of Buchanan and Tazewell counties, Virginia, and McDowell County, West Virginia. This is a very

Pilgrim's Rest Church and cars lining Peapatch Road, during the Elkhorn Primitive Baptist Association's Annual Session, 1994.

mountainous region that shelters a number of Elkhorn Association and Washington Association churches—Pilgrim's Rest, Hale Creek, Slate Creek, Bee Branch, Macedonia, Mount Olive, and Salem.

Old-timers in this region of Virginia and West Virginia know the immediate section of State Line Ridge that supports Pilgrim's Rest as "Wimmer Gap." They also know as "Peapatch" the knob 2,848 feet high that lies a couple of miles east of the church. The continuance of the ridge beyond Peapatch is called "Bearwallow." From Peapatch, which is relatively clear of view-obstructing vegetation, a visitor can look north down toward Bradshaw, West Virginia, and into the Dry Fork region of the Tug Fork–Big Sandy watershed system. The view to the south reveals the ridges and coves that route streams toward Dismal River[4] in one direction, or toward Big Creek and Indian Creek in another direction; the former drains eventually into Louisa Fork of Big Sandy, and the latter empties down the south face of Smith Ridge into the Clinch River basin.

The Pilgrim's Rest segment of State Line Ridge is especially narrow, providing absolutely no room other than what is needed for the church building, for a few feet of grass on each side of the facility, for the tight two lanes of the main roadbed, and for a driveway that circles the church on the north side, below the level of the church. South of the road, the land slides steeply away, down toward either the Linn Camp Branch cove or the Betsey Branch cove. To the north, there is an equally precipitous surface plunge in the direction of the Middle Fork of Bradshaw Creek. Rain that falls on the metal roof of the Pilgrim's Rest meetinghouse runs off it to one watershed or the other.

Anyone seeking to locate this spot on a map of Central Appalachia should start by drawing an imaginary line between Whitewood, in Buchanan County, Virginia, and Jolo, in McDowell County, West Virginia. That reference mark will intersect State Line Ridge at or near the crossing of Routes 635 and 616, the precise geographical point identified as Wimmer Gap. East of that crossing—five-tenths of a mile, to be exact—the Pilgrim's Rest facility stands on the north side of Route 616.

Motorists who reach this particular spot in Central Appalachia do so by traveling complicated networks of narrow roads—usually paved, but sometimes not—that twist up and down tight mountain coves and through those ridge gaps that became so necessary to the back-country migrations of early settlers. These mountain-top depressions now carry such names as Short Gap, Low Gap, Flat Gap, Panther Gap, Bearwallow Gap, and Wimmer Gap. In addition, these high-country roadways frequently parallel one of the region's ever-present creeks or branches—fast-flowing streams to which those early settlers also gave such colorful titles as Slate Creek, Indian Creek, Contrary Creek, Dismal River, Long Branch, Camp Branch, Wolfpen Branch, or Mudlick Branch. Sometimes a road will run the back of a ridge—called, perhaps, Smith Ridge, Chicken Ridge, Brushtop Ridge, Horse Ridge, or Compton Ridge.

This is coal country, and savaging of the landscape by this extraction industry is evident in almost any direction a traveler looks. However, residents of the region seldom complain about the coal industry's uglifying nature, since its jobs provide almost the only major money flow in this area of Virginia and West Virginia.

State Line Ridge, nevertheless, is an especially scenic region of Central Appalachia, and those who drive the snakelike line of asphalt or crushed rock separating states are rewarded by vistas that often are as inspiring as those found in the Great Smokies. Indeed, the very mining industry that has reduced the value of this region for resort development has allowed land ownership—absent mineral rights, of course—to remain with families whose lack of affluence might not permit them to keep possession of such beauty were it located in the Blue Ridge Parkway areas of Southern Appalachia. In these latter areas, skyrocketing land prices and resulting increases in taxes often drive the original owners off the land—a scenario that seems less likely to be played out in this land between the Virginias. Such are the ironies of coal country.

The easiest directions for a Virginia-side ascent to Pilgrim's Rest Church would have the motorist leave Highway 460 at Richlands, Virginia; travel Highway 67 past the community of Jewell Ridge, until reaching the crest of Smith Ridge; turn right onto Route 616; then, one mile later, turn left onto 636. After another five or six miles, this last road crosses Dismal River and connects with Route 638, where a left turn points the traveler toward the old mining town of Whitewood, Virginia. Just past Whitewood, 638 meets Route 635; a right turn onto 635 allows the motorist to begin an adventurous climb up to that high saddle known as Wimmer Gap, where a hairpin maneuver to the right will return the traveler's vehicle to what then will be the upper end of Route 616 (Peapatch Road). From that point, driving east five-tenths of a mile will place the traveler beside Pilgrim's Rest.

From the West Virginia side, the route is simpler. The traveler arrives in Jolo on Highway 83 and from that point travels Route 635 south, up the Middle Fork of Bradshaw Creek and along a winding course five or six miles, to the north side of Wimmer Gap. There, a soft left moves the traveler again onto Peapatch Road.

My Introduction to the No-Hellers

The beginning of the next chapter will introduce the reader to Hale Creek Church, also located in this particular part of "No-Heller Country." Now, however, I want to tell about my own introduction to the PBU people, their churches, and their doctrine.

Readers should remember that the term "No-Heller" is not a title that Primitive Baptist Universalists have chosen for themselves. In fact, it is a name they diligently try to avoid, believing strongly that the phrase creates confusion concerning their basic theology. I agree with the premise underlying that concern; most of the non-PBU Appalachians with whom I have talked about this faith do perceive these people as rejecting the entire concept of hell. Yet, so far as I know, never in the history of their specific Universalist doctrine have they done that.

As stated in chapter 1, Primitive Universalists believe that hell does exist, but as a temporal-world condition rather than as an afterlife place. Hell, for the Primitive Baptist Universalists, is an "absence from God's blessing," a punishment applied in the temporal world to all humans who sin and turn their backs on the deity.[5] It is a state of great torment that results from all transgressions of God's will, but this punishment is received in the present life for sins in the present life.[6]

While I understand this part of PBU doctrine, I have found it difficult to abandon the "No-Heller" term altogether, primarily because the phrase has become so fixed in the Central Appalachian lexicon of religious terms. If Central Appalachians are aware of anything at all about this faith, they generally know only that, at some time, a group of the region's Primitives split into the "Heller side" and the "No-Heller side" and that fellowships representing the camps of that original split continue to exist. Therefore, the title still is employed. I, however, try to use it sparingly, and almost always place it within quotation marks.

I first became aware of a religious group identified as the "No-Hellers" when I was involved in an ethnographic study of the Old Regular Baptists, especially when I visited Old Regular congregations in southwest Virginia—around Wise, Clintwood, Haysi, Vansant, Grundy, and the like; but the only information that I recall being given about the faith was that its adherents rejected the idea of hell. It was also suggested that the Old Regulars and the "Heller-Side" Primitives held this particular Old-Time Baptist division in special disdain, believing as they did that any doctrine that rejected an eternal hell was an extremely dangerous heresy. How could anyone, they argued, be motivated toward goodness without a fear of eternal consequences for badness?

That was the level at which my understanding of this subdenomination rested until the summer of 1992, when I first attended a service at Point Truth Church, near Nickelsville, Scott County, Virginia. Even at the time of that initial visit, I did not know that this was a PBU fellowship; I thought I was visiting a Group I Primitive affiliate. Like so many of my other introductions to interesting aspects of Appalachian religion, there was a serendipitous quality about this first encounter with the Primitive Baptist Universalists. Indeed, to be forthright, I have to say that I simply stumbled into my first contact with the PBUs.

Having just finished a book manuscript that was in press, I was looking around for another field research project. At the time, I was interested in examining the entire range of Central Appalachian Primitive Baptists, knowing that something needed to be written to delineate clearly the various groups. The mere fact that many of these Primitive Baptist associations did not recognize each other's legitimacy told me that *they* saw theological or practice differences among themselves. I wanted to understand those differences. I thought that I might write a monograph solely on the Appalachian Primitives.

I already had made limited contacts with the Senter Association, the Mount Zion Association, the Mountain District Association, the St. Clair's Bottom Association, the Sand-Lick Association, the Eastern District Association, and the Original Mates Creek Association, few of which corresponded with any other member of this group. So I mentioned to Darvin Marshall—a friend, fellow researcher, and guide during the Old Regular project—that I was interested in getting all these groups of Primitive Baptists sorted out, doctrinally and behaviorally. Marshall suggested that I start with the Point Truth Church, a member of the Three Forks of Powell's River Association. Some of his own ancestors had been members of that church and were buried in its cemetery.

As a result of that suggestion, on the second Sunday in August 1992, Marshall and I visited Point Truth, for what just happened to be that church's union meeting. There I met, among others, Elder Jennings Shortt, moderator of the Three Forks Association; and Elder Roy McGlothlin (now recently deceased), a member of the Regular Primitive Baptist Washington Association and the second elder to whom this book is dedicated. From these two individuals I received invitations to attend the 1992 sessions of their respective associations. Then, at the Three Forks session, I was invited to attend Elkhorn's annual meeting. On that second Sunday in August 1992, however, I still did not realize that I had made contact with the Primitive Baptist Universalists—the "No-Hellers."

Nevertheless, the contact had been made, and at a propitious time. Each year these three PBU fellowship clusters hold their annual "Association Times" during consecutive weekends, in each instance beginning on Friday and closing on Sunday. Three Forks' session begins on Friday before the fourth Saturday in August; Elkhorn follows, on Friday before the first Saturday in September; and Washington then closes out the series, beginning on Friday before the second Saturday in September. I was set to

Elder Roy McGlothlin "in the stand" during the Regular Primitive Baptist Washington District Association's Annual Session, 1994, Hale Creek, Virginia.

make my first cycle of these events, traveling first to Delphia Church near Dante in Dickenson County, Virginia; then to Pilgrim's Rest Church, up on State Line Ridge; and finally to Hope Church near Gray in Washington County, Tennessee.

AN INFORMAL DEBATE AT DELPHIA CHURCH

On Friday, August 22, 1992, Darvin Marshall and I arrived at Delphia Church around 9 A.M. and found a crowd already gathering under and around two funeral-home canopies erected on one side of the church. The session was not scheduled to begin until 10:30 that morning, but these early arrivals were there to help with final arrangement of the church and grounds or just to talk, to socialize, to be a friend, to debate, to be a part of developing association movements (whatever they might be), and in some cases to catch up with people not seen for several months.

The first day of one of these three-weekend cycles is apt to be an especially celebratory day, in part because some of these people have come from Ohio, Pennsylvania, Indiana, Maryland, or elsewhere outside the main PBU zone and indeed may be greeting people whom they have not seen since the previous August or September. There are no PBU churches in either Indiana or Maryland, but in both these states there are individual PBU families who have remained very dedicated to the faith and its occasions. The main reason for the high spirits on this day, however, is the fact that this is the beginning of a rising three-week tide of happy emotions, a tide that builds as the group moves the next weekend to Pilgrim's Rest, where the Elkhorn Association's meeting usually is staged, and crests on the last day of the Washington Association's session, wherever that meeting is held. Year after year, the expectation of these people is that the second Sunday in September will close out their religious year with an explosion of emotions that will sustain them during the ensuing winter.

As is the case within the entire Old-Time Baptist family, these annual "Association Times" generate a high degree of spiritual excitement. These are the times when things happen that become parts of the larger legend of the faith—the times when a particular elder assumes his position as moderator of the association, when another elder becomes so "carried out" that he preaches a rousing introductory sermon, when a particular sister gets to shouting so wonderfully that she electrifies the entire meeting, when a brother long troubled receives the call to go down to the water. Important happenings such as these do take place during the course of the regular church year, but "Association Time" brings such intensity to every event that the congregational mood becomes charged in anticipation of all types of religious drama. More than anything else, "Association Times" are happy times, rejoicing times, celebrating times; when three of these events are strung together in quick succession, it seems only natural that a kind of crescendo effect will develop.

After arriving at Delphia Church, I plunged into my usual routine of meeting people, making contact with a number of the PBU leaders who would be very helpful during the next three years of ethnographic field-work. One individual whom I encountered was a past acquaintance, Elder Bob Fields of Mendota, Virginia, an Old Regular Baptist preacher whom I had met during my work with that group of Old-Time Baptists. Fields is a member of the Original Mountain Liberty Association of Old Regular Baptists, and I first had gotten to know him when I attended a service at the Holston Old Regular Baptist Church, which stands beside the North Fork of Holston River, just east of where Highway 58A crosses that water course. This Holston Old Regular church should not be confused with the Holston PBU meetinghouse introduced in chapter 1, as the former is located considerably upstream from the latter.

The presence of this Old Regular Baptist elder, Bob Fields, at a PBU association session is an excellent example of a phenomenon I have encountered occasionally during my two decades of working with Old-Time Baptists. As chapter 1 suggests, the love of doctrinal debate is so strong among these people that they sometimes enjoy visiting each other's gatherings just to discuss theological positions that diverge from their own. This tradition may have originated in those more formal nineteenth-century great debates, like the one in Fulton, Kentucky, between Elders Throgmorton and Potter. On the other hand, the tradition could have arisen in those early union meetings, when, supposedly, elders occasionally faced interrogations concerning the doctrinal positions from which they had been exhorting. Then there always have been the debates that preceded and followed major splits. The missionary-antimissionary controversy alone precipitated years of theological forensics.

Anyway, Elder Bob Fields was at Delphia Church, and, before long, he was engaged in theological discussions with a number of PBU spokesmen, taking on one at a time or interacting with them in groups of three or four. The list of PBU advocates involved in these dialogues included: Elder Farley "Ronnie" Beavers, of Tazewell, Virginia; Elder Danny Davis, Hyden, Kentucky; Elder Roy Flanary, Keokee, Virginia; Elder Lewis Hill, Coeburn, Virginia; Elder Jack Horne, Jolo, West Virginia; Elder Roy McGlothlin (now deceased), Blountville, Tennessee; Elder Reece Maggard, Mayking, Kentucky; and Elder Willard Owens, Vansant, Virginia. There may have been others as well.

At the beginning of these discussions, I still had not realized that I was among the "No-Hellers." As the discourse on both sides of that informal debate proceeded, however, I quickly became aware that I was not hearing the doctrines of the more traditional Primitive Baptist faith, those Group I doctrines I had expected. Eventually I found an opportunity to ask Elder Farley Beavers a direct question: "Who are you folks?"

"Well, they call us the No-Hellers," Beavers replied, "but that name's not right."

With the assistance of several other discussion participants, Beavers went on to explain that their faith pronounced hell to be a factor of temporal life, but denounced the idea of an afterlife divided into heaven and hell. Thus, during that weekend, I gradually learned the most basic tenets of the Primitive Baptist Universalist faith; at that time, however, I would not have been able to outline the ten PBU tenets listed in chapter 1. My confidence in those ten statements, as being representative of PBU doctrine, has emerged only after literally hundreds of hours of discussions with various PBU elders, augmented by the limited body of printed literature produced within the movement. This theology has become primarily an oral one, heavily dependent upon word-of-mouth transmission from one generation to the next; and my efforts to delineate its tenets for myself were not without some frustrations.

Only one past PBU writer, Charles F. Nickels (1881–1948) of Nickelsville, Virginia, attempted anything approaching a detailed written exposition of the theology; his essay, "Salvation of All Mankind," occupies only nineteen published pages.[7] That work will be examined in chapter 4, along with two circular letters written by Elder E. M. Evans[8] and one by Elder G. H. Coleman.[9] These four documents constitute the only written materials on PBU doctrines, other than the three associations' articles of faith, that I have uncovered. A significant problem arises in connection with the articles of faith, as they are remarkably similar in wording to the articles of faith of the "Heller Side" of Washington Association, the group from whom the "No-Hellers" split in 1924. The difference develops out of how those articles are interpreted.

My own approach, when faced with this paucity of written explications of PBU theology, has been to listen closely to my sources, convert my understandings into written tenets, and then submit those understandings back to my sources for clarification or correction. The ten tenets recorded above have been read and reread by a number of contemporary PBU elders, to the point that I am comfortable in asserting that they represent the movement's beliefs.

Within the framework of an oral tradition, however, written words can become problematical, in the sense that they make scrutiny of meaning more intense and variations in interpretation more diverse. Ask any person to verbalize a belief. Then try capturing that belief in written form, and return it to that individual. You are apt to find yourself doing at least a couple of revisions. That is the difficulty presented by this study, a difficulty that is compounded by the number of oral sources used.

Some of these tenets I first discovered in the back-and-forth flow of dialectics precipitated by Elder Fields. Those discussions also suggested why the Old Regulars and other Old-Time Baptists were so threatened by PBU doctrine. What follows is loose paraphrasing of some of the arguments that took place on that August Sunday in 1992. That informal dispute was not tape-recorded; but later I wrote down my version of what I heard, and then I consulted the respective participants as to the accuracy of my reports of their arguments. I cannot verify the sequence in which these statements were made. Here, therefore, are those statements which the individual communicants agreed they said, though not necessarily in the order in which they made them:

> Elder Bob Fields: "I don't understand you people. You want everybody to go to heaven regardless of how bad they've been. Where's the justice in that? I can't believe in a God who simply ignores all the evil we do. Isn't there a general judgment?"

> Elder Reece Maggard: "There is a general judgment, but it's here and now. This is where God rewards us for righteousness, and the Elect will always know when the rewards stop—when they are in hell."

> Fields: "If I believed the way you people do, I could do anything I wanted to do—no punishments making me do otherwise."

> Elder Willard Owens: "Not so. If I do something wrong I'm punished right now—in this world. Besides, there are also the present-moment joys of doing good. We follow God because it is joyous to do so, not because we fear some eternal punishment in an aterlife."

> Fields: "There are too many people who are just plain evil. Without a clear system of eternal punishment, how can those people be controlled?"

> Owens: "By hell operating in the present life. I don't know about you, but I know when I've gotten out of step with God. I'm in hell and feel it."

Later that morning, Elder Farley Beavers, known in PBU circles as "Ronnie," told me that there were some people who were so hardened by sin that they were not always aware of the "hell" they were in. Still, they were being punished, he argued. The suggestion, it seemed, was that this temporal-world hell hit hardest those whose lives ordinarily followed a godly course.

> Elder Farley Beavers: "The righteous, however, will always know the hell into which they have slipped due to their own momentary failings. They've got something wonderful to compare that hell to."

Elder Roy McGlothlin: "Some Baptists take delight in assigning sinners to an eternity in hell. We're happy that everybody escapes that kind of eternity."

Maggard: "That's the reason Christ died, so *all* mankind can benefit."

McGlothlin: "That death on the cross was for us all, and we can't escape its blessing, no matter how sinful we are."

Elders Beavers, Hill, McGlothlin, Maggard, Owens, and others each made it clear that they believed that *all* transgressions of God's will really were punished in the present life. They were concerned that people like Fields viewed their theology as easy on sin, as implying that somehow people got a free ride straight to heaven. That was not the case, they argued. Hell in the present life was a very real thing, a horrible thing.

"But what about someone like Jeffrey Dahmer?" I asked, observing that outwardly he had seemed to communicate little or no remorse concerning the crimes he committed. Was he in hell while he lived? What was the nature of his torment? Yes, he was in hell, they all insisted, suffering more torment than any of them could imagine. Indeed, such people as Dahmer, Charles Manson, Hitler, "Son of Sam," and the like became, in their conversations, symbols for the type of person who was so completely removed from "God's blessing" that he or she had no hope of experiencing the joys of a temporal life properly aligned with God's will. What could be more horrible, they asked, than the loss of that hope? The metaphor that kept emerging in this discussion was "death"—not a literal death of the natural body, but a temporal-world death of the spirit.

Thoughts at Chapter's End

Sometime during that first visit to Point Truth Church, Elder Roy McGlothlin gave Darvin Marshall a copy of Nickels's publication, *Salvation of All Mankind*. This short work—to be examined in detail later— received a very limited private printing, probably in 1937, and now is owned primarily by members of the Nickels family. Indeed, it is not even widely held in contemporary PBU households, and, so far as I know, it does not form part of any collections of Primitive Baptist materials, including the Primitive Baptist Library at Elon College, North Carolina, and the Primitive Baptist Library at Carthage, Illinois. Furthermore, the WorldCat electronic data base of publications shows no such work housed in any library that participates in that catalog listing. Nevertheless, this brief treatise provides the only reasonably complete written explication of PBU doctrine. By providing me with a photocopy of the booklet, Darvin Marshall enabled me to obtain my first overview of the sect's theology.

The following week, while attending the Elkhorn Association's annual session, I sat in the back of Pilgrim's Rest Church with Elders Farley Beavers and Lewis Hill and began my first really fruitful explorations of PBU beliefs, using Nickels as my guide. It is not clear what effect using such a procedure had upon my pursuit of a theology largely maintained orally. Nickels provided my initial structuring of PBU thought, and, in doing so, he obviously determined many of the questions I was to ask during the next three years of my ethnographic work. Were there additional questions that I could have or should have pursued? I have no difficulty accepting that probably there were.

Nickel's short work did leave numerous issues essentially unexamined, including those represented by the following queries:

1. What is the role of Satan? Will he cease to exist in the eternal life? Is he a creature of God's making, or does he exist as a totally independent counterforce to God? These questions Nickels simply did not explore.

2. Who precisely are the elect? Will they have a higher status in the afterlife than that held by the nonelect? Nickels touched on this but declared that he had no wisdom concerning the issue.

3. How does PBU doctrine depict the Resurrection? Will this be only a spiritual Resurrection, or will it be a physical one? Although the 1937 essay did not address this issue, we do see evidence—explored in chapter 4—that Nickels struggled with this question. However, he appears not to have arrived at an answer that satisfied him.

4. What is predestined—only election, or the totality of human experience? Nickels avoided this issue, perhaps because it was a thorny one.

5. What is the meaning of human suffering? Is it all to be explained by the principle of hell in the temporal world? Here Nickels gave no hint of his thinking.

These were not the only questions I initially asked concerning PBU doctrine, but they illustrate issues that I sought to clarify in my interviews during the next three years, as I traveled among the Primitive Baptist Universalists of Central Appalachia. I did not always discover consistency of thought among PBU elders concerning some of these questions, and I became intrigued by the fact that far greater diversity was tolerated in some doctrinal areas than in others. Wider variance seemed to be acceptable, for example, on the predestination question than on the question of the nature of Resurrection. The reader will be exposed—in chapter 9—to painful evidence of that fact.

3 THE SPLIT BETWEEN "HELLERS" AND "NO-HELLERS"

Approximately a mile and a half due west of Wimmer Gap, State Line Ridge takes a sharp northerly turn; shortly beyond that position, it angles off in a northwesterly direction toward Paynesville, West Virginia. At the point of that northern turn, another ridge, known as Compton Mountain, runs off to the southwest and begins a slow, twisting, downward slide toward Highway 83, the meandering two lanes of asphalt that run from Grundy, Virginia (and points south), across State Line Ridge to Paynesville, Jolo, and Bradshaw, West Virginia. From the southern face of Compton Mountain drop a couple of lesser crests, plus one branch and several creeks: Harry Branch; Left, Middle, and Right Fork of Spruce Pine Creek; and Hale Creek. On Compton Mountain's northern side, Slate Creek collects water from several smaller tributaries and carries that flow northwest, toward its intersection with the Highway 83 corridor, and from there continues almost due west toward Grundy and Levisa Fork of Big Sandy.

The area is a wonderful maze of streams, hollows, and minor ridges that twist the topography into undulating works of art, in the process folding into seclusion elements of both the sublime and the ugly. Three geographical components of this larger scene have figured prominently in PBU history: Compton Mountain, named after the family of a PBU elder mentioned in this chapter; Slate Creek, the location and namesake of one of the PBU Washington Association churches, to be treated later in this chapter; and Hale Creek, upon which my attention will focus now.

Hale Creek Church sits near the mouth of Hale Creek, where this stream joins Dismal River. This facility was the first specifically mentioned in the annual minutes of the Washington District Primitive Baptist Association as having sheltered Primitive Baptist Universalist doctrine— preached in that instance by Elder M. L. Compton, whose forebears gave their name to the mountain that rises above the church.

In that first Washington District's account of the theology's presence within the association, there is a suggestion that other congregations might have allowed Universalist ideas to be preached, but only Hale Creek and Elder Compton are singled out by name:

> Resolved, that whereas, we have been troubled with the doctrine of uni-
> versalism that we advise the churches that if they have any elders preach-
> ing such heresies, or members arguing it, that they admonish them to
> quit preaching it or talking it, and if they fail to hear them to withdraw
> fellowship from such, and especially we admonish Hale Creek church
> to admonish Elder M. L. Compton to refrain from such doctrine.[1]

Since this 1907 statement constitutes the first mentioning of Universalism within any of the associations currently composing the PBU camp, that fact could suggest that Hale Creek is the mother church of this subdenomination. Nevertheless it hastily should be noted that Universalist doctrines flourished in Washington County, Tennessee, long before 1907 (more about that in chapter 5). Furthermore, PBU elders would argue at this point that this doctrine has maintained an unbroken lineage from "Gospel times," making the 1907 incident—in their eyes—just another one of those moments when the "true vine" began to break away from some heretical group.[2]

THE HALE CREEK MEETINGHOUSE

To reach the Hale Creek meetinghouse from Wimmer Gap, one would travel back down Route 635 to the place where that road connects with Route 638. A right turn at that point would take one in the direction of the Hale Creek facility, which rests on the right side of Route 638, approximately three miles northwest of the small community of Pilgrim's Knob. Southwest of this point, Route 638 moves on along Dismal River until the latter empties into Levisa Fork and Route 638 intersects Highway 460 a few miles east of Vansant, Virginia. A morning drive along this route in early fall often will provide an explanation for the stream's name, Dismal River; on such mornings, a serpentine trail of dense fog hangs low over the entire course of this water channel.

Hale Creek Church is one of those unadorned, wood-framed, Old-Time Baptist structures described in chapter 2. It snuggles lengthwise against the southwestern base of Compton Mountain, huddled as if to protect itself against the cold of Appalachian winter. On its east side sits a one-room log building that once served as both church and schoolhouse. The congregation currently uses this century-old structure as a storage facility, housing various objects for use outdoors (picnic tables, benches, and the like) that are needed when "Association Time" is held at this church. Hale Creek members also speak of plans to restore the old structure.

The present meetinghouse—only one hundred or so feet west of the log facility—is wedged between the mountain and Route 638, leaving only three or four feet on the southern side for a grass-covered passageway.

Hale Creek meetinghouse, Buchanan County, Virginia, spring 1994.

Here men of the congregation sometimes stand, leaning against the outside wall of the facility, to smoke, to chew tobacco, and to talk of church and association matters. It's a spot that catches the warming rays of the morning sun as they cut through the Route 638 clearing in the mountain foliage.

Immediately west of the meetinghouse is the mouth of the tight mountain flume through which runs Hale Creek, a stream that flows down to this point from its northern headwaters at the west end of Compton Mountain. A narrow and extremely winding road runs up the east side of this hollow, past a handful of private homes and the Hale Creek Old Regular Baptist Church, with which I had become acquainted during my study of that Old-Time Baptist subdenomination. A sign on the front of this Old Regular facility says only "Hale Creek Regular Baptist"; this church, like a number of others in the region, drops the "Old" but really is an Old Regular meetinghouse. The congregation is affiliated with the Union Association of Old Regular Baptists and in 1994 claimed a membership of twenty-seven people.[3] That same year, the Hale Creek Primitive Universalist community numbered twenty-six.[4] At some time in the past, these two church fellowships were one, but the unity within the Hale Creek

The old log Hale Creek meetinghouse, Buchanan County, Virginia, spring 1994.

THE SPLIT BETWEEN "HELLERS" AND "NO-HELLERS"   53

Baptist community ended decades ago as a consequence of one of the many splits that have plagued this region of Central Appalachia.

North of this Old Regular structure, the Hale Creek road stops running parallel to the creek and cuts across one of the westward extremities of Compton Mountain, to drop down into the Slate Creek–Highway 83 corridor. Some West Virginia Primitive Universalists reach the Hale Creek meetinghouse by traveling this road, but in winter it can be treacherous.

Although it has been widened slightly by centuries of silt-depositing stream overflows, the mountain basin at the confluence of Hale Creek and Dismal River still is tightly circumscribed by sharply rising topographical features. Nevertheless, because this spot marked not only the convergence of the two streams but also the meeting of two narrow valleys, it once provided space for a Hale Creek community, including a number of private homes, Ethel Matney's store, and the two churches. When I wrote the first draft of this chapter, the old store was closed, its windows and doors boarded up and its Royal Crown Cola sign beginning to rust. Now, however, that structure has been removed, and only a scattering of private homes remain in the area, sharing the basin with an electric utility substation.

Approximately fifty yards up the Hale Creek road, one small house has been abandoned, is partially overgrown with vegetation, and is slowly decaying into ruin; but in front of the structure stands a hand-lettered sign, the message composed by Elmer Matney, the house's previous owner or occupant. Its words protest the payment offered by the State of Virginia's Department of Transportation for the additional footage demanded when the road was widened and paved, a road that now squeezes the small home between asphalt and creek bed, apparently making continued occupancy unacceptable to Elmer Matney. However, his hand-lettered, faltering, but impassioned rhetoric still cries out against the overpowering bureaucracy that this particular Appalachian engaged in battle. Matney's land did not end up under a TVA lake, but his front yard was decimated, perhaps along with his memories of the blooms of roses, mountain laurel, dogwood, rhododendron, and the like.

As indicated earlier, the Hale Creek church upon which we are focusing belongs to the Regular Primitive Baptist Washington District Association, as opposed to Elkhorn Primitive Baptist Association, with which Pilgrim's Rest is affiliated. Both of these meetinghouses are favorite locations for their respective associations' annual sessions; when such an event is staged at Hale Creek, the business meetings are held in the

The protest of Elmer Matney, Hale Creek community, Buchanan County, Virginia, spring 1994.

meetinghouse, and the accompanying rounds of preaching and singing are staged under an open arbor or shed that sits across the road from the church, adjacent to the chain-link fence that surrounds the utility company's substation.

When the church members built this preaching arbor, anchoring it to a slab of concrete approximately 1,800 feet square, they made the mistake of extending part of the structure onto the utility company's land. For a while it looked as if the company would require the structure to be rebuilt—the concrete slab to be broken up and the entire shed moved back toward the meetinghouse. The company's position later was reversed, however, allowing this particular Appalachian little-person's battle to be won by the church.

A typical "Association Time" sponsored by Hale Creek and the Washington District will find perhaps two hundred people crowded under the metal roof of this arbor or standing around its perimeter. Cars, pickups, vans, and even an occasional recreational vehicle will line the road and surround that outdoor preaching space, providing tailgates and hoods upon which the plates of dinner-on-the-grounds will be placed. It was under this arbor or shed, during the 1995 Regular Primitive Baptist Washington District Association's annual session, that I last heard Elder Wallace Cooper preach. Many of those in the audience were sobbing convulsively, for no other reason than that this aging elder once more had been able to "take the stand."

While such an episode of preaching or singing is at its height, accompanied by all the shouting that such peak moments frequently engender, it is interesting to move up the Hale Creek road or in either direction along Route 638, to measure the distances these hallelujah sounds travel in this tight little three-pointed valley. Such celebratory vibrations float equally well in all directions along Dismal River and Hale Creek, flooding the basin with the "joyful noise" commanded by Psalm 100, while also inadvertently "singing 'em in," as earlier works have described.[5] Although these Primitive Universalists disavow any evangelistic intent or effort, they always seem pleased when a nonmember wanders into their exuberant celebrations.

The Formal Washington District Split

After that 1907 statement that Universalism was being preached at Hale Creek by Elder Compton, the Washington Association took no further action concerning this emerging doctrinal difference until 1921. In September of that year, the association met at New Garden Church, near Honaker in Russell County, Virginia, for what was to be the organization's 110th annual session. That year's minutes reported the following: "[W]e say in answer to the query from Salem church, concerning the heresy of no everlasting punishment, that if there come any unto you with this heresy that such church, after admonishing them the second time, and the offender still persists in such heresy, to reject them and notify the church unto whom they belong of their disorderly conduct."[6]

Although "Universalism" was not mentioned in this query response as it had been in the 1907 resolution, the association was dealing with the same issue. At that time—as is true today of the "Heller" side of Washington Association—the tenth article in the "Abstract of Principles" read as follows: "We believe in [the] resurrection of the dead, both of the just and the unjust, and a general judgment, and that the joys of the righteous and the punishment of the wicked will be everlasting."[7] However, the Primitive Universalists and their "Heller" side brethren were interpreting this statement very differently.

The Universalists were arguing—in agreement with the doctrine mentioned in chapter 1—that the "general judgment" was in the temporal world and that "everlasting" applied to the ongoing time of that temporal world. Resurrection would begin something very different, the culmination of Christ's atonement for *all* humankind. For the "Heller" side advocates, on the other hand, such a statement proclaimed "everlasting punishment," a literal afterlife hell into which all unregenerate sinners would be cast.

To clarify the Universalist position, the Regular Primitive Baptist Washington District Association (the PBU side) since has modified its tenth article to read as follows: "We believe there *now* [emphasis added] is a general judgment and the punishment of the wicked is everlasting and the happiness of the righteous is eternal." Then this association's eleventh article of faith further clarifies the doctrine: "We believe there will be a resurrection of the dead bodies of *all* [emphasis added] people when Christ shall change these vile bodies of ours like unto His most glorious body."[8]

The Elkhorn Association's "Abstract of Principles" makes the Primitive Universalists' position on the general judgment even clearer: "We believe there is a judgment, and we are living in the judgment now."[9] The fellowships of Three Forks of Powell's River Association have adopted the following language relative to *all* persons being raised at resurrection: "We believe that there shall be a resurrection of the dead, both of the just and the unjust; the dead shall be raised incorruptible."[10]

Although no mention was made of his name, the 1921 Washington Association action may have been directed towards Elder John Hankins, a Salem Church member who was having a doctrinal dispute with that fellowship's moderator, Elder T. W. Osborne, later to become one of the main instigators, on the "Heller" side, of the 1924 Washington District split. In 1922, the Hankins-Osborne discord had caused Osborne to step down from his position as moderator, presumably leaving that fellowship under a Universalist majority. Prior to stepping down, however, Osborne apparently had been the person who filed the 1921 Salem Church query with the Washington Association, precipitating the second admonition the association issued against the preaching of Universalism.[11]

This second admonition was critical, since Old-Time Baptists believe strongly in following the procedural formula established in Matthew 18:15–17, a formula that mandates two attempts to bring an offending brother back into a state of correct behavior before taking final action in a church or association. The 1907 action, of course, was considered as the first admonition.

Elder Osborne's resignation from the post of moderator at Salem Church resulted in Elder E. M. Evans—who in 1921 had been the clerk of the Elkhorn Association—being invited to assume the vacated moderator position. In an apparently unrelated action, Evans earlier had moved from Lex, West Virginia, to Honaker, Virginia, and had transferred his membership to New Garden Church, placing him within the Washington District Association. It should be noted, however, that Evans was not required to be an actual member of the Salem fellowship in order to be the church's moderator. In fact, elders often moderate two or three churches but maintain their memberships, as they must, in just one fellowship. By the time all of this moving about transpired, Evans already had become identified with the Universalist doctrine. Consequently, he was acceptable to the Universalist majority that now controlled Salem Church.

The reader should remember that Salem Church is located in the same region of Central Appalachia as the Hale Creek meetinghouse and the Pilgrim's Rest meetinghouse. Indeed, the Salem facility rests in Tazewell County, Virginia, only about twenty miles "as the crow flies" from the spot where Elder Compton, in 1907, was alleged to have preached his Universalist sermons. Therefore it appears that this particular section of southwestern Virginia did spawn much of the early PBU movement.

After resigning the Salem moderator post, Elder Osborne did not exit from the church's controversies, but instead continued to oppose both Salem's Universalist faction and that fellowship's new moderator, Elder E. M. Evans. Osborne's ongoing agitation within the church, and some abusive language he was alleged to have used against the Salem congregation, resulted in his expulsion from that church in September 1921.[12] Since Osborne was never restored to Salem Church's membership, he could not legally have represented that fellowship in the 1924 association session. Nevertheless, Osborne ultimately became one of the "sound members" of Salem Church whom the Washington Association accepted as delegates from that fellowship to the association's 1924 session. In addition, it appears that, perhaps more than any other tensions existing at the time between "Hellers" and "No-Hellers," Osborne's activities at Salem Church became the impetus for the 1924 Washington Association confrontation between the Universalists and their opponents.

Concerning Salem Church alone, here is what apparently happened on that critical Friday morning, September 12, 1924. Elder Osborne, with the support of only three other former members of Salem Church (like

Salem Church meetinghouse, Tazewell County, Virginia, summer 1995.

Osborne, they had been expelled), arrived at the association meeting with a letter that he claimed represented the will of the Salem congregation. However, Elder E. M. Evans also arrived with a Salem Church letter, which appears to have been supported fully by the membership still officially in the church. Nevertheless, the two letters initially were given equal standing and were referred to the Committee on Arrangements for Saturday morning action. When the two conflicting documents were considered, the session accepted what apparently was only a four-person faction, headed by Osborne, as the legitimate Salem Church, effectively excluding from the association the main body of the congregation: "With reference to the churches with two letters, received and seated Elder T. W. Osborn[e] and the sound members, and rejected the others until they set themselves in order."[13]

Although no specific mention is made of other churches having two letters, the plural "churches" suggests that two other congregations, Looney's Creek and Sumac Grove, also may have been represented by two letters; in both of those cases, the association also accepted only a few "sound members" and rejected the rest. Those situations in those two churches may have been identical to the Salem Church scenario. The constitutionality of these maneuvers is discussed below.

THE TOTAL IMPACT OF THE 1924 SPLIT

In 1923, Washington District Association was an alliance of twenty-four Primitive Baptist fellowships, located in eastern Tennessee and southwestern Virginia. Eleven of these churches (Big Creek, Concord, Duty View, Johnson Bottom, Mill Creek, Miller View, Mount Zion, Reed's Valley, Sand-Lick, Sulphur Spring, and Union) apparently had solid "Heller" majorities, while nine of the fellowships (Hale Creek, Jerusalem, Looney's Creek, New Garden, Pilgrim's Rest, Prater Creek, Salem, Slate Creek, and Sumac Grove) were just as solidly in the "No-Heller" camp. The Pilgrim's Rest church mentioned here apparently was a different church from the one in the Elkhorn Association, since the 1924 Elkhorn minutes also reported a Pilgrim's Rest church.[14] In addition, New Garden Church apparently did split into "Heller" and "No-Heller" factions, but the actual physical church remained with the Universalists.

Today both sides of the Washington Association have New Garden fellowships, Slate Creek fellowships, and Salem fellowships,[15] but the physical structures for all three of these congregations ended up in the Universalist camp. Therefore, it appears that the "Heller" side had some church building to do after 1925.

There was a tenth fellowship, Pine Creek, that seems to have had, in 1924, a Universalist majority; but this church did not even bother to "letter up" to the 1924 "Heller" side session, choosing instead to report to the 1924 "No-Heller" side session. Of the remaining churches that had been listed in Washington District's 1923 statistical table (Harmony, Macedonia, and Spruce Pine Grove), only Harmony appears to have rested squarely on the "Heller" side.

Interestingly, Mount Olive Church, which in 1923 had not been on the Washington District list, materialized in 1924 on both the "Heller" and "No-Heller" tables, each time with fourteen members. Today, however, Mount Olive clearly is in the Universalist camp, and no Mount Olive is in the present "Heller" side of the Washington District. Therefore, in 1924, the "Heller" side may have been claiming this church either in error or because the fellowship had not decided which way it would go. Furthermore, Mount Olive became one of four churches officially expelled from the "Heller" side in 1925. The other three were Macedonia, Pine Creek, and Spruce Pine Grove.[16]

It is difficult to determine precisely how the many adherents fell on each side in this split, because in three cases (Macedonia, Mount Olive, and Spruce Pine Grove), the 1924 minutes for both sides show exactly the same membership counts for a fellowship that had split, suggesting that both sides were still claiming the entire congregation of the respective church; and in two cases (New Garden and Salem), the Universalist side reported significantly larger 1924 memberships than earlier counts had shown. It would have been possible, however, that some memberships grew, since some of the "Heller" side churches that did not formally split still lost some members to other churches that were on the Universalist side. For example, in his history of the Sand-Lick Church—one of the Washington District churches that did not split—Elihu Jasper Sutherland acknowledges that Sand-Lick lost seven members to the Universalist camp.[17] Sutherland also authored a history of the "Heller" side of the Washington Association, and in both works he expressed intense disdain for the Universalists and a belief that the split showed a considerable numerical superiority on the side of the "Hellers."[18] However, Sutherland's claims for significant "Heller" majorities may have been exaggerated. Consider the following facts.

The "Heller" side's statistical table for 1924 reported a total of 983 members, with that table omitting only the four churches that had been formally dismissed (Hale Creek, Jerusalem, Pilgrim's Rest, and Prater Creek); while the Universalist side—meeting a month later—after the churches had had time to obtain a more accurate count of their members—reported 635 members, with the four "dismissed" churches accounting for only 203 of that total. Washington District's membership total for 1923 (before the split) showed only 1,239, but if the two sides' 1924 totals are added together, the sum is 1,618 members in all.[19]

Where did all those extra members come from? It seems possible that Sutherland severely understated the impact of the split upon the "Heller" ranks. Consider the "Heller" side's 1925 membership total—857. By then, that side of the split would have had time to obtain a more accurate count of its membership. Thus the 1924 division may have been approximately 57 to 43 percent, with the Universalists having the smaller of the two percentages. Nevertheless, a division of 57 to 43 percent represents a picture very different from the one painted by the "great majority" language employed in both the "Heller" side's 1932 resolution and E. J. Sutherland's 1952 history of Washington District.[20]

In 1924, probably neither side had a firm idea of how the split would finally work out, since there was considerable movement back and forth between the two camps, as individual church members and entire congregations decided which side to support. For example, between 1924 and 1929, the "Heller" camp experienced considerable volatility in its count of both churches and total memberships. In 1924, it reported 983 in twenty churches; in 1925, 857 in sixteen churches; in 1926, 981 in nineteen churches; in 1927, 889 in nineteen churches; in 1928, 904 in twenty-two churches; and in 1929, 742 in twenty-one churches. What was causing these rises or falls of one hundred or more members from one year to the next? The answer appears to be that it took a number of years for this split to "shake itself out."

Why Did This Split Not Occur Earlier?

If the numerical analysis provided above seems valid, why would an association that had become so badly divided stay together for as long as it did? Between 1907 and 1921, a period of fourteen years, no mention of Universalist doctrine appears in the Washington District minutes. Does that mean that the issue died after the 1907 session and was not reborn until 1921? That explanation does not appear to be logical, in part because of information Sutherland reported in his history of the Washington Association:

> Elders E. M. Evans, Thomas Grimsley, and J. J. Childress, all aged, able and respected ministers in the Association, were the chief leaders of the new doctrine [Universalism] in the bounds of the Association. They were aided and abetted by preachers from Stony Creek [no longer extant as an association], Three Forks of Powell's River and Elkhorn Associations, especially Ewell Goode, William M. Robinette, John C. Smith, Noah Adair and Samuel F. Adair.[21]

Thomas Grimsley was indeed an "aged, able and respected" elder in the association when it split in 1924. He had served as moderator of the Washington District Association during the 1881 session and then again in 1883, 1884, 1888, and 1889.[22] Thus he probably had been a highly influential association leader when, according to Sutherland, "prior to 1907," Universalism "was brought into the bounds of the Washington Association." When Washington District met at the New Garden church for the 1921 session, Thomas Grimsley was there as one of the delegates from the Pilgrim's Rest church, and J. J. Childress was present as a delegate from the Slate Creek fellowship.[23] With such "respected" Washington District elders having been in the Universalism camp for so long a time, why had there not been more frequent association actions concerning the doctrinal division?

Obviously, association splits are painful and very destructive to every aspect of church and association life. Indeed, the pain and destructiveness do not stop—as we shall see—at the association's own boundaries; instead they spread to those other fellowship clusters with which the splintered group corresponds. Such a split, therefore, has broad repercussions, as was illustrated by the Old Regular Baptist Indian Bottom division of 1960.[24]

Splits invariably are precipitated by "ordained authorities" (elders and deacons), but frequently they are felt much more intensely by the laity, especially women, who undoubtedly feel compelled to suffer in silence the consequences of men's actions. These divisions often drive wedges between families, and sometimes between individual members of one family. They precipitate distrust that can be felt for years, and they erect solid barriers separating elements within communities. Most of all, however, they engender anger, guilt, revenge, tears, and a host of other negative emotions that often linger for a lifetime. Therefore, such destructiveness and pain often will be delayed as long as possible, in the hope that a division in the ranks somehow can be healed. Such is especially the tendency when a strong association moderator is in charge, one who does not want to see his collection of churches reduced in number and strength, and one who most of all does not want to induce pain.

Elder William B. Sutherland apparently was such a moderator. He had been at the helm of the Washington District Association since 1897 and would stay at that post, on the "Heller" side, through the session of 1943, a forty-seven-year tenure. The Washington District moderator with the next longest tenure was Elder John Wallis, who moderated the association in 1845–46, 1848–50, and finally 1852–75, for a total of twenty-nine years. For comparison, look at Elder J. C. Swindall in the Old-Time Baptist subdenomination; he moderated the Union Association of Old Regulars from 1896 to 1938, forty-two years.[25]

It is a matter of pride when such Old-Time Baptist leaders manage to keep their associations together throughout their tenures, and it is very likely that Sutherland wanted to do just that. Therefore, it is probable that he exerted every effort to keep the divergent doctrinal partisans from each other's throats. In those efforts, he must have had to discipline his own inclinations to debate doctrines that diverged from his own. Nevertheless, even a very forceful moderator cannot always keep combative factions from battling.

It is unclear what brought the Universalist issue to the forefront in 1907. No name of a church or an individual is listed as having sponsored the resolution that was passed admonishing Hale Creek and Elder Compton. It is interesting, however, that Elder Grimsley was not named in that action, given that Sutherland had labeled him as one of the major preachers of the Universalist camp. Indeed, Grimsley's absence from the 1907 record suggests either that, at the time, he had not yet become identified with Universalism, or that his status as the association's former moderator precluded his having such an admonition directed at him. In the fact that both Grimsley and Childress (who also occupied, as early as 1907, a very high-status role) were not mentioned, we may have evidence that someone was trying to keep the confrontation at a relatively low level. It is unclear, however, why indicting Hale Creek and Elder Compton might have been considered a lower level of confrontation. In any case, by the time the 1921 query was filed, considerable confrontation had already taken place, as the dispute erupted at Salem Church. If Elder William Sutherland had been trying to control the controversy, he now became unable to do so. Elder T. W. Osborne seemed determined to bring grief to those of Salem Church who had excluded him, including Elder E. M. Evans.

A QUESTION OF CONSTITUTIONALITY

When the 1924 Washington District split finally erupted, it did so in response to a "Heller" maneuver that should have made Moderator William Sutherland worry about the legitimacy of his side's behavior. By that year, Sutherland had served twenty-seven years as moderator. He was sixty-three years old, and he certainly was experienced enough in Washington District leadership to recognize that what transpired at the 1924 session was of questionable constitutionality.

As its first item of business, the 1924 Washington District session accepted the letters of only eleven (Big Creek, Duty View, Harmony, Johnson Bottom, Miller's View, Mount Zion, New Garden, Reed's Valley, Sand-Lick, Sulphur Springs, and Union) of its twenty-four listed churches. A "letter" is an annual report to the association on matters of membership and finances, and it announces the "delegates" sent by the respective church to represent it at the larger body's session. Therefore, by immediately accepting the letters of only these eleven churches, the association made those delegates the initial working body of the 1924 session. That initial working body then proceeded to accept or reject the remaining letters, considering them later that Friday morning or referring them to the Arrangements Committee for placement on the Saturday agenda.[26]

On Friday, some delegates for Macedonia, Mount Olive, and Spruce Pine Grove apparently were seated later, but the "Heller" side minutes do not make this clear. Nevertheless, by having their letters referred to the Committee on Arrangements, the obviously Universalist fellowships were disfranchised and left at the mercy of the seated delegates, who evidently were solidly in the "Heller" camp.

Elder E. M. Evans later would complain that, in addition to being unconstitutional, all of this was achieved through a violation of one of Washington District's traditions concerning the order of seating delegates. According to Evans—and no written procedural rules existed to verify his claim—the tradition had been for entering delegations to stack their letters in a single pile on the clerk's desk. Then, when the letters were to be read and the delegates seated, the clerk would start with the letter on top of that stack and move in succession down to the bottom of the pile. On that Friday morning, however, the clerk selected out the "Heller" fellowships and read their letters first, the delegates being seated as he went along. Then, when the letters of the allegedly "unsound" churches were read, their delegates immediately were challenged, with the obvious voting results.[27]

No other action angered the Universalist side as much as these arbitrary rejections of a church's letter. Elder Evans argued, even during this first 1924 session, that such an action was a clear violation of Washington District's constitution. Article 2 of that constitution prescribed then, as it does now, the following restrictions concerning session delegates: "The Association shall be composed of members chosen by the different churches in our union and duly sent to represent them in the Association, who shall be members who they judge best qualified for the purpose, and producing letters from their respective churches certifying their appointment, shall be entitled to a seat."[28]

This article, as included in the 1993 "Heller" side Washington Association's minutes, has only two changes: the insertion of a comma after "union" in the second line, and the changing of "who" to "whom" in the third line.[29]

This is a very traditional article, one that shows up almost verbatim in many, if not most, Old-Time Baptist association minutes:

> The Association shall be composed of members chosen by the different churches in our union and duly sent to represent them in the Association, who shall be members whom they judge best qualified for that purpose, and producing letters from their respective churches, certifying to their appointment, these shall be entitled to a seat.[30]

> The Association shall be composed of members chosen by the different churches in our union, and duly sent to represent them in the Association, who shall be members whom they judge best qualified for the purpose, and, producing letters from their respective churches certifying their appointment, shall be entitled to a seat.[31]

The clause also receives an interpretation that is remarkably consistent within Old-Time Baptist circles: first, the local church determines its own association delegates; and, second, once that determination is made, the association must seat those delegates. It stipulates an individual-fellowship right that churches have closely guarded, not wishing to relinquish this power to their associations.

It was a double affront to Salem Church when its association accepted as delegates individuals who had been excluded from the Salem membership. Heretofore, in the Washington District, when a church excluded a member, that member could not be accepted into membership in another Washington District church until that individual had gone back to her or his original congregation and been restored to membership. That is the policy followed by the vast majority of Old-Time Baptist associations, one enforced with great regularity in Old Regular Baptist churches. It is also the policy followed by the current PBU associations.

The only justification ever given by the "Heller" side for this 1924 delegate-seating procedure came in a lengthy resolution passed by the 1932 Washington District Association. What follows are passages from that resolution, the only ones treating this question of constitutionality:

> Whereas, at that association [session,] certain persons *claiming to be messengers from several churches* [emphasis added] were rejected on the ground that they permitted the doctrine of Universalism to be preached in their churches, some contesting messengers were rejected for the same

reason, and the association withdrew its fellowship from the churches which had declined to drive this heresy from their pulpits.

The association of 1924 was made up of messengers from the various churches belonging to the association as was usual and proper in our annual meetings. No effort was made by *the orthodox and regular members* [emphasis added] to "pack the association" or "by ruling over and riding over" the constitution of the association.

The proceedings of said association strictly followed the Constitution and Rules of Decorum of the association. No messenger was denied any privilege or right *to which he was entitled*. There was no disorderly or illegal act *on the part of the regular members,* who were in great majority. [Emphasis added][32]

It seems obvious that the "Heller" side, with regard to the debate over constitutionality, satisfied itself by arguing that these protesting individuals were not legitimate messengers and therefore had no Washington Association constitutional rights. The Universalists appeared to be in a far better position, arguing simply that the individual churches had been given the right to determine their messengers and that such a right had been acknowledged in the past.

FORMATION OF THE UNIVERSALIST SIDE OF WASHINGTON ASSOCIATION

When the dust settled from all the combat at that rancorous 1924 session, the "Heller" side was in firm control of the "Washington District Association of Primitive Baptists." Churches representing the Universalist side had been deprived of representation in the association or dismissed altogether, but in several cases it was unclear which side remained in possession of the respective physical church. Indeed, the tug-of-wars over trustees, and their legal control over these facilities, apparently went on for several years before the present ownership configurations emerged.[33]

Nevertheless, by October 5, 1924, the Universalist forces had regrouped sufficiently to be able to stage what they then would claim to be the official completion of their 1924 session. Initially naming themselves the "Old Constitutional Washington District Association," delegates from fourteen fellowships met at Mount Olive Church in Tazewell County, Virginia, and elected Elder E. M. Evans as their moderator. Two years later, the Old Constitutional Washington District of Primitive Baptist changed its name to the Regular Primitive Baptist Washington District Association, arguing in the process that it was the "true vine" of the original association.

Split Aftershocks

As is typical in Old-Time Baptist eruptions of this sort, the "Heller" side of this split was slow to accept the fact that it had lost almost half of its churches and a similar proportion of its total individual members. Demands were made that the Universalists vacate church buildings, and threats of legal action were issued in an attempt to prevent the Universalists from assuming any part of the Washington District Association name. In addition, notice was given that the Universalist leaders were in "disorder" and should not be allowed in the stand of any church or association with which the "Heller" side still corresponded:

> Resolved that we publish to all whom it may concern that the following elders are preaching in disorder and that we have withdrawn our fellowship from them. They are not preaching under our patronage, to-wit: Elders T. Grimsley, E. M. Evans, J. J. Childress, H. C. Mullins, John Hawkins, Columbus Owens, R. Honaker, T. H. McGlothlin, John Sizemore, Tyra McFaddin, and that a copy of this be furnished The Lone Pilgrim, and The Advocate and Messenger.[34]

Elders Grimsley, Evans, and Childress already have been identified. Mullins (spelled Mullens in the 1924 Old Constitutional Washington District Minutes) was a minister at Hale Creek. "Hawkins" appears to have been a misprint, since no individual of this name shows up in the Universalist records. This probably was John Hankins, the elder at Salem Church who had had the doctrinal dispute with Elder T. W. Osborne; although, strangely enough, John Hankins is listed in the 1925 "Heller" side minutes as the lone delegate from Salem Church. In 1926, that listing changed to R. J. Hankins, one of the Salem members expelled with Osborne in 1922. In the meanwhile, John Hankins was being recorded in the Universalist side minutes as a loyal minister of that camp.

Elder Columbus Owens was a PBU minister at Sumac Grove Church, while Elder Honaker was an elder affiliated with Spruce Pine Grove

Church. Sizemore and McGlothlin both were with the Jerusalem fellowship, but McFaddin does not appear at all in the Universalist side's 1924 minutes as one of that camp's ministers. However, McFaddin was listed in the 1921 Washington District minutes as being an elder from Vicy, Virginia.[35]

In 1926, the "Heller" side stepped up its efforts to acquire full ownership of the Washington District name:

> Resolved, that in answer to the queries and requests from New Garden, Harmony, Miller View and the Salem churches in regard to the people who were excluded from us for the heresies of Universalism, . . . those people having organized and using part of our name and our date of organization, we say that they are a fraud and an imposition on the public, being unconstitutionally organized. We therefore appoint Elders Wm. B. Sutherland, A. R. Singleton, J. J. Counts and Elder J. T. Stinson a committee to ask them to desist from the further use of any part of our name, and that said committee report to us what they have done at our next association.[36]

Since a majority of the members of New Garden and Salem, along with twenty-six members of the original Harmony congregation, were then affiliated with the Universalists, these queries and requests came from those portions of the pre-1924 fellowships that now had aligned themselves with the "Heller" side. When a split such as this occurs, individual members often find themselves stripped of the church facility they previously thought was theirs, and a legal battle develops, not only over the association name but also over church properties. The alignment of trustees and fellowship majorities becomes critical in this process, along with the question of who actually owns the church structure and property (occasionally a private individual or family). Harmony's meetinghouse went to the "Hellers," while the meetinghouses of New Garden and Salem went to the Universalists.

Elder Sutherland and the other members of the committee mentioned above performed their delegated assignment, but their efforts were not productive: "The committee appointed last year to see those heretics who are using part of our name, reported that they had prepared a notice to them and have not received any answer from them. It was agreed that the matter be referred to our next association, and that the committee . . . report the same to our next association."[37]

By September 1928, the Sutherland committee still had received no response, and that year the association authorized these men to remain active in their efforts "indefinitely." The 1929 association meeting time then came and went with no additional mention of the matter. Not until 1932 did the "Heller" side abandon the entire issue, through its thousand-word resolution summing up that camp's entire argument concerning the split, including its answer to the constitutionality question. In short, this resolution asserted that, as "heretics," the Universalists had no rights at all in the 1924 session; and that, following that session, they had acted as usurpers of the association's name and properties, "in many instances securing the appointment of church trustees of their own faith by gross and willful misrepresentations to the courts."[38]

This was a bitter statement that seemed to close officially the various events of a bitter split. A year before, however, the Universalist side had met at Slate Creek Church in Buchanan County, Virginia, for what it claimed was the 120th annual session of the "Washington Regular Primitive Baptist Association," that year reporting the aforementioned 728 members in sixteen churches. At Slate Creek, the gathered crowd heard Elder E. M. Evans present a lengthy circular letter in which he explicated the PBU positions on sin, death, hell, atonement, and salvation, explications that will be examined in detail in the next chapter.[39]

The Other Associations

During these critical years, the PBU movement by no means was restricted to the Washington District Association. This study focuses on that PBU setting simply because the Washington split became the one event that clearly demarcated the "Heller" and "No-Heller" camps. It was the Washington split that created a clearly defined Primitive Baptist Universalist faith. Nevertheless, it should always be remembered that PBU advocates claim a continuous chain of Primitive Baptist Universalist doctrine and kinship from Adam and Eve to the present moment.

As for the other associations that aligned themselves with this PBU doctrine, Washington District first denounced Three Forks of Powell's River and Stony Creek:

> Resolved that whereas, it is commonly reported that ministers of the Three Forks and Stony Creek associations are preaching Universalism and sowing the seed of discord among our brethren, and as we have twice

before admonished and protested against this heresy we therefore ask you to take some steps to have them cease preaching these heresies, for it is sorely distressing and grieving us.[40]

This resolution was quickly followed in 1925, as the Washington "Heller" side took action to withdraw formally from its "correspondence and fellowship" with both Three Forks and Stony Creek.[41] E. J. Sutherland reported that this severing of correspondence with Stony Creek was a particularly sad step, since that association had been Washington's "first offspring."[42] Washington District, however, continued its recognition of and fellowship with the Elkhorn group of churches, despite the fact that Elder Evans had come from that cluster of congregations. Apparently Elkhorn's fellowships were divided concerning which way that association would go; but, by 1931, when Evans delivered his circular letter, Elkhorn had a contingency of congregations firmly connected to the other Universalist associations.

Stony Creek Association officially remained a PBU cluster of fellowships until the organization's demise in 1949, as a result of yet another split (covered in chapter 4). In this 1949 case, however, the controversy did not center on Universalism. Instead, the key question was the nature of that which was resurrected—the physical body or only the spiritual body? Universalists have not always agreed on this issue, but Elder Farley Beavers argues that in 1995 PBU elders believe that the entire physical body, though changed, is resurrected.[43]

Closing Comments

In many ways, the Washington District split is representative of the multitude of divisions that have occurred in Old-Time Baptist associations of Central Appalachia. In two ways, however, it does not conform to the usual pattern: the split did not derive from a struggle between two or more parties warring for the moderator position; and it did not arise from a competition between two powerful churches, each striving for dominance in the association. In 1924, Elder William Sutherland's role as leader of Washington District went unchallenged. He was experienced, apparently well loved, and at an age that usually guarantees respect within Old-Time Baptist circles. In addition, up to this point he had been successful in unifying the association.

Nor were two churches squared off against each other, with a long history of animosities and intrigues. Both the "Heller" and the "No-Heller" doctrines were distributed throughout the association, as is suggested by two facts: (1) after the split, there was considerable movement of members from church to church, as the process of settling into camps became finalized; and (2) the split ended up being a relatively even one, close to a fifty-fifty division.

In fact, the confrontation that occurred was almost as pure a doctrinal dispute as one could imagine. Two very different theologies existed within the same association, and it could not be expected that such a difference would be tolerated forever. Indeed, there appeared to be almost no common ground between the Universalism of the Grimsley-Evans side and the traditional Calvinistic doctrines of the Sutherland side, making that long period of coexistence seem even more surprising. Nevertheless, had it not been for some bitter words spoken at Salem Church, who knows how long this coexistence of strange bedfellows might have continued? Perhaps at that point, Moderator Sutherland began to realize that he might not be able to harmonize the divergence of thought that had developed within his association.

4 "SALVATION FOR ALL"

The Stoney (spelled with an "e") Creek Primitive Baptist meetinghouse, lying just off Highway 91 in Carter County, Tennessee, rests beside Carter Branch, one of the many narrow streams that flow from the south side of Holston Mountain into Stony Creek (spelled without the "e"). This structure is smaller than the usual PBU facility; when filled to capacity, it holds approximately seventy-five celebrants. The building is another of those starkly simple wood-framed houses of worship that Old-Time Baptists cherish so profoundly. It is especially loved by the ten Primitive Baptist Universalists who hold their memberships with this fellowship, an affiliate of the Regular Primitive Baptist Washington District Association, the PBU organization whose beginning was detailed in the last chapter.

Constructed sometime in the 1930s, as the successor to two earlier structures, the Stoney Creek meetinghouse has been renovated a number of times. The exterior, however, has maintained its original image of simplicity, functionality, unpretentiousness, and anonymity. There is only one small, hard-to-see sign, which is nailed above the front entrance to the church and which becomes readable only upon close approach to the building. This refusal to proclaim a church's identity has always suggested to me a message that might read something like the following: "If you find us, it is because you are already among us, or because some unseen guide is leading you to our door. We will not shout out our presence; we will not entice you to visit; but if you find your way to us, we will make you welcome."

To find your way to Stoney Creek Church, you will need to drive northwest from Elizabethton on Highway 91, travel approximately twelve and a half miles to the Carter community, and then watch for Carter Branch Road, which will run at right angles into Highway 91 on your left. Turn left there, and about five hundred yards more of roadway will lead you directly to the front of the Stoney Creek meetinghouse.

The plot of land surrounding the meetinghouse contains all the features traditional in such Old-Time Baptist environments: large and usually aged shade trees; a creek nearby for "living water" baptisms; one moderately spacious opening to facilitate dinners on the grounds; additional areas—tucked all around the church—for parking; and the outhouses, which fellowships seldom remove even after more modern facilities have been provided inside the church.

Stoney Creek Church meetinghouse, Carter County, Tenn., summer 1994.

At Stoney Creek, tables are set up for dinner-on-the-grounds under a row of shade trees that lines the banks of Carter Branch, a bubbling stream that adds much to the sense of traditionalism hovering about this place. This line of trees provides a cool and inviting atmosphere for these after-service meals that are so tied to past and place. Old benches are brought out from somewhere, and a few people bring their own folding chairs or even a rare collapsible picnic table. Old-Time Baptists take pride in the informality of dinner-on-the-grounds and stand ready to adjust to any circumstance that may arise.

Stoney Creek's interior gives evidence—as do most of these PBU meetinghouses—of its membership's considerable sacrifice to make the worship space modern, attractive, and comfortable, but the result has been a loss of those older architectural features which most students of traditionalism would like to see preserved. Tongue-and-groove planking once covered both the walls and ceiling; that rich, dark, and poorly insulated interior now has been overlaid with drywall plasterboards, sealed and painted. The bottom third of the enclosure has been covered with an inexpensive wood wainscoting. Cushioned pads make the aging plank benches more comfortable; carpet covers the original hardwood flooring, adding supplementary insulation.

Apparently the old tongue-and-groove planking reached up to the pinnacle of the inner roof line; today a dropped ceiling makes the structure easier to heat in the wintertime. That heat once was supplied by a free-standing wood stove, but two sets of electric thermal coils have been installed beneath grates in the floor of the center aisle, and the warmth from these units is augmented by a baseboard heater running behind the center pews in the stand area. New window units and venetian blinds also help to keep out both heat and cold. One of the days on which I visited this PBU fellowship was a cold, rainy Sunday in April 1995. The thirty-eight members and visitors who composed that morning's congregation were snugly protected from an early spring Appalachian morning that was bone-chilling in its dampness. Indeed, the protection was so complete that, midway through the service, all of the heating units had to be turned off. In addition, the fervor of the morning's worship resulted in even jackets being discarded.

As suggested above, purists bemoan such modern renovations of these old church structures, and, when I am placing tradition above people, I tend to think that way, too. Appalachian congregations, however, appreciate the labor savings afforded by such modern touches, including the vinyl siding on the exterior; and they insist on the right to make their sanctuaries as comfortable as the those of mainline churches. At Stoney Creek, however, the renovations have not destroyed the atmosphere of plainness that is so well suited to the old-time ways of PBU worship. The plank benches are still there; the standard configuration of the worship space has been preserved; and the colors of all interior elements remain simple, muted, and unpretentious—natural wood tones, subdued earth shades, and off-white.

This Stoney Creek Church was organized in 1820 in Carter County, Tennessee, arming off the Sinking Creek Church, soon to be discussed.[1] Nineteen years earlier, another Stony Creek Church (this time spelled without the "e") had been organized in Scott County, Virginia; and during the initial phase of my study of the history of the PBU movement, I kept getting these two mixed up. The Virginia Stony Creek Church was a member of the now-defunct Stony Creek Association, mentioned at the close of chapter 3 as one of the other associations that joined the PBU movement soon after the 1924 Washington Association split. Like the Stony Creek Association, its namesake church is no longer extant. A building still stands, but it has long since become the home of another religious group. The Carter County church, on the other hand, though small in membership, remains as a vital unit of the Washington Association.

Chapter 5 examines in some detail the circumstances that may have led to the introduction of Universalist doctrine in the East Tennessee region. For now, suffice it to say that Hale Creek in Buchanan County, Virginia, probably was not the point of origin for PBU theology. Instead, it seems more likely that the East Tennessee counties of Washington, Sullivan, and Carter may have constituted the seedbed of this interesting subdivision of Primitive Baptist thinking. Therefore, it seems appropriate that Stoney Creek Church preface the following brief discussion of Baptist beginnings in northeastern Tennessee. An understanding of those beginnings should render more meaningful the later discussion, in chapter 5, of the emergence of Universalism in Washington County, Tennessee.

ARRIVAL OF BAPTISTS IN THE AREA THAT IS NOW EAST TENNESSEE

Johnson City, Tennessee, the largest municipality in Washington County, and Elizabethton, Tennessee, seat of Carter County, sit in an elongated mountain basin that serves as the meeting place of three ridge-draining waterways—the Watauga River, the Doe River, and Stony Creek. The widest and longest of these streams, the Watauga, approaches Elizabethton from the east, twisting its way down from headwaters in North Carolina and flowing through the Tennessee Valley Authority's artificially created Watauga Lake, before squeezing in succession past the gates of Watauga Dam and Wilbur Dam, both lying at the southwestern end of Iron Mountain. Arching around the north side of Elizabethton, the Watauga River then meanders on a predominantly northwestward course past Johnson City, until it merges—in Boone Lake—with the flows of the South Fork of the Holston River. These mingled North Carolina, Virginia, and Tennessee waters then spill through the controls of yet another TVA dam, Boone Dam. The once turbulent and untrammeled streams of East Tennessee now serve the region's needs for flood control, hydroelectric power, recreational lakes, commercial marinas, and lakeside homes; but in the process, the streams have become a "far cry" from the wild waterways the Cherokee knew.

Doe River approaches Elizabethton from the south, having gathered its watery flow from tributary streams on the north side of Roan Mountain and from a network of branches that feed Laurel Fork, as the latter drains the tight little valley between White Rocks Mountain and Pond Mountain. Finally, Stony Creek rushes into this basin from the northeast, maneuvering between Holston Mountain on the north and Iron Mountain on the south. Iron Mountain is the higher of these two ridges and provides a part of the lengthy Appalachian Trail. As noted earlier, it is into this third stream, Stony Creek, that Carter Branch flows, close to the spot where Stoney Creek Church sits.

Settlers coming into this particular "western frontier" sector during the last quarter of the eighteenth century would have connected, for the most part, with the Holston River gateway, after having arrived in southwestern Virginia via the Shenandoah or James River corridors. A few, however, cut directly across from North Carolina, following the twisting course of the Watauga River and settling lower elevations that lay between the Holston and the Nolichucky rivers. Both routes funneled early Baptists into the region. The Shenandoah and the James River routes evidently brought to the region Regular Baptists who were connected to either the Philadelphia or the Ketocton Association, and the North Carolina and southern Virginia currents of migration apparently contained some Separate Baptists with ties to the Sandy Creek Association.[2] Indeed, the Battle of Alamance in 1771, before the Revolutionary War, and the subsequent defeat of the North Carolina Regulators, set quite a number of Separate Baptists moving westward toward East Tennessee.[3]

By the mid-1770s, Baptists had begun to cluster in what are now Washington and Carter counties in Tennessee, and the first two Baptist churches of the area had been organized. Sinking Creek Church was established in Carter County between present-day Johnson City and Elizabethton; and the Buffalo Ridge Church was first established eight miles north of present-day Jonesboro, in Washington County.[4] Although controversy exists concerning which of these two is the older, both O. W. Taylor, in his *Early Tennessee Baptists,* and Frank Merritt, in his *Early History of Carter County, 1760–1861,* present convincing arguments that this title should go to Sinking Creek.[5] Apparently Sinking Creek Church was first established in 1775, while Buffalo Ridge Church followed in 1779. Buffalo Ridge's founding members evidently came directly out of the Sandy Creek Association and thus were Separate Baptists.[6] In contrast, the Sinking Creek fellowship members were decidedly Regular Baptist in their leanings, even though that church lay closer to the Watauga River corridor that routed some Separates into the region.[7]

As indicated in chapter 1, when the Holston Association was instituted in 1786, this action had the effect of merging many of the Separates and Regulars of southwestern Virginia and northeastern Tennessee, with the Separates apparently being in the majority.[8] That Separate majority, however, did not preclude Holston's adoption of the Philadelphia Confession, with certain interpretative concessions made to that majority.[9] The result was a union of Baptists who agreed to disagree concerning the absolutes of Regular atonement doctrine.

It should be noted, however, that the period from the 1770s through the first two decades of the nineteenth century was a relatively peaceful one for Central Appalachian Baptists. The mood definitely was one of union rather than separation, in part because the frontier environment encouraged Baptists to find religious kinship wherever and whenever they could. In addition, during much of this time, an exhilaration and a growing sense of freedom and importance appears to have existed among this denomination. For these Baptists, life on the frontier often differed greatly from life in the former colonies, where persecution and ridicule frequently had been their lot, especially in Virginia.[10] The year the Holston Association was organized, 1786, was also the year that saw the signing of Virginia's bill to establish religious freedom, finally giving the Baptists of that state the liberties vital to their more rapid organization and growth.

That new law, coupled with the revivalistic enthusiasm that began to emerge in Virginia as early as 1783[11] and which had spread to the Cumberland Mountains by the close of the century,[12] significantly increased the number of Baptists who joined the steady flow of early-nineteenth-century westward migration.

By 1811, the original seven-church Holston Association had grown into a twenty-one-church alliance and had become spread over an expansive mountainous region of eastern Tennessee and southwestern Virginia. As this territory was largely devoid of wagon roads or even horse and mule trails, the association had trouble bringing its churches together for union meetings or even for annual association sessions. The former were devised as a method of maintaining both vitality in worship and consistency in doctrine and practice; and the latter, of course, were organized to conduct the business of the association. To ease the difficulties encountered in staging these coming-together events, Holston instituted an amicable division within its ranks, separating off seven congregations that drew their memberships from settlements along the Virginia sides of the three forks of Holston River.[13] In 1812, this divided-off cluster of fellowships assumed the name "Washington Association of Baptists," officially becoming the organization featured in chapter 3. Like its mother association, the new alliance organized itself as part of the Regular Baptist tradition, again accepting the Philadelphia Confession. All previous Separate influences appear to have been forgotten.[14]

By 1812, the heated controversy that would produce the missionary-antimissionary split had not yet materialized, so the first decade of Washington Association's existence was one of relative unity and peace. At the turn of the century, the Great Western Revival had swelled and then subsided; but, as noted in chapter 1, it had multiplied the number of western frontier Baptists of Virginia, Tennessee, and Kentucky and left them relatively unified.[15] The old division between the Regulars and the Separates ceased to be a problem, and among the Baptists, peace prevailed across most of Central Appalachia until the beginning of the third decade of the century. Then the missionary-antimissionary controversy shattered that harmony.

Two years after Washington Association was founded, the Baptists of Virginia instituted a "Foreign Mission Society," which was to exist independently of the Virginia General Baptist Association and with which individual associations could affiliate or not, as they chose. The year 1816 saw the Washington cluster of fellowships agreeing to "correspond" with this missionary society, but by 1821 that position had been reversed, clearly consigning the Washington Association to the "Old School" Baptist course it soon was to follow.[16]

Although the Washington District Association ceased cooperating with the Virginia Foreign Mission Society in 1821, it remained in correspondence with the pro-mission General Baptist Association of Virginia until 1845. At that time, the antimissionary elements in Washington District had achieved a majority status sufficient for the accomplishment of four goals: to elect a new moderator, one favorable to the antimissionary cause; to drive away four fellowships that had been supportive of the pro-mission side; to break allegiance to the General Association; and to sever correspondence with the Washington District Association's pro-mission mother, the Holston Association.[17] Thus, by 1845, the Washington District had become firmly fixed as part of that segment of Baptists who would constitute the "Old School" or "Primitive" movement.

Six years after Washington District's missionary-antimissionary split, the association responded to its burgeoning growth—and to its continuing problems in traveling between churches—by arming off nine fellowships to form the Stony Creek Association. These churches lay in Lee, Russell, and Scott counties, Virginia, and in areas of the state that later were to become Wise and Dickenson counties. Thus, in 1851, another association came into being that—at least from 1924 until its demise in 1949—would figure prominently in the PBU movement. Indeed, as this chapter will demonstrate, it was the Stony Creek Association that supplied—through a publication of its clerk, Charles F. Nickels—the most significant written version of PBU theology.

Today only two of the Stony Creek Association churches remain in the PBU camp: Holston Church, previously mentioned as lying on the western side of Cherokee Lake in Grainger County, Tennessee; and Point Truth Church, lying southeast of Dungannon in Scott County, Virginia. Both of these fellowships severed their affiliations with the Stony Creek Association in the 1940s—Holston in 1945 and Point Truth in 1949. As indicated earlier, at issue was the nature of the resurrected body: Would that body be purely spiritual, or would it be a natural body, even if returned to some earlier condition of physical health?[18]

The issue brought considerable discord to the Stony Creek Association throughout the early 1940s, and, by the 1945 annual session, the "spiritual body" side of the division had gained control of the association. Thus, "natural body" Holston Church and Point Truth Church eventually were driven to request affiliation with Three Forks of Powell's River Association. As mentioned above, those requests were granted in 1945 and 1949, respectively. Then, in 1946, Three Forks of Powell's River severed all correspondence with the Stony Creek Association.[19]

The other two PBU associations, Washington and Elkhorn, also terminated their correspondence with the Stony Creek Association, and the latter, after 1949, fell into complete disarray and ceased functioning. Suffice it to say that, following that year, this particular cluster of Old-Time Baptist fellowships—except for the two churches that had withdrawn and affiliated with Three Forks—no longer could be counted in the PBU ranks. Nevertheless, the Stony Creek Association, Point Truth Church, and the latter's longtime clerk, Brother Charles F. Nickels, must be counted as critical elements in the PBU story. Nickels, as already stated, contributed the only reasonably complete, published exposition of PBU theology, a nineteen-page essay entitled "The Salvation of All Mankind."

Published as the title piece in a larger seven-essay booklet—only two of the contributions were authored by Nickels—"Salvation of All Mankind" became Charles F. Nickel's definitive statement concerning his universal-atonement faith. The second Nickels essay, "A Bequest to Old School Baptists," constituted a limited will and testament in which this man spelled out in detail how a violin that he purchased in 1905—and which he evidently believed was of substantial value—was to be passed down through his family for four hundred years before being sold. The proceeds then were to be contributed to those "Old School Baptists" who at that time still adhered to his theological positions—presumably the Point Truth Church of that date, the year 2337.[20] The sad thing about this "bequest" is that Nickels had nine children (two of whom preceded their father in death), and, at his demise, his personal, business, and religious possessions quickly became scattered, with the result that present descendants have no idea what happened to the violin. Curious as to what he might have read from the works of eighteenth- and nineteenth-century Universalists, especially the writings of Hosea Ballou, I tried to track down Nickels's library, but that effort was in vain. This "bequest" story, however, is not the only feature that makes Charles F. Nickels an intriguing element in the PBU saga.

Born on December 26, 1881, Charles F. Nickels lived all of his sixty-eight years in the region of his birth, making his greatest contribution to Scott County, Virginia, as a professional photographer. In Nickelsville, Virginia, he operated a commercial photography business which he named

"The Rural Studio," capturing on those old turn-of-the-century glass plates a wide-ranging collection of southwestern Virginia personae.[21] A self-educated man, Nickels developed a number of intellectual interests, including Primitive Baptist theology; and his writing skills made him a "natural" as a clerk, not only of the Point Truth Church but also of the Stony Creek Association. He never, however, professed a "call" to preach, and all of the Stony Creek Association session records and the Point Truth Church minutes refer to him only as "Brother Nickels" and never as "Elder Nickels," this despite the fact that his publication places "Elder" before his name.

The lack of the latter title must have limited his influence at both the church and association levels, even though his writings suggest that he would have been well qualified to engage in any doctrinal discourse of the moment. In Old-Time Baptist hierarchies, however, there has always been a wide gap between the world of the ordained elder and that of the ordinary church brother, the former being not only "called" to preach but

Headstone for graves of Charles F. Nickels and his wife, Loula V. Nickels, at Point Truth Cemetery, near Nickelsville, Virginia, summer 1995.

"blessed" to do so, suggesting at least the possibility that God speaks through an elder. Such assumptions give to the voice of the "elder" an authority not generally assigned to the voice of the "brother," especially on matters of doctrine.

There is some evidence that Nickels experienced the frustrations of such restrictions upon his influence when, during the Stony Creek Association's debates over resurrection of the body versus resurrection of the spirit, he tried to play a role as keeper of the peace. On July 1, 1946, in expectation of a heated association session for that year, he wrote the following letter to Stony Creek affiliated churches and sent copies to the other three PBU associations:

> To the Churches of our membership and all the Associations with which we correspond when assembled with the church at Stony Creek in Carter County, Tenn. On August 16, 1946:
>
> Dear Brethren: I have been going in and out among you for many years, being devoted to the Old School Baptists since my earliest recollections, even before I had lawful fellowship with the church. When I first came to know and meet with the Church in her solemn gatherings, there did not seem to be any strife or contention among them. . . . It seemed that they nearly all were of one mind and worshipped together in harmony, peace, and love. But in my observations, in the last fifty years, to my sorrow, I have seen a declension from the peace and fellowship that formerly existed among us. I have seen the rise and fall of many issues involving different points of Doctrine, some debated with bitterness and striving about words to no profit [and] resulting in divisions and separation of our members. Some of these questions have been reconciled then another would spring up. We are now aware, there is a vitally important question among us disturbing our peace: The Resurrection of the Dead. Which, as evidenced in our Associational gatherings last year, produced some friction and I fear unkind feelings among our Brethren, which things ought not so to be. This sublime subject has been viewed from so many angles; if we are made to agree on what the scriptures teach concerning it, I exhort you, Brethren, to be charitable and forbearing with each other. Remembering that it has not pleased our God to make us all believe the same things in the same way. . . . And I am persuaded that any difference existing between us, as in some mysterious way by the purpose of our God, and if embraced in His Will, will be reconciled in His Own time and way. . . . Now, Brethren and

Sisters all, I pray that you will do nothing of [the] fellowship that has for so long time bound us together. On this . . . incomprehensible subject, I unhesitatingly affirm, I believe in the Resurrection of the Dead. But, frankly confess, I do not know how it will be. . . . How this great change shall be accomplished, I do not have the faintest knowledge, but rejoice to know that we shall be like Jesus, and that we shall appear with Him in Glory. Brethren, I beg you to stop, look, and listen; forbear, and do not devour each other, or destroy our loving fellowship. This subject is shrouded in such deep mystery, I cannot explain it, but if the Resurrection be as you believe, when we attain it, I shall rejoice as much as you, and if it be according to my convictions, you shall rejoice as much as I. And if [it] be as neither of us believe, then it shall [be so] by the Power and the Purpose of Our God and so shall we ever be with the Lord.

Brethren, farewell: I pray that you may be brought together in meekness, forbearance, humility, and love. And that God will reveal Himself in a Manifestation of his Power and Love, put us in remembrance of Him, and enable us to observe His Commandment; that "Ye love one another," and "Let Brotherly Love Continue." Yours in affliction in Gospel Bonds,

Chas. F. Nickels[22]

After pouring his heart out in this well-meant effort, Nickels experienced the disappointment of having his letter "rejected" by the Stony Creek Association, apparently meaning that it was not even read and considered. In addition, some members of his home church, Point Truth, criticized him for having submitted the letter in the first instance, arguing that it created "confusion."

Indications are that Nickels wanted to save the Stony Creek Association from the disorder into which it eventually fell. Clearly his letter indicated his own willingness to live with the theological differences that had developed within the alliance. However, that tolerance was not shared by all of the Point Truth membership, some of whom apparently wanted the fellowship to move ahead (as Holston Church already had done) and separate from the "spiritual body resurrection" faction that had gained control of the association. Nickels, of course, lost this battle, with the consequence that Point Truth did follow Holston Church's action, but not before the 1948 death of this longtime clerk of both Point Truth and Stony Creek.

A decade before all these happenings, however, Nickels published his "Salvation of All Mankind" essay.

No publication date is provided in Nickels's booklet, *Salvation of All Mankind and Treatise on Predestination, the Resurrection of the Dead, and a Bequest*, but the date that he signed his "Bequest" was February 15, 1937, and it is likely that the larger document was printed sometime that year. Nickels may have been motivated to publish this work by early distress over the Stony Creek Association's long and destructive debate concerning natural-body versus spiritual-body resurrection, since one of the essays included in the booklet deals with that issue. "The Resurrection of the Dead," by Elder Charles M. Weaver, Illmo, Missouri,[23] argues a "resurrection of the natural body" perspective. The inclusion of this essay in Nickels's work shows that the Point Truth clerk supported the natural-body perspective, in spite of the fact he seemed to take an "undecided" position in his 1946 letter to the Stony Creek churches.

Other essays included in the booklet—pulled from such periodicals as the *Sectarian, Signs of the Time,* the *Predestinarian Baptist,* and the *Lone Pilgrim*—suggest that Nickels believed in, or at least had a strong leaning toward, absolute predestination. This latter belief belonged to that "double predestination" theology discussed in chapter 1 as identified with what Elder Robert Webb calls the Group II division of Primitive Baptists.

Included in the booklet were, for example, "Predestination and Obedience," by Elder W. I. Carnell; "Absolute Predestination," by Elder S. M. Smoot; and "Absolute Predestination of All Things," by Elder Gilbert Beebe. Along with Charles W. Weaver, Carnell became a controversial figure among midwestern Primitive Baptists during the first couple of decades of the twentieth century. Weaver and Carnell founded the *Predestinarian Baptist,* but their theological interests ranged far beyond the mere issue of predestination. Allegedly they promoted a doctrine suggesting that "after the resurrection the wicked would be entirely destroyed—annihilated."[24] It appears, therefore, that Weaver and Carnell could have been called "No-Hellers," in the sense that no such place would be needed to house the wicked for eternity, as they would have been totally exterminated after the Resurrection. Such a doctrine, of course, is far removed from the PBU theology treated in this book.

Upon acquiring Charles F. Nickels's booklet, I assumed that these other contributors—Weaver, Carnell, Smoot, and Beebe—must have been Primitive Baptist Universalists, too. The possibility existed, then, that PBU elements might be found in the Midwest, where all but Smoot (a Virginian) had operated. That thought provided part of the motivation for my summer 1994 visit with Elder Robert Webb at his Primitive Baptist Library in Carthage, Illinois. Elder Webb helped me track down information on Weaver, Carnell, Smoot, and Beebe, and then he allowed me access to what has become one of the largest collections of minutes of Primitive Baptist associations, particularly in the Midwest. At the beginning of that search, Elder Webb expressed doubt that I would locate any evidence that Universalism influenced any Primitive association outside Appalachia, and so far he has been correct.

A More Detailed Look at the Ten Tenets of PBU Theology

Nickels's small essay now will become very important to my discussion, since the extant published material on PBU doctrine is so limited: the Nickels piece, two circular letters composed by Elder E. M. Evans, several other less helpful circular letters, and the sketchy materials that have been included in the minutes of both sides of the 1924 split between "Hellers" and "No-Hellers." This small body of printed works has been augmented by the oral explications of PBU doctrines garnered in three years of discussions with contemporary PBU elders. While these elders have not always been in total agreement, a general consensus seems to exist concerning the ten statements about to be explored. In some instances I shall be forced to report variances, ambiguities, or simply blank spaces in the exegeses of doctrine. Contemporary PBU elders appear not to be greatly disturbed or highly defensive concerning these inconsistencies or unknowns, however, for they believe that the inconsistencies simply reflect humanity's limitations when it comes to expressing God's truths ("This is only what God has allowed me to understand") and that the unknowns signify nothing more than the presence of the unrevealed.

One important point to keep in mind during the discussions that follow is that PBU theologians are not biblical literalists. The movement readily accepts the thesis that much of Scripture speaks in parables, is prophetically abstract, or is subject to interpretations tied to historical settings and understandings. Given that starting point, PBU elders are able, with ease, to make such Scriptural accounts as the Lazarus story and the "lake of fire" language of Revelations 19:20 mesh with their "no hell in the afterlife" creeds.

1. Because of Adamic sin, all humankind is inherently sinful; therefore, sinfulness is a standard characteristic of "natural man."

There seems to be nothing unusual in this first PBU premise. It captures the traditional understanding of the doctrine of "original sin," which argues that no member of the human family escapes this condition, even the members of "the elect." "The elect" are those individuals chosen "before the beginning of time" to constitute "The Church."[25] Furthermore, since human nature is axiomatically corrupt, we have a logical explanation for all the imperfections of human society.

Concerning the "original sin" nature of even the elect, there is some disagreement among the Appalachian Old-Time Baptists. Many elders—including a majority of PBU preachers—argue that the propensity to be sinful prevails in all of humankind; while others assert that if a church member falls into corruption, then that circumstance serves only to prove that the individual in question was not elected. In his 1931 circular letter to the Washington Regular Primitive Baptist Association, Elder E. M. Evans suggested that he saw *all* humankind—the progeny of Adam—as innately sinful. Evans explained the consequences of Adam's "fall" in this manner:

To my mind it is figurative, where the word garden appears, which means an inclosure of God's protection around the man as long as he stands in obedience of His law, but as soon as he violated the law, the Lord God turned him out of the garden. And now, lest he put forth his hand and independently eat of the tree of life and live forever, the Lord has turned him out of his favor, which means the garden. For it cannot be denied, before he violated the law, he could walk and talk with God, and was in fellowship with God. Doubtless the essence and love of His Spirit shone on him. But the very day he violated the law, and was beguiled by the serpent, his nature became corrupted, and he became a slave to the power and works of the flesh, which led him to a deathly state from the fellowship and love and smiles of his Creator.[26]

2. Satan is nothing more than natural man, warring with "spiritual man," and thus will have no existence beyond the temporal world.

"Satan" has been an inconsistent metaphor in both Christian theology and western literary invention, "his" depiction ranging from an incredibly awesome power for evil (a force equal with God, who commands the universe's dark side, rules over his own dominion of lesser devils, and manages that allegedly eternal underworld of fire and brimstone, where all sinners ultimately go) to a rather impish and "wimpy" little devil whose artifice in seduction is easily recognized and just as easily thwarted, particularly by the pure and innocent, no matter how limited they may be in maturity, intelligence, learning, or sophistication. Nevertheless, Christian thinking usually has made Satan an everlasting figure, operating in the temporal world to tempt and beguile, and serving in the afterlife as an administrator of earned punishment. Indeed, the imagery of Satan and hell frequently emerges as an element essential to universal justice: without the two, contrasted with God and heaven, there would not exist a balance of retribution and reward. According to such thinking, Satan and hell are just as important in explaining and responding to evil, as God and heaven seem crucial to explaining and responding to good. Furthermore, traditional interpretations of hell and Satan assert that they are eternal; were rewards to be eternal and retributions not, says this thinking, then the entire system of justice would be thrown out of symmetry, and the motivation for righteousness would be lost.

Nothing within the paragraph above, however, relates to PBU doctrine, which completely removes hell in the afterlife from the formula. Nickels, for example, argued that it would be an amazingly insensitive and unjust God who would first assign to all humans a wholly corrupt nature, and then condemn any or all of these humans to eternal punishment in hell for exhibiting behaviors arising from that assigned nature:

> In my survey and meditation on the theory of hellfire and damnation, or a living, conscious, Eternal punishment after death, for any of the creatures of His Powerful Hand, I find that it is not compatible with the Holy Nature of the High and Lofty One that inhabiteth Eternity. And if true, would bar, and exclude Him from the Divine Attributes of Love, Justice, and Mercy with which He is so magnanimously endowed. God is Love. We cannot conceive of Him violating all the Holy faculties of His Person, by consigning any part of His helpless creation to interminable torture. It would rob Him of Justice, since man was created without any choice, or will in the matter, and violated the Divine Law by reason of the evil propensities of the nature given him. It would also bar Him from extending Mercy to his poor helpless fallen creatures. "For all have sinned, and come short of the Glory of God." But thanks

be to His Holy Name, the transgression of His creature, man, only brought death on the human family, and not Eternal punishment.[27]

We shall return to Nickel's argument in chapter 5, which examines some of the American antecedents of the PBU movement, for this "nature given him" and "justice" rationale had an earlier life, in the writings of Hosea Ballou.[28] For now, however, let us continue to explore the image of Satan in PBU doctrine, asking the following questions: If hell is not to be a feature of eternity, does that mean that Satan is to play only a temporal role? If so, what role is that to be? Indeed, who or what is Satan?

Neither Nickels nor Evans addressed these issues in the published writings uncovered in this study, but contemporary PBU elders provide what appear to be an internally consistent set of three responses, which have been extracted from their discussions of Satan: (1) Satan is not a being, but a nature, the corrupted temperament of natural man. (2) This nature is ultimately under the control of God, since it is a creation of God. Nevertheless, (3) Satan (humankind's natural state) will continue to determine much of human experience until Resurrection, when all consequences of Adamic sin will be terminated.[29]

Concerning the first of these three statements, Elder Farley Beavers is fond of quoting the comic-strip character, Pogo, when talking about Satan: "We have met the enemy, and he is us."[30] Thus he simply asserts that all the evils we have traditionally assigned to Satan should be attributed to our own basic inner nature, a nature that PBU doctrine views as "fallen." Concerning the second statement above, Elder Landon Colley argues succinctly: "There was only one creator; therefore, anything that exists must have been created by Him."[31] Supporting the third statement, Elder Lewis Hill remarked, "After Resurrection, that old fellow is totally out of the picture."[32]

3. In addition to the creation of "sinfulness" (the given nature of natural man), this Adamic transgression also instituted "punishment" (the "general judgment" hell of the temporal world, the torment of absence from God's blessing that sin generates) and "death" (humankind's ultimate punishment for Adamic sin).

While addressing Christ's atonement for *all* of the sins of *all* humankind, Nickels made it clear that a system of punishment still prevails in the temporal world:

This [universal atonement] is not a licentious doctrine, for God punishes the transgressor. For truly the way of the transgressor is hard. The Apostle was not forgetful that men would be punished here in TIME for the sins done in the body, by saying: "Be not deceived; God is not mocked: for whatsoever a man soweth, that shall he also reap."—Gal. vi, 7. But [it] is evident he reaps where he sows, and not in the world to come.[33]

Nickels also made it clear that PBU theology includes "death" among the consequences of Adamic sin: "Yet by transgression of God's Divine law, Adam brought death on all the human family."[34] However, for both Nickels and contemporary PBU elders, "death" is a dual metaphor, referring not only to literal death but also to that separation-from-God death which is the consequence of temporal-world sin.[35] The latter, declare these elders, is a condition that is greatly to be feared.

4. Humankind cannot possibly extricate itself from this state of natural sin and so requires Christ's atonement.

The Articles of Faith published annually in the minutes of the three PBU associations being examined in this book contain clear statements of this doctrine:

We believe that all mankind is in a fallen state, by reason of sin and transgressions, and consequently, is in a state of condemnation and that man cannot recover himself from that fallen state by his own free will and ability.[36]

We believe man was created upright but has ruined himself by the fallen state he is in, and it is impossible for him to recover by himself by his own free will and ability.[37]

We believe that all mankind is in a fallen state by reason of sin and transgression, and consequently, is in a state of condemnation; that man cannot recover himself from that fallen state by his own free will or ability.[38]

These statements emphasize not only that an external atonement is needed, but also that man's will and independent actions are totally inoperative in the process. The most important argument here is that humans are helpless to initiate any action in pursuit of their own regeneration, in contrast with the Arminian thesis that Christ's church is composed of persons who exercise their free will to believe and to follow.

The PBU interpretation of the articles of faith provided above contrasts sharply with the position taken by most traditional single-predestination and double-predestination Primitives. Regular Primitive Baptist Sand-Lick (today's spelling) District Association, a group of Primitive fellowships that are in correspondence with the "Heller" side of Washington District, includes in its articles of faith essentially the same clause as the one provided above: "We believe that all mankind is in a fallen state by nature, and consequently in a state of condemnation, and that man cannot recover himself from this state by his own free will and ability."[39] However, Sand-Lick churches believe in an atonement doctrine tied to the principle of the elect: only the elect are chosen for extrication from this fallen state and for reunion with God in heaven. The remainder of the human family ultimately goes to an eternal (afterlife) hell. That huge difference in beliefs leads us to an examination of the next tenet.

5. Christ's atonement was for all humankind and at Resurrection will irrevocably come to pass for all humankind; just as, irrevocably, Adam's transgression earlier had condemned all to the sinful state of natural man.

PBU doctrine belongs to what Ernest Cassara has called "Ultra-Universalism," in the sense that the theology allows no exception to the universal atonement principle. There is "no punishment whatsoever in the afterlife"; at Resurrection all humans go directly to heaven; and there will be no way to avoid this blessing, just as there was no way to avoid the curse of Adamic sin.[40] The Scriptural rallying cry becomes 1 Cor. 15:22: "For as in Adam all die, even so in Christ all shall be made alive." Furthermore, when this text is read or quoted, "all"—in both instances—is strongly underscored.

In his essay, Nickels was determined to show that "all" meant not only the elect but also the nonelect—the complete history of humankind, from Adam until the moment of Resurrection:

> Having shown that all the posterity of Adam is under sentence of death, we desire to prove by the irrefutable testimony of the Scriptures, that the same number who died because of the transgression of the first man Adam . . . shall be made alive by the last Adam, the quickening Spirit, the Lord from heaven.[41]

We now further proceed to show that Salvation is not confined to a limited number, but is innumerable in comparison as the sands of the sea, or the stars of heaven, and that embraces the WHOLE world.[42]

"And we have seen and do testify that the Father sent the Son to be the Saviour of the World."—1 John iv,14. "And He is the propitiation for our sins; and not for ours only, but also for the sins of the WHOLE WORLD."—John ii,2. The great Preacher John is here addressing his brethren, but after assuring them of the certainty of the atonement for their sins, stoutly declared it did not cease there, but included the sins of the WHOLE world, the human race.[43]

My discussions with contemporary PBU elders have strongly confirmed their acceptance of the inclusiveness of this atonement. Elder Reece Maggard stated the principle most succinctly when, at Colly Creek Church in Letcher County, Kentucky, he told me, "Nobody gets away from this one." His meaning was clear: As far as Christ's atonement is concerned, there's no choosing it or rejecting it; every human—past, present, or future—is included in this dispensation.[44]

6. However, there is an "elect," Christ's church (the established Primitive Baptist Universalists and perhaps others not known to the movement), which has been "separated from the rest of God's people here in time," chosen to be a witness for Christ and an earthly preserver of his righteousness, and "kept by the power of God through faith," never finally to fall away.

Once again the articles of faith, for the three PBU associations under examination, make clear the movement's acceptance of "election":

> We believe in the Doctrine of Election according to the foreknowledge of God, the Father, through sanctification of the spirit and belief of the Truth; and that the church was chosen in Christ before the world began, separated from the rest of God's people here in time.[45]

> We believe the Doctrine of Election according to the foreknowledge of God, the Father, through sanctification of the Spirit, and the belief of the truth. God made his choice before the world began and reaches us here in the church and not in eternity.[46]

We believe in the doctrine of election according to the foreknowledge of God, the Father, through sanctification of the Spirit and belief of the Spirit and belief of the truth; and that the church was chosen in Christ before the world began, separated from the rest of God's people here in time.[47]

The first point that must be made clear about the PBU interpretation of "election" it that the doctrine has nothing to do with the issue of who are to be the beneficiaries of Christ's atonement. That question is answered by tenet no. 5: *Everyone*. Instead, in PBU election doctrine, two other issues are being addressed: (1) What is the role or duty to which the Church is elected? (2) Does "election" carry any special benefits at all?

Nickels stated—with no apparent uncertainty—that the role to which he believed "The Church" was elected was that of witnessing: "I desire before closing this article, to notice a peculiar chosen people that were witnesses for His Name's Sake, to bear testimony to His Great and Matchless Name, in all ages, past, present, and future." In addition, he also stated pointedly who he believed "The Church" was:

This Church so faithfully represented by figures, and beautifully depicted in the prophecy of the Scriptures, and made manifest in Christ's Ministry, I verily believe to be the Old School Primitive Baptist Church of Christ. So designated in contradistinction from all orders, and institutions of earth and men. Of which I have had the happy privilege of being numbered in fellowship, and membership for many years. From my earliest memories [I] have been [an] adherent to this Precious Faith. In fact [I] was an Old School Baptist before I was born. . . . Therefore, I conclude, and am certain that my name was known of God before I was born.[48]

Elder E. M. Evans evidently envisioned a second role for the elect, that of preserving in the temporal world a certain level of godly order and righteousness. Employing the metaphor, from Psalms 127:1, of a house built by god, Evans compared the elect to that house—a house not built *for*, but built *of*, all those "sinners" who have been "killed to all" of their "worldly pleasures":

This house is built out of men and women that the Lord has selected and chosen out of the field which belongs to Him. He built it on His own premises, out of His own material, and placed every member in the house as it pleased Him, and if any man . . . undertakes to place a stick in this building, he will labor in vain. . . .

This great building, which is the Church of the Lord, rests upon the seven spirits or attributes of God. This Church is built out of believers who are baptized on profession of their faith in Christ. This house is still in building, because every time the Lord quickens or changes the heart of a poor sinner who has been killed to all his worldly pleasures, wilts as a tree cut from the stump, and falls submissive to the Great Builder, he comes as material for this house by way of floats, which is baptism, and the Lord places him in the building of his own choice, whether he is a minister or deacon, and she is a singer or prayer.[49]

At the close of the first paragraph above, Evans spoke to all Arminian or Freewill thinkers, when he threw in his "labor in vain" statement. He wanted it understood that, when it came to the concept of "election," PBU doctrine was deterministic; God has already chosen "the Church," and when Arminian evangelists attempt to "win souls" to that body, they are engaged in futile acts.

Before ending this discussion of tenet no. 6, let us focus on the "never finally fall away" thesis. This is a doctrine that is addressed clearly in all three articles of faith:

We believe that the saints are kept by the power of God through faith unto salvation, and that they never fall away.[50]

We believe the Saints will be preserved through Grace and never finally fall away.[51]

We believe that the saints are kept by the power of God through faith unto salvation.[52]

If an individual declares a call to redemption, is baptized, joins the church, and then returns permanently to a lifestyle inappropriate to a "saint," he or she usually is not spoken of as "fallen away" or as a "backslider." The judgment could be that he or she was never truly "called" in the first place. God never makes a mistake when "electing," says this argument, but humans make them all the time. Elder Farley Beavers does believe, however, that individuals can "slide so far" that their names "are removed from the Book of Life." His argument is that the "never finally fall away" principle applies to "the Church" collectively but not necessarily to the individual.[53]

7. So these elected individuals can sin, and in doing so, they suffer the hell on earth that a separation from God's blessing institutes. Probably they feel that hell more intensely than the nonelect, simply because the elect have a sharply contrasting experience for comparison.

One of the first things I was told at Delphia Church, on the day of my initial introduction to PBU doctrine, was that the elect can sink into that temporal-world hell, probably only temporarily, but in the process they suffer an intense sense of loss, having fallen out of alignment with God. PBU believers speak with considerable pain about these moments of estrangement from their deity, feeling—they say—shut off and alone, deprived of the "joy" and the "fellowship" they know they experienced in the past.

Elder Landon Colley, moderator of Washington District Association, spoke to me briefly, one Sunday afternoon, about "hell" and the PBU contention that some sinners seem so "dead" that they appear incapable of knowing that they are experiencing the state. In this conversation Colley speculated about the late Jeffrey Dahmer, a case that I suggested he explore. Was Dahmer's a situation in which "sin" became so destructive of ordinary sensibilities that the punitive value of "hell" was lost? Elder Colley seemed to have no "stamp-your-foot" answer to this query, but his one unwavering assertion was that had he (Colley) been in Dahmer's skin, he would have experienced the purest form of torment, the worst type of hell.

Elder Colley and I were sitting in the stand area of Point Truth Church, and, in that setting, it was not difficult to understand that he viewed the joy and comfort that his faith had brought him as being so essential to his present happiness that any substantial loss of that joy and comfort would constitute an unbearable hell. This is the type of pain that PBU enthusiasts have sought to conceptualize for me when they have spoken of individual periods of hell they believe they have experienced.

8. At Resurrection, however, all temporal existence will terminate, for both the dead and the still living, bringing an end to all "sin" (that given nature of humankind), to the "general judgment" (the sentence imposed upon humans for Adamic sin), to "punishment" (the hell on earth, the absence from God's blessing, that is instituted by sin), and to "death" (the ultimate punishment for Adamic sin).

There is not much to be said concerning this tenet except to note that it is consistently supported by contemporary PBU elders. It does, however, raise some interesting issues, such as the question of what has transpired with the dead in the long interim between expiration and resurrection.

The dead, asserts Elder Farley Beavers, sleep, unaware of the great passage of time between the exact moment of death and the moment of Resurrection.[54] It will be the living, says PBU doctrine, who will experience the greatest shock imaginable, the sudden termination of all temporal life forms and practices, including the cessation of all "sin."

The post-Adam temporal world will be no more, proclaims the doctrine, and all relationship between a transgression and those evils that ensued will end. Therefore, sin, punishment, and death will have no more meaning; and God will return humankind to a purified and immortal state, prepared for an eternity of fellowship with Him in heaven. "Things won't be as we have known them," said the late Elder Roy McGlothlin. "We will have our bodies, but all of the corruptions of natural man will be gone."[55]

9. At Resurrection, all humankind will go to a totally egalitarian heaven, the culmination of Christ's universal atonement.

On this tenet there may be some disagreement (or indecision) concerning the argument that heaven will have no rankings. The contention is, for example, that there will not be one level for the elect and another level for the nonelect. When Nickels treated this question, he admitted that he simply did not know the truth in this matter:

> . . . after this fleeting transitory existence in this present evil world, . . . ALL mankind will possess Eternal Life, the Life of God, and His Son Jesus Christ. (Though it has not been revealed to me whether they all will occupy the same station.) But we are assured ALL will be heirs with Christ, and be satisfied and God glorified.[56]

Evans seems not to have addressed this question, but the consensus among contemporary PBU elders appears to be that heaven will be—as far as humankind is concerned—a wholly egalitarian place, meaning that Christ's atonement was so inclusive and so complete that all of God's children—the good, bad, and otherwise—will stand on an equal footing in eternity. Elder Jennings Shortt, on the other hand, in a 1993 conversation at Little Stone Gap Church, seemed to join Nickels in saying that he simply did not know what the exact situation in heaven would be, except that everyone would be there. In a 1995 conversation with me at Jerusalem Church, Buchanan County, Virginia, Elder Farley Beavers made it clear that he believed heaven would be a wholly egalitarian place.[57]

10. Since punishment is a factor solely of the temporal world, there will be no hell after Resurrection.

This is the tenet, of course, that earned for Primitive Baptist Universalists the pejorative title "No-Hellers," and it is also the tenet which earns PBUs the most scorn from the rest of the Old-Time Baptist family—Regulars, Old Regulars, Uniteds, Group I and Group II Primitives, and the like. Finally, it is the tenet which receives the most vehement scripturally-based attacks, particularly those drawing upon the Lazarus story of Luke 16:19–31 and the "lake of fire" language of Revelations 19:20.

Evans viewed the statements in the nineteenth chapter of Revelations as being both figurative and restrictive, applicable only to the ancient prophecies concerning the Jewish nation:

> The great judgment is spoken of in Revelations 19:16–18, 20–21. . . . The language here is doubtless figurative. The wrath of God is here compared to a lake, those that were cast in had feelings, for they were cast in alive. The word brimstone refers to the added wrath that surrounds them as poured out in their guilty consciences. The sword that proceeded out of his mouth, represents his power and the influence of the spirit, that was Titus, Captain of the Roman army, and all those that fought under his banner. They were inspired by him whose sword proceeded out of the mouth of him who sat upon the horse, in the execution of this great judgment. A writer says that the blood ran for a hundred forty and four furloughs, even to the horses bridles.
> The . . . language is visionary and is a symbol yet, of that which was actual, and referred to the destruction of the Jews, which God showed He would pour out on them for their sins.[58]

Nickels dealt with the Lazarus story by including in his collection of essays an article authored by Elder Charles M. Weaver. Weaver was not, of course, a Primitive Baptist Universalist, but he did advance an interpretation of Luke 16:19–31 that can be viewed as compatible with PBU doctrine. Weaver argued, first of all, that the story was a parable and therefore was not to be taken literally. Next, the two deaths (that of the rich man and that of Lazarus) were not actual and permanent deaths, but metaphors for the two very different situations of the Jews and the Gentiles during New Testament time. Moreover, the story had "no reference to future punishment, or [to] the condition of man between death and resurrection." Finally, the rich man represented the privileged Pharisees (or the Jews), while Lazarus represented the Gentiles. "The attempt to make this an historical account of events in the lives of two literal men," concluded Weaver, "seems to break down at every point when carefully considered, and there is the best of evidence to show it is a parable given to the Pharisees."[59]

Contemporary PBU elders have offered only a few explanations of the Lazarus story, and all have been general in nature, noting that the account was a parable and could not be used as proof of an afterlife hell. A good example would be the sermon delivered by Elder Aaron Williams, a young PBU preacher from Portland, Indiana, at the Sulphur Springs meetinghouse in Wise County, Virginia, on July 16, 1995. Williams's explanation of the Lazarus narrative focused on the nature of the tale as a parable, but Williams also ventured an analysis that had Christ using the story to illustrate how a sense of remorse can place one in hell in the temporal world: The rich man knew that he had wronged Lazarus and was experiencing the "hell" derived from that sense of guilt. Neither had actually died, and no literal hell in the afterlife was being depicted.

A CLOSING COMMENT

Were I to move beyond these ten basic tenets, I would be in danger of examining doctrine concerning which I have found no PBU consensus. The astute reader, therefore, will notice that a wide variety of traditional Christian theological questions have not been addressed. The following are merely examples: the question of the Trinity, the question of millennialism (apparently not applicable to this doctrine), the question of the precise nature of morality or goodness, the question of predestination beyond the identification of the elect, the question of natural law versus spiritual law, and the question of the absolute sovereignty of God versus the free will of man.

Despite these lacunae, the ten statements examined above seem to constitute the basic bedrock for the beliefs of this faith. The doctrines are not multitudinous, and they are not intricately detailed; but it seems logical that such would be the norm in a theology that is largely oral in tradition. Furthermore, I can imagine, somewhere out there in the reading audience, a voice advising: "Don't push for great exactitude. You're apt to cause trouble. When it comes to theology, keep it simple. The more you elaborate, the more you alienate." Given the Old-Time Baptist history of painful splits, that advice appears to embody considerable common sense.

5 THE "HAPPIFYING" OF GOD

Keokee, Lee County, Virginia, is anchored to the southern face of Little Black Mountain, about two miles from the crest of the ridge that United States Geological Survey maps identify as the Tennessee Valley Divide, meaning that streams to the south of that line flow into the Powell and Clinch river system, while streams to the north flow into tributaries and forks of the Cumberland River. Until 1905, the small community of Keokee was known as Crab Orchard, but that year a coal company leased the land upon which the unincorporated village sat, and the wife of one of the company managers volunteered her name, Native American in origin, for both the town and the company. Thus was born Keokee, Virginia, and Keokee Coal and Coke Company.[1]

The asphalt of Virginia's Secondary Highway 624 moves northwestward out of Keokee, follows a switchback path that climbs up two miles—maybe three—to the top of that state-dividing ridge, where it connects with Kentucky Route 38. It then drops down towards the Clover Fork of the Cumberland River, in Harlan County. Northeast of town, Virginia Highway 606 and then Virginia Highway 68 mark another zigzag course, in this case moving toward Appalachia, Virginia. Due south of Keokee there are no paved roads, but creeks and branches flow in constantly changing directions down to the North Fork of Powell River. The latter stream has created the long and rugged valley between Little Black Mountain and Stone Mountain. Virginia Highway 610 heads southwestward out of Keokee, winding along a lower ledge of Little Black Mountain over toward Rawhide, Shepherd Hill, and Robbins Chapel.

As was indicated earlier, Keokee, Virginia, is the home of another Primitive Baptist Universalist church, Oak Grove, an affiliate of Three Forks of Powell's River Regular Primitive Baptist Association. In terms of membership (46), Oak Grove is the largest PBU fellowship of this particular cluster. The church was established in 1882 by Elder Morgan Tennessee Lipps, mentioned in chapter 1 as being buried in the Holston Church cemetery. Under Elder William M. Robinette, the moderator who served this congregation longest (1893–1934), Oak Grove became a strong leader on the Universalist side in the 1924–25 split between "Hellers" and "No-Hellers."[2]

Elder Lipps merits further attention here, not only because he has been credited as establishing several Primitive Baptist churches in East Tennessee and southwestern Virginia, but because he was the first clerk of court of Wise County, Virginia, serving in that role from July 1856 to February 1869.[3] As of 1995, Lipps's portrait still hangs in the courthouse in Wise, Virginia.

Lipps died in 1894 and thus predated the period, 1907–25, when controversy raged within Tennessee and Virginia Primitive Baptist circles over the rise of Universalism. Nor have I discovered any statement linking him to this movement. E. J. Sutherland's history of Washington Association (the "Heller" side), however, places Elder Robinette right up there with Elders Noah Adair, Samuel F. Adair, J. J. Childress, E. M. Evans, Ewell Goode, Thomas Grimsley, and John C. Smith as a leader in the 1924–25 PBU insurgency.[4] So it seems safe to assume that, under Robinette, Oak Grove Church definitely was pro-Universalism during that troubled period.

In more recent years, Oak Grove's membership has thought so well of Elder Robinette that they have preserved an old cane with which he walked. The cane hangs, along with a photograph of Robinette, on the church wall behind the stand. Another photograph on that wall depicts Elder John C. Smith. So this church is an important one for PBU heritage.

OAK GROVE MEETINGHOUSE

One can reach Keokee, Virginia, and the Oak Grove meetinghouse by traveling southwest from Appalachia, Virginia, on Highway Alternate 58, then connecting with Virginia Highway 68 and finally with Virginia

Highway 606 for that climb almost due west up to Lower Exetor, Exetor, and then Keokee. Shortly after entering the latter community, one sees a narrow lane that turns off to the left and passes between seven or eight houses before reaching a dead end in front of the church. Large oaks line this short street, providing the justification for the church's name.

The meetinghouse actually sits on the southern lip of a hill, one that falls off sharply at the rear of the structure. In all likelihood, the church once occupied this rise all by itself, but now the several homes block all view of the facility from Route 606. These homes, and their attractive oak-shaded yards, also severely restrict parking space in front of the church, forcing the congregation—especially on union meeting Sundays—to jam vehicles right up against the building, and to move them when anyone wants to exit early.

Several years ago, the Oak Grove membership covered the old building in brick veneer and apparently reroofed the structure at about the same time. Soon the tops of the two long walls began to pull outward, causing the crown of the roof to sag visibly. The problem of the outward movement was solved by two cables that stretch across the interior of the church at the base of the ceiling, tethering those walls to each other; but the sag in the roof remains, causing a short, boxy bell steeple that rests on the front point of the roof line to tilt toward the rear of the structure. The effect is not unlike some cartoonist's rendering of a church with a jauntily cocky attitude, moving forward in animated fashion. I have found myself hoping that the building is never restored to its earlier, more respectable, straight-and-narrow state. In the spirit of that imagined cartoonist, I accept this structure as a symbol of the zestful, radical character of the PBU movement, which dares to assert a conception of God that does not require any threat of eternal fire and brimstone as a means of controlling the creatures He created.

On October 2–3, 1982, Oak Grove Church staged a centennial service and marked the event by placing an engraved plaque on the wall behind the stand. There hang a number of framed photographs of past leaders, including the two already mentioned. Among other statements, the engraving records a verse from 1 Cor. 15:22, which, as the last chapter noted, has become the PBU scriptural motto: "For as in Adam all die, even so in Christ all shall be made alive."

This back wall also provides space for a large wooden placard detailing some of the history of the church, including the tenures of all of the church's moderators, beginning with Elder Lipps and ending with Elder

Roy Flanary, who has served the fellowship since 1955. Like most Old-Time Baptists, Primitive Baptist Universalists usually remain loyal to a church or association moderator, allowing that individual to stay in position until illness or death decrees otherwise, or until that person steps down of his own volition. Moderator shifts not in accord with this model typically indicate that trouble has been brewing somewhere.

As of this writing in 1995, no trouble seems to be brewing at Oak Grove Church. The Old-Time Baptist ideal of a fellowship's peace and harmony appears to prevail, and members from other PBU congregations imply, by their frequent visits, that all is well under its sassy sagging roof. Elder Roy Flanary may be a critical factor in whatever formula for PBU success is operative in this situation. A warmly hospitable man who smiles broadly and who stands ready to welcome any visitor to his church, Flanary presides over a spirit of congregational fellowship that is quite affable, affectionate, fervent, genuine, and open. Oak Grove, for example, was one of the first PBU congregations to allow me, apparently without reservation,

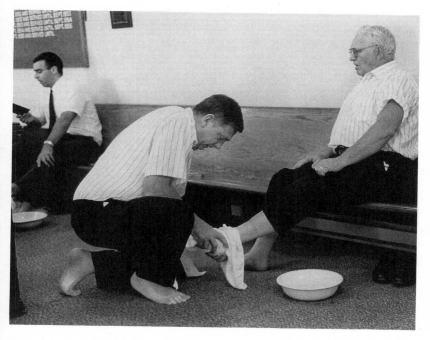

Footwashing at Oak Grove Church, Keokee, Virginia, spring 1995. Elder Keith Bowers washes the feet of Elder Roy Flanary.

to photograph their communion and footwashing services. Many Old-Time Baptist churches will not countenance such an intrusive and distracting procedure.

My observation has been that a particular moderator's personality is a factor that heavily influences the spirit of any given Old-Time Baptist church. This dynamic became obvious especially during my eight years of fieldwork among the Old Regular Baptists. In that subdenomination, certain congregations were far more tolerant of my probing investigations than others, simply because of the openness of the particular moderator. I especially remember Elder James O'Quinn, who, during those years, served as moderator of Tivis Chapel.[5] Such variations are not as sharp among PBU fellowships as they seemed to be among the Old Regulars, in part because the PBU movement is much smaller than the Old Regular phenomenon, but in part, too, because PBU doctrine has a decided effect upon how the faithful view outsiders. This issue will be discussed further in chapter 9.

Also affecting the openness of fellowships is the fact that, among the twenty-eight churches in the three PBU associations under examination, only thirteen elders, according to 1995 statistics, serve as moderators. A number of these men, then, officiate at more than one church; indeed, two elders moderate four fellowships each, one moderates three, and seven moderate two.[6] The fact that leadership is concentrated in few hands delimits the leadership styles dominant in these associations. In truth, none of the church moderators in this movement conforms to the old Appalachian stereotype of steely-eyed hostility towards the outsider. Three or four conform to the stereotype even less than the rest; Elder Flanary just happens to be one of those three or four.

As is the case with all Old-Time Baptist subdenominations, each individual church elects its own moderator, who then serves at the pleasure of the particular congregation. In turn, the moderator of an association is elected by the church delegates to the association session in question. The process, in theory, is a very democratic one, and, if all works well, it does produce church leaders who represent the wills of local church majorities. Elder Roy Flanary, then, is not supposed to *lead* the Oak Grove membership so much as *serve* it, officiating over church business meetings and worship services and in general functioning as the congregation's spiritual mentor.

Oak Grove was selected to introduce this chapter for two reasons. First, I like Keokee, the church facility, and the congregation's spirit. Second, this fellowship's ties to both Lipps and Robinette suggest a bridge between the two lives of this church, and indeed between the two lives of all the other churches within the current PBU faith. One life predated the 1924–25 split and any formal identification with Universalism, even though the theology certainly was in circulation. The second life falls under the explicit title, Primitive Baptist Universalism, with all the commitment devoted to that cause.

The remainder of this chapter attempts to suggest a third and earlier life—not of the churches, but of the basic doctrine that constitutes PBU theology. It also advances a possible explanation of Universalism's presence in Central Appalachia, a linkage between one branch of America's eighteenth- and nineteenth-century Universalist theology and the Primitive Baptist Universalist doctrines of today.

America's Universalist Antecedents to the PBU Phenomenon

Hosea Ballou (1771–1852), an early-nineteenth-century Baptist turned Universalist, decried the wrathful and vengeful image of God that he believed had affixed itself to much of New England theology:

> It is well known, and will be acknowledged by every candid person, that the human heart is capable of becoming soft, or hard; kind, or unkind; merciful, or unmerciful, by education and habit. On this principle we contend, that the infernal torments, which false religion has placed in the future world, and which ministers have, with an overflowing zeal, so constantly held up to the people, and urged with all their learning and eloquence, have tended to harden the hearts of the professors of this religion, that they have exercised, towards their fellow-creatures, a spirit of enmity, which but too well corresponds with the restless cruelty of their doctrine, and the wrath which they have imagined to exist in our heavenly father.[7]

Although Ballou was not addressing directly the rhetoric of any specific cleric, he may have had in mind one particular sermon that, during the Great Awakening, was preached by Jonathan Edwards (1703–1758). A highly respected Congregationalist cleric, theologian, and philosopher, who became—shortly before his death—president of Princeton College, later Princeton University,[8] Edwards delivered his "Sinners in the Hands of an Angry God" on July 8, 1741, in Enfield, Connecticut, as part of a Great Awakening revival. Through fierce pronouncements about sin, punishment, and the absolute wrath of God—such as those examples given below—Edwards reportedly reduced his Enfield audience to such a state of distress that they wept profusely,[9] responding quite fearfully to a rhetoric depicting divine vengeance directed at universally iniquitous humankind.[10] Inundating these audiences with the darkest assertions about human depravity and God's intolerance of such wickedness, Edwards drew a picture of a deity who to Universalists appeared totally devoid of love and compassion.

> [T]hus it is that natural men are held in the hand of God, over the pit of hell; they have deserved the fiery pit, and are already sentenced to it; and God is dreadfully provoked, his anger is as great towards them as to those who are actually suffering the executions of the fierceness of his wrath in hell . . . ; the devil is waiting for them, hell is gaping for them, the flames gather and flash about them, and would fain lay hold of them, and swallow them. . . . In short, they have no refuge, nothing to take hold of; all that preserves them every moment is the mere arbitrary will, and uncovenanted, unobliged forbearance of an incensed God. . . .
>
> The God that holds you over the pit of hell, much as one holds a spider, or some loathsome insect over the fire, abhors you, and is dreadfully provoked; his wrath towards you burns like fire; he looks upon you as worthy of nothing else, but to be cast into fire; he is of purer eyes than to bear to have you in his sight; you are ten times more abominable in his eyes, than the most hateful venomous serpent is in ours.[11]

The deity emerging in Edwards's rhetoric was, for such Universalists as Ballou, mean-spirited, vindictive, and—worst of all—"arbitrary," ready to allow interminable suffering to be visited upon those he created, and prepared to justify such an eternity of horror on the grounds of his absolute loathing for these works of his own hands. Indeed, Edwards's God held "natural men" in such contempt that he (God) found it difficult even to gaze upon them. Thus the "Sinners in the Hands of an Angry God" deity seemed close to the Old Testament God of Jer. 5:20–29, bellowing threats of vengeance at his people, rather than winning them with his love.

Repelled by such depictions of the deity, Ballou announced that the task to which he was dedicated was that of "happifying" God,[12] as he reasoned that no enlightened person could believe in such a hateful divinity, one who showed no feeling—other than anger, hatred, and contempt—for the products of his own will. "Such notions have, in my opinion," announced Ballou, "served to darken the human understanding and obscure the gospel of eternal life; and have rendered, what I esteem as revelation, a subject of discredit to thousands, who, I believe, would never have condemned the scriptures, had it not been for those gross absurdities being contended for, and the scriptures forced to bend to such significations."[13]

Ballou's effort to "happify God," therefore, was fused with his larger goal of reforming Christianity by making the Christian deity rational. Laboring under the assumption that it was neither rational nor just for an omnipotent creator to condemn his own creations to an eternity of excruciating suffering as punishment for the sinful human nature this deity either created or allowed to develop, Ballou defended a universal atonement doctrine that promised heaven to all, an eternity with a "happy" divinity, in the sense that God would rejoice in the ultimate glorification of all his creations. Thus the term *happy*, as employed by Ballou, should be interpreted as suggesting a kind of loving paternal delight and exaltation, a sanguinity generated by knowledge of an eventual paradise for all, a spiritual kingdom in which mankind returns to the sinless nature that existed before "the Fall."

EIGHTEENTH-CENTURY AMERICAN UNIVERSALISTS

Eighteenth-century American religious thought took three distinctly different avenues of response to those elements of harshness and arbitrariness present in some of the century's theology. *Deism*, which lauded human reason as the path to an understanding of all natural law and spiritual truth, cast aside what the movement judged to be the barbarism of Scriptural mythology but retained the teachings of Jesus, which were viewed as being not only humane but rational. *Unitarianism*, in celebration of the avowed wisdom and potential goodness of man, sought—among other objectives—to unify the Godhead and to make more inclusive His domain. Then *Universalism*, in defense of God as a loving creator, sought to reform traditional Christian dogma by adopting an atonement doctrine applicable to all of humankind, a doctrine which would proclaim that *all* of God's children ultimately would be liberated from the judgment Adam's transgression had engendered. Ernest Cassara has reasoned that both Unitarianism and Universalism were "compromises between Christianity (especially in its Calvinistic form) and Deism";[14] but it seems fair to say that, between these two, Universalism held closer to its traditional Christian base, often preserving the doctrine of original sin in relative purity. Unitarianism, on the other hand, placed considerable emphasis upon enlightened humanity's ability to reason a way into social and spiritual goodness. That judgment, as we shall see in Ballou's theology, has not always been a feature of Universalism.

Universalism was very much a product of the Enlightenment and sought to make Christian thought not only rational but also consistent with those humane tenets of social justice that had emerged with the movement. Concerning rationality, the question arose: if humankind were so bestial, so depraved, so deserving of an eternal hell as Edwards's rhetoric seemed to suggest, how could such creatures have been created by a perfect deity? Concerning social justice, the question was: if God were a loving parent, how could He inflict such seemingly indiscriminate eternal punishment on any portion of his children, especially if—as the Calvinists contended— a few of these children were to be "elected" out of this torment to a temporal-world goodness and an eternal-world salvation? If Christian doctrines were to have any validity, they must have internal consistency, just as the laws of the natural world that God created appeared to have internal consistency.

New Jersey's British import, John Murray (1741–1815), usually is thought of as the father of American Universalism. Murray landed at Barnegat Bay in 1770, bringing with him to the colonies a theology that he had borrowed largely from Londoner James Relly, author of the Universalist work, *Union, or, the Consanguinity of Christ and His Church,* later published in Boston under the slightly expanded title, *Union; or a Treatise on the Consanguinity and Affinity between Christ and His Church* (1779).[15]

After coming to America, Murray traveled widely in New England and the Middle Colonies, introducing—with a missionary's zeal—his universal-salvation theology wherever he went, especially in Boston and Philadelphia. The theology in question was one that took most of the traditional Christian doctrines as they had been, but universalized Christ's atonement by making all of humankind the elect.[16] In England, Murray had identified himself with the Methodist movement, but his influence in America was denominationally diverse, touching Baptists, Congregationalists, and Presbyterians, among others. This denominational diversity was also present in the backgrounds of the cadre of American Universalist spokespersons who emerged during the eighteenth and nineteenth centuries: George De Benneville (linked to the pietism of the

German Lutheran movement), Elhanan Winchester and Hosea Ballou (both from Baptist ranks), and Charles Chauncy and Jonathan Mayhew (Congregationalists).

The discussion of these Universalist spokespersons will be selective, focusing on three individuals who made distinctly different contributions to the American Universalist phenomenon: Elhanan Winchester, Charles Chauncy, and Hosea Ballou.

The Restorationist Universalism of Elhanan Winchester

The theology of Elhanan Winchester (1751–1797) already has been mentioned as having influenced religious traditions in Central Appalachia. Generally identified as "Restorationist" theology, Winchester's universalist doctrine argued that temporal-world sin was significant and would be punished in the afterlife. This punishment, however, would not be eternal, meaning that once the sinner had spent her or his deserved period of time in an after-world purgatory, he or she would be "restored" to the loving fellowship of God and under that final condition would spend eternity in heaven.[17]

Winchester's autobiographical accounts of his early years in the Baptist faith show him vacillating between a highly Arminian and even open-communion doctrine and the more staunchly Calvinistic thinking he adopted in his early preaching.[18] He had begun his ministerial career in his native Massachusetts, but it was while he served a church at Welch Neck on the Great Pee Dee River in South Carolina that he first encountered Universalism, the restorationist doctrine of the Dutch theologian Paul Siegvolk. Siegvolk during the sixteenth century had published a work which carries the shortened title *The Everlasting Gospel*. An edition of this work had been published in Germantown, Pennsylvania, in 1753, and had received a limited circulation in the American colonies near the close of the pre-Revolutionary period. Winchester first became acquainted with the book in 1778.[19]

After this first introduction to Restorationist doctrine, Winchester continued to ponder its implications. Two years later, soon after beginning his ministry at St. Paul Baptist Church in Philadelphia, he read a work by the English theologian, George Stonehouse. This book, *Universal Restitution, A Scripture Doctrine* (1761), served to move Winchester more completely toward his eventual Restorationist position; and by 1781 he had become recognized in Philadelphia as a popular spokesman for that doctrine.[20]

Winchester's Restorationist preaching, however, split his Philadelphia Baptist congregation and caused a disturbance that reached deeply into the Philadelphia Association. The result was the emergence in that city of a movement identified as "Universal Baptists."[21] Even before Winchester's congregation had divided over this issue, Restorationist thinking had reached the confines of the South Kentucky Association, being preached—according to J. H. Spencer—by Elders John Bailey and William Bledsoe, and recognized as "hell redemption doctrine." Old-Time Baptist association minutes have also referred to Restorationist theology as the "short hell doctrine."[22]

Arminian Universalism of Charles Chauncy

In 1784, Charles Chauncy (1705–1789) published—anonymously—his Universalist volume, *The Mystery Hid from Ages and Generations, Made Manifest by the Gospel-Revelation: or, The Salvation of All Men,* having with considerable reserve—perhaps even timidity or fear—withheld the manuscript from release for a decade.[23] A Congregationalist cleric, Chauncy was for sixty years pastor of the influential First Church of Boston. He had served as a strong and frequent voice raised in opposition to the frenzied emotionalism of the Great Awakening, especially as generated by the hortatory rhetoric of James Davenport, Gilbert Tennent, and George Whitefield;[24] but his caution and apparent deep concern over being labeled a doctrinal extremist kept him from assuming a forceful position of advocacy concerning his version of Universalism.[25]

The Salvation of All Men lays out a Universalist theology that rejects Calvinistic determinism and works in tandem with the freewill tenets of Arminianism.[26] It shares with the Restorationism of Winchester, the idea that especially vile souls might spend some time in afterlife punishment, but it suggests that the all-loving God will continue, even during that stage, to win rebellious spirits to his benevolent fellowship. Indeed, the claim is that God eventually will win in all of these struggles, with the result that "All Men" will attain salvation.

In essence, Chauncy argued that God would not force the particularly stubborn sinner to accept the benevolent "salvation for all" that he (God) held forth as a redemptive grace.

> [I]t ought to be particularly remembered, and considered, that the future misery, though not everlasting, . . . may yet be awfully heightened in

degree, and protracted in continuance; which I . . . mention, lest any should take occasion, from the doctrine here advanced, to encourage themselves in their evil ways. Let not any say, if we shall finally be saved, we may then live as we list. For, according to the scheme we are illustrating, there will be no salvation for those, in the next state, who habitually indulge in lust in this; but they must be unavoidably miserable, notwithstanding the infinite benevolence of the Deity, and to a great degree of severity, God only knows how long, in proportion to the number and greatness of their vices. And this ought, in all reason, to be a powerful motive to refrain men from making themselves vile: Though *it be a truth, that in the final result of things, they shall be happy* [emphasis added].[27]

The significant difference between the Universalism of Winchester and the Universalism of Chauncy is that the latter preserved for humankind the maximum degree of free will, stopping short only of that end in which the Deity's benevolent resolution would itself be thwarted. God will win, but the volition of stubbornly sinful man will be honored. Indeed, the impression is left that this victory will be one of love, not tyranny.[28]

The Ultra-Universalism of Hosea Ballou

Ballou first released his *A Treatise on Atonement* in 1805, and then he continued to revise it throughout his lifetime, in the process moving more and more toward what Ernest Cassara has labeled "ultra-Universalism."[29] Retaining one aspect of his earlier Calvinistic bent, Ballou conceptualized a version of atonement that was absolute and irrevocable, a feature of God's supreme will. Like PBU doctrine today, this scheme mandated that all of the human family, past and present, be redeemed from Adamic sin by an expiation that admitted no exception to the rule of universal application. Ballou could not imagine God's loving design for man's salvation being compromised in any fashion.[30]

In addition, Ballou's theology upheld two ideas about sin that have become fixed features of PBU doctrine. One is that sin is sufficiently punished in the temporal world. The other is that avoiding sin is more pleasurable—productive of happiness—than yielding to it. In support of these contentions, Ballou argued that Scripture made it clear that God intended to punish all sin in the real world of its commission,[31] and that the Christian pulpit's traditional—but erroneous—rhetorical treatment of sin as pleasure only served to obscure the truth of its being just the opposite:

A mistaken idea has been entertained of sin. . . . I have often heard sincere ministers preach . . . that it is the greatest folly in the world for people to forego salvation in a future state for the comforts and pleasures of sin in this. Such exhortations really defeat their intentions. The wish of the honest preacher is that the wicked should repent of their sins and do better; but, at the same time, he indicates that sin, at present, is more productive of happiness than righteousness. . . . Sin deprives us of every rational enjoyment, so far as it captivates the mind; it was never able to furnish one drop of cordial for the soul; her tender mercies are cruelty, and her breasts of consolation are gall and wormwood. Sin is a false mirror, by which the sinner is deceived in everything on which his mind contemplates. . . . In a word, sin is of a torment-giving nature to every faculty of the soul, and it is the moral death of the mind.[32]

These three tenets—especially the absolutism of atonement—made Ballou's doctrine more palatable to election-leaning Baptists than was Chauncy's Arminian-Freewill version of Universalism. God was in control and allowed no human being a license to go her or his own way into eternal perdition. The latter, argued Ballou, simply could not happen.

Universalism Crosses the Allegheny Mountains

Ernest Cassara argues that Ballou's thinking dominated American Universalist doctrine from 1817 until 1852, the year of Ballou's death.[33] If that indeed was the case, it probably was Ballou's theology that was planted in western Kentucky in 1819, with the establishment of the Consolation Universalist Church, supposedly the first institution of this faith organized west of the Allegheny Mountains.[34]

Founded in Christian County, Kentucky, Consolation did not have a continuous existence, having to be reorganized in 1836.[35] Neither a building nor a membership under the name Consolation Church are extant today. Nevertheless, its establishment initiated a rich Universalist tradition that officially was alive in this part of the Bluegrass State until 1992. The church's former location is presently memorialized by a Kentucky Historical Society marker that stands beside Highway 109 between Hopkinsville and Macedonia.

Consolation Church became the first of twelve Universalist fellowships organized in western Kentucky during the 1800s. Three of the physical structures still stand—one near Crofton, off Highway 41; the second in

UNIVERSALIST CHURCH

Near this site, the Consolation
Universalist Church was organized
by a traveling preacher, Wm. Lowe,
in home of James E. Clark in May,
1819. It was first Universalist
Church organized west of Allegheny
Mountains. Early ministers were:
L. T. Brasher, J. E. McCord,
D. M. Wooldridge, W. E. McCord,
Joab Clark and L. M. Pope.

Presented by the Kentucky Universalists

Historical marker at the site of Consolation Church, on Highway 109 between Hopkinsville and Macedonia, Kentucky, summer 1994.

Fruithill, off Route 800; and the third, the largest and most modern, on South Main Street in Hopkinsville. Established in 1887, the Hopkinsville church was the last of the twelve to become the home of a purely Universalist fellowship. Only in 1992 did it become Unitarian Universalist, in line with the 1961 consolidation of these two faiths.[36]

Hopkinsville's Universalist community apparently remained relatively strong through the 1930s and 1940s, before beginning to experience sharp membership drops in the 1950s. The fellowship voted in 1955 to locate a Unitarian congregation with which to consolidate. That action predated by one year the decision of the national organizations of the Unitarians and the Universalists to create a Commission on Merger to study the feasibility of unifying the two denominations. In 1961, the actual nationwide unification took place. However, in 1955, no such Unitarian group could be found within a reasonable driving distance of Hopkinsville, Kentucky; therefore, enrollment continued to drop, primarily by attrition, and in 1982 the fellowship lost its last minister. That was five years before the church was due to celebrate its one hundredth anniversary.[37]

Old Universalist Church, near Croften, Kentucky, summer 1994.

The 1987 centennial celebration took place, with the help of Universalist interests outside of Kentucky; but by that year there were only five aging members of the Hopkinsville congregation. They had begun to explore various options for use of a church facility that seemed destined to emptiness but structurally appeared worth saving. Finally, a proposal came from a civic organization, known as "The Heart of Hopkinsville," that would have transformed the sturdy brick building into a community museum.

That is how the situation stood when, in August 1992, Gwendolyn Wilkins received a call from Cleo Hogan. Wilkins then was one of the three remaining Hopkinsville Universalist members, and she was a trustee for the church. Hogan was an attorney living just across the state line in Clarksville, Tennessee, and was a leader of a Unitarian fellowship of twenty-two persons that had been organized only recently in Clarksville. The Clarksville group was searching for a physical home and wondered if it were too late to propose a merger between the Clarksville and the Hopkinsville fellowships. Apparently no papers had been signed concerning the earlier Heart of Hopkinsville proposal, and Wilkins and the other two Universalist trustees eagerly accepted this opportunity to maintain the viability of this century-old religious institution.[38]

Hopkinsville Unitarian Universalist Church, Hopkinsville, Kentucky, summer 1994.

Having accepted an invitation to speak in August 1994 at a Sunday evening meeting of this amalgamated fellowship, I stood before an audience of thirty-four Unitarian Universalists, only one of whom—Gwendolyn Wilkins—remained from that tradition begun in 1819 with the establishment of the Consolation Universalist Church. I could not avoid drawing a parallel between this woman and that last aging member of Holston Primitive Baptist Church in Grainger County, Tennessee.

Universalism's Possible Route to Washington County, Tennessee

From its initial implantation in Kentucky, it is possible that Ballou's theology backtracked eastward through Tennessee, as Universalist societies were founded—and survived at least for short periods—in Glimpsville, Knoxville, Harriman, Chattanooga, and Free Hill in Washington County.[39] Glimpsville, now no longer shown on a Tennessee map, was in Lauderdale County in the extreme western part of the state; but the fellowship there flourished until about 1910, occupying a church built in 1836.

In addition, the meetinghouse apparently was the site of a debate that took place on November 29–December 1, 1887, between Daniel Bragg Clayton, a Universalist, and Elder J. N. Ball, a Missionary Baptist from Fulton, Kentucky. Clayton was a South Carolina Universalist who traveled widely (Alabama, Georgia, Mississippi, North Carolina, South Carolina, and Tennessee), preaching the faith and debating all who were willing to meet him in theological argument.[40]

However, of these Tennessee Universalist churches, the one at Harriman became the best established, having been instituted in 1891 with strong financial backing and an active congregation. This society maintained a viable program "until the late 1920s" in a building that was paid for in part by funds raised by the Universalist Young People's Society of Boston and by generous contributions from the Ohio oatmeal tycoon, Ferdinand Schumacher. Grace Universalist Church, situated on Cumberland Street in Harriman ("the town that temperance built"), became not only a show place in that community but also a national symbol to the larger denomination that the faith could prosper outside of Boston and Philadelphia.[41] Completed in 1892, the church attracted as its pastor W. H. McGlauflin, who came to Harriman from the Universalist fellowship in Rochester, New York. The following is an 1896 newspaper account of the church and its program:

> The Universalist Society [in Harriman] was charted by the State September 1891. Out of its members Grace Church was formed in January 1892. The "society" is the legal body; the "church," the religious. The auxiliary bodies are a flourishing Sunday School and a Young People's Christian Union, neither of which has missed a single Sunday since first organized in the autumn of 1892. There is a Woman's Missionary Circle, and the usual committees on benevolence, temperance, etc. The church has had but one pastor, W. H. McGlauflin, who began his ministry in August 1891. The edifice and furnishings cost $8,500.[42]

W. H. McGlauflin also was influential in the creation of small Universalist communities in Knoxville and Chattanooga, the Knoxville society having had its formal inception in 1895. However, McGlauflin left Tennessee in 1896, and the Knoxville missionary effort did not remain strong after that date. Chattanooga's Universalist community was more stable and long-lived. With the aid of the Young People's Christian Union the national Universalist youth organization that had raised money to help establish the Harriman church, a Universalist church building finally was dedicated in Chattanooga in 1917.[43]

Like the Harriman congregation, however, neither the Knoxville nor the Chattanooga Universalist community continued to exist after the second decade of the twentieth century,[44] and the movement eventually died out in these areas, just as it did in Christian County, Kentucky, to be revived only slightly after the 1961 merger of Unitarianism and Universalism. The Tennessee Universalist experience most relevant to the PBU story, however, may have been the one in Washington County.

UNIVERSALISM COMES TO WASHINGTON COUNTY, TENNESSEE

It is entirely possible that the Universalist societies in Chattanooga, Harriman, and Knoxville had some impact upon Universalism in Washington County; but it is also possible that the faith reached this last area of East Tennessee before it reached the other two locations. Indeed, a small cluster of Universalists may have been active in the Limestone community of Washington County as early as the 1820s.[45] However, if one or two Universalist families did reside in Limestone, apparently they did not establish a church and their presence was of short duration. Nevertheless, it has been firmly established by the Universalist Historical Society at Tufts University, that Dr. William Hale, a physician of Free Hill (near Gray in Washington County), was licensed as a Universalist "lay preacher" in 1877.[46] Therefore, Universalism definitely existed in the county by this last date.

William Hale (1838–1906) came into Universalism from a Methodist background, after having developed a profession as a medical doctor. The account provided by the Hale family is that William was introduced to this doctrine by his father, Hiram Decatur Hale, and by his uncle, Aman Hale, the latter a circuit-riding Methodist preacher who applied Universalism to the teaching of this Wesleyan faith. The father, however, apparently was the more influential of these two.

According to an oft-repeated family story, the father acquired a Universalist tract "out of Kentucky" and began to devote considerable time to investigating the work's contentions.[47] Shortly thereafter, Hiram became a dedicated believer in Universalism, possessing a missionary zeal to reveal his new doctrinal find to all who came near. An article that ran in the *Universalist Herald* on July 15, 1879, credited Hiram with giving Universalism a hefty push in East Tennessee:

Then [following Hiram's introduction to Universalism] the Bible became his hourly companion and the all-absorbing subject [Universalism] was laid before his neighbors in such serious and unanswerable arguments, that many became interested and would listen for hours to the old man as he read and commented on this new and astonishing doctrine; new only because it was uncommon here and astonishingly reasonable and true.[48]

The Hale family story goes on to relate that, during the early period of Hiram Hale's intense interest in Universalism, his son, William, visited his father to find out what was transpiring in the old man's life. William, who had married and was living in Sullivan County, Tennessee, at the time, called on his father at the family's Free Hill farm and discovered the elderly enthusiast plowing a field, the previously mentioned Kentucky tract secured to one handle of the plow and a Bible to the other.[49]

There is no Hale family record of when this introduction to the faith "out in the field" actually occurred, but Dr. William Hale evidently became a fervent disciple of his father's newfound belief, even traveling in 1874 to St. Lawrence University Theological School for a summer training session in the tenets of the denomination, and evidently also in ministering in the faith.[50] Universalist records archived at Tufts University indicate that by 1877 he was licensed to preach the doctrine and that by 1879 he was in the process of organizing a church in the Free Hill vicinity. In addition, those records show that in 1880 a Free Hill Universalist society was established, containing twelve members. That number grew to fifteen in 1881 and then to twenty-five in 1886. Hale's lay-preacher license was renewed in 1881, 1886, and 1892.[51]

Hale family stories also tell of the doctor's frequently being on the road during these years, traveling as far south as Atlanta and Birmingham to attend Universalist meetings or to participate in debates, all of this very much to his wife's vexation.[52] In 1877, when Hale first was licensed to preach, he was the only known Universalist minister in Tennessee, and the singularity of his position may have intensified his missionary zeal.

It would be difficult to say how widely the influence of this father-son pair of believers reached. It is entirely possible that their number of converts to Universalism went far beyond the limited group that constituted the Free Hill Universalist Society.

The church in which Hale preached to his small Universalist congregation was actually a "union" church, meaning in this case that the

Home of Dr. William Hale, Free Hill, Tennessee, summer 1993.

society shared the structure with three other denominational factions. Each first Sunday of the month was the Universalists' turn, and Hale apparently divided the preaching between himself and another lay preacher, A. C. Bowers.[53] Union churches frequently were seen in the religious life of early Central Appalachia, but each of the four supposedly separate congregations would not necessarily ignore the church's other three Sundays. Therefore, Hale and Bowers occasionally may have preached to a Methodist, Baptist, or Presbyterian.

Free Hill's Universalist Society was short-lived, existing only from 1881 through 1896. Russell E. Miller of the Universalist Historical Society notes that, after that latter date, the society was listed as "dormant." Miller also reports that, after Hale's death in 1906, no mention is found in Universalist records of the Free Hill experience.[54] Hiram had died in 1891.

Ida Metz Hyland of Johnson City, Tennessee, an author with a long family connection with Universalism, has chronicled the story of the Hale family and the Free Hill Universalists. She believes that this small society depended so heavily upon the enthusiasm of this father-son pair that, after the two died, the drive went out of the movement.[55] The absence of any formal Universalist denomination after 1906 appears to support Hyland's thesis.

Headstone for graves of Dr. William Hale and his wife, Lucy Hale, Free Hill, Tennessee, summer 1993.

As of this writing in 1995, the only presence of a continuing Universalist faith in Washington County, Tennessee, is found in the activities of two very divergent congregations. One is the Holston Valley Unitarian Universalist Church, which sits to the east side of Interstate Highway 181, midway between Johnson City and Kingsport. The second is Hope Church, a PBU affiliate of the Regular Primitive Baptist Washington District Association, ironically resting only a couple of miles away from Holston Valley Church, on the west side of Interstate 181.

Until June 12, 1994, when I addressed the Holston Valley Unitarian Universalist congregation about the PBU faith, neither church was aware of the other's tie to this common heritage. Now a kind of intellectual interest in each other exists, but the two fellowships are separated by vast differences in both their secular and their religious backgrounds. Hope Church definitely is an Old-Time Baptist congregation, preserving all of those characteristics of worship and practice discussed in chapter 1; while the Holston Valley fellowship seems very representative of the cultural and spiritual mix that one usually encounters in a contemporary Unitarian Universalist congregation—intellectual, liberal, humanistic, and omnidirectional in terms of actual religious doctrine. Hope Church practices an impassioned form of worship that, in styles of preaching, singing, and fellowship interaction, bears little resemblance to the more structured, aesthetically aware, yet sincere religious expression heard two miles away. Therefore, it is difficult to imagine that these two traditions could find any really comfortable middle ground upon which seriously to mingle.

Nevertheless, back around the turn of the century, some happenings may have taken place in Washington County, Tennessee, that constitute a common heritage for these two churches. In addition, there may have been a string of circumstances—stretching from Boston and Philadelphia to Christian County, Kentucky, and back eastward through Tennessee—that explains the similarity between the thinking of Hosea Ballou and that of Charles F. Nickels, and that led to the 1907—or earlier—emergence of Universalism in the preaching of Elder M. L. Compton and other Washington Association "No-Heller" preachers.

6
"CARRIED OUT"

New Garden Church sits to the right of Highway 80 just east of Honaker, Russell County, Virginia. This area of southwestern Virginia constitutes the upper middle region of the Clinch River Valley and is fed by waters from a multitude of streams that flow down the east face of the Tennessee Valley Divide—Lewis Creek, Swords Creek, Pine Creek, Lick Creek, Mill Creek, Coal Creek, and others. The first of these, Lewis Creek, runs closest to the New Garden meetinghouse.

Of all the PBU churches, New Garden arguably is the most historic, having been constructed shortly before the Civil War and—according to local accounts—having served for a brief period during that conflict as a field hospital,[1] supposedly under the on-site direction of Clara Barton. I have been unable to verify this Clara Barton connection with New Garden, but there appears to be a possibility that she was in southwestern Virginia in the fall of 1862.[2] An old cemetery located on a rise just west of the church is rumored to contain some human remains from that field hospital; however, the older graves in this area are marked with native stones that lack inscriptions, and I have been unable to establish that any of these burials marked with native stone dates back to the Civil War. Still, the story that Clara Barton performed some of her work as an "angel of the battlefield" at this church is a lasting part of the oral history of this PBU fellowship, and the account may have some validity. The New Garden membership memorializes that history with a picture of Clara Barton secured to the church wall behind the stand.

Also hanging on that wall is a photograph of Elder E. M. (Elexious Musick) Evans, II, so strongly related to the events and doctrines treated in chapters 3 and 4. During those critical years after the 1924–25 split, Evans moderated not only Salem Church, but also, off and on, New Garden, Johnson Bottom, Macedonia, and Reed's Valley churches. Indeed, it seems fair to say that, during the first decade of its formal existence, the PBU movement was led primarily by Elder E. M. Evans—despite the fact that he could not write. This last fact was verified by Evans's daughter, Ethel Evans Albert, when she submitted the following to the Historical Society of Southwest Virginia:

> Born in 1862 in McDowell County, Virginia/West Virginia, he did not learn to read until after he was called to preach at age 24. . . . He was a member of the Regular Baptist Church called Primitive Baptist and became an avid reader. Before learning to read print, he began memorizing the Bible as he heard others read passages of scripture aloud. He continued that practice until he could recite the Bible from memory. He did not learn to write anything except his own signature. He dictated epistles patterned after those of the early apostles called Circular Letters which we younger offspring and others wrote in long hand for him.[3]

Therefore, Evans's contributions to PBU doctrine—which may have been significant—were made despite his inability to write. He could read, apparently with ease; but the 1931 and 1939 circular letters quoted in chapter 4—along with his lengthy account of the 1924 split, published in the Old Constitutional Washington District Association Minutes—evidently were dictated to other individuals—family members or perhaps the association clerk serving at the time of the writing. Charles F. Nickels also was a self-educated man, but he was able to write.

Because of Evans's connection with New Garden Church, a strong majority of that fellowship sided with the "No-Hellers" during the 1924–25 unrest. In fact, at the 1924 PBU annual session, this church reported a membership of 154, twelve more than it had reported in 1923.[4] As mentioned in chapter 3, such a change in membership totals between 1923 and 1924 might not have been unusual. During the month between the September 1924 meeting of Washington District (where the first actions of the split occurred) and the meeting of the Old Constitutional Washington District (as the PBU fellowships initially called themselves) in October 1924, apparently there was considerable shifting of membership back and forth between churches. Where majorities remained "Heller," "No-Hellers" probably found sanctuary in a church on the PBU side; where majorities became "No-Heller," "Hellers" undoubtedly shifted to churches on the anti-PBU side.

In the case of New Garden Church, the big win for the PBU movement was their preservation of control over that physical facility, a proud old structure that both sides evidently sought to retain. In splits of this kind, at least one legal battle over church property usually is waged, and there always is a fight over which side should retain the original association name.[5] Concerning any struggle for the New Garden meetinghouse and property, E. M. Evans's leadership in the fellowship no doubt was helpful in keeping the New Garden trustees in the PBU camp.

When the PBU Washington District held its 1994 annual session at this church, the reverence that these fellowships held for New Garden meetinghouse was palpable. Not only was that event well attended, with many people telling me how they enjoyed returning to the old New Garden church; but an inordinate number of people seemed to want to relate their favorite stories about this church and its past moderators. There seemed to exist a special level of dedication to this facility and its heritage.

Because of its age, the New Garden meetinghouse preserves one significant characteristic of turn-of-the-century or earlier Old-Time Baptist structures: two front doors, one originally used only by men and the other originally used only by women. This architectural feature relates back to a time when gender separation was an absolute in these churches—the men usually occupying the right and the women the left. In PBU congregations today, most of this tradition now belongs to the past. Only a slight tendency to maintain some gender segregation is observable among older members, and in these cases it is difficult to judge whether what is seen relates to the old tradition or merely to natural social clustering. The separations that do occur seem spotty and unstructured, varying greatly from one church to another. When working with the Old Regulars, I developed the habit of walking into a meetinghouse and immediately monitoring the gender plan (the tradition still being very much in evidence in many of those fellowships), but that procedure has been unnecessary during my PBU visitations.

New Garden Regular Primitive Baptist Church meetinghouse, located near Honaker in Russell County, Virginia, fall 1994.

The front of New Garden Church sits several feet off the ground, as a result of the facility's having been constructed on a slight slope. To accommodate the numerous individuals within the three associations who now are confined to wheelchairs, the membership has provided a long ramp that rises to the building's right door. In fact, almost every meetinghouse within the PBU movement has been compelled to make similar entrance adjustments, in recognition of the fact that so many of its worshipers are growing old and physically impaired.

One of the first things I noticed about this old church was that, at some earlier time, the windows had been rather lofty, reaching ten to twelve feet above their sills. Now, however, those openings have been diminished considerably, allowing the ceiling to be lowered and the interior walls reduced in height to ten feet. Thus the worship area today is much easier to heat. Those interior walls presently are veneered with the traditional wood paneling and crowned by a modern system of suspended ceiling tiles and fluorescent lighting.

All of this remodeling has produced a worship space that is neat, effi
cient, and economical, but markedly different from the original antebe
lum interior that architectural historians and other preservationists ur
doubtedly would like to see restored. Except for the lowered windows, th
access ramp at the front, and a number of other modern touches, the e:
terior of the old church retains much of its original flavor; but the interi
environment differs markedly from its state during the old field-hospit
days.

At the rear of the church is a roofed, open-sided shed, similar to th
ones found at Hale Creek, Oak Grove, Macedonia, and Pilgrim's Res
During normal summer monthly meetings, this facility is used as a ser
ing area for dinner-on-the-grounds. On those second-Saturday weeken
in September, when New Garden hosts Association Time, however, th
structure becomes an outdoor stand area, under which auxiliary preacl
ing services are conducted while the business meetings transpire inside th
meetinghouse. For these special events, the New Garden congregatic

*The Washington Association's Annual Session, 1994, at New Garden Church, Russell Coun
Virginia.*

creates amphitheater seating for this outdoor stand by placing benches—improvised from two-by-twelve planking resting on concrete blocks—on the upward-sloping, curved rear perimeter of the church yard.

The arrangement accommodates perhaps three hundred people, and on Association Time Sunday afternoons at New Garden, when three weeks of annual sessions (Three Forks, Elkhorn, and then Washington) are climaxing with a final dinner-on-the-grounds, this amphitheater area is packed with an especially celebratory crowd of PBU members and followers. That certainly was the case in September 1994, when, after eating, the crowd seemed particularly reluctant to leave the scene, as it continued to visit, then broke into hymn singing, and finally provided the audience for a concluding round of apparently unplanned preaching.

PBU PREACHING AND CONGREGATIONAL RESPONSES: "CARRIED OUT"

This chapter is devoted to two topics: first, PBU preaching and the corresponding congregational responses; and, second, the arrangement of PBU worship.

Preaching shed, New Garden Church, Russell County, Virginia, fall 1994.

Since Appalachian preaching first captured my interest in 1971,[6] this aspect of the Appalachian religious tradition has been a strong focus of my research. That focus certainly has been in evidence during this PBU study. Old-Time Baptist preaching—and PBU sermonics definitely fall under this heading—can be characterized by five attributes or claims:

1. *Extemporization,* the total yielding of oneself to a spur-of-the-moment speaking process, with the understanding that only unplanned and unprepared sermons allow God's thoughts to be revealed.

2. *Distinctive delivery modes,* featuring exaggerated and dramatic cadence, chant, song, and inflection, with the understanding that a more prosaic expression generally is "without blessing."

3. *Emotionality* that demands that the speaker yield to tears, shouts, wails, laughter, or other forms of deeply felt personal responses, with the understanding that one who is unmoved is unsanctified.

4. *Physicality,* the delivery being enhanced by dynamic gestures, pronounced strides and leaps, constant movement of some kind, and frequent support contact with other elders, with the understanding that "blessed" preaching is both an individual and a group expression, with physical activity forming part of both types.

5. *Transcendence,* the claim being that the "blessed" preacher is "carried out," lifted above the natural state to a very special status of communication, with the understanding that at these moments God takes control of a message that then loses any causal relationship with either the special skills or the deserving nature of the particular exhorter.

In addition, congregations engage in reciprocal responses that mirror and extend these characteristics, and thus—at times—listeners might themselves be labeled as "carried out."

Extemporization

This Old-Time Baptist preaching characteristic has received attention in all three of my earlier volumes on Appalachian religion and more particularly in one journal article.[7] Therefore, only what is essential to the current discussion is repeated here, and this discussion will relate specifically to PBU preaching. Succinctly, PBU elders agree with the mainstream of Old-Time Baptist thought in pronouncing prepared sermonics as the speaking of man and extemporaneous "blessed" preaching as the speaking of God. Two things are required for the latter: the preacher must yield himself completely to the uncertainties of improvisational expression, and he must be "blessed" during the key moments of that improvisation.

Four metaphorical terms are employed in PBU circles to address that second requirement. The terms *blessed* and *carried out* already have been introduced, and third and fourth key terms are *alive* and *quickened*. Contrasting metaphors include *dead, cold,* and *unblessed*, among others. The first set of terms signifies that state of transcendence when the speaker is lifted above his natural form of expression, and the second set, of course, suggests the absence of such transcendence.

Being "carried out" is a profoundly critical state for a PBU elder. He does not enter it every time he gets into the stand; therefore, he is painfully aware when the condition is absent. In fact, he may go for an extended time—even months—without a "blessing," resulting in an almost explosive expression of joy when the period of "death" ends. "It's been a long dry spell for me," exuberantly proclaimed Elder Willard Owens, after a "carried out" sermon delivered at a family memorial in Thompson Valley, near Tazewell, Virginia. "I thought I might have lost it permanently."[8]

Elder Owens' pronouncement illustrates the deep distress PBU preachers occasionally experience after several "unblessed" periods in the stand. During these times, they frequently speak of being "dead" and somehow immune to God's "quickening" touch. This temporary immunity is not equated with current sinfulness or with any other inadequacy of the natural being. It simply is a factor of God's will and cannot be explained other than by the understanding that some divine plan is in operation.

One of the most poignant expressions of this concern over periods of "deadness" was offered by Elder Keith Bowers during his preaching at Stoney Creek's 1995 union meeting. When Bowers rose to take his position in the stand, he began by telling the congregation that he was troubled by the fact that so frequently he was "dead." An unpretentious and deeply honest man, Elder Bowers spoke of his pain with convincing sincerity. He even confessed that he had tried to do what he knew he should not do, prepare some thoughts ahead of time, thinking that doing so would "jump-start" the inspiration process. The technique, however, had not worked, leaving him feeling worse about the situation than he otherwise might have felt, adding a sense of guilt to his perception of being "unblessed."

Elder Willard Owens, "in the stand" at Harrison-Beavers Family Reunion and Memorial, Thompson Valley, Virginia, 1995.

Bowers also mentioned that, in the past, he had been called to union services at one of the three Ohio churches (Little Flock at Greenfield; Little Village, Continental; and Rich Hill, near Centerburg) or at the Pennsylvania church (Mount Grove, near Airville). "After traveling three hundred to five hundred miles," he said, "I expected the Lord to give me a three-hundred- to five-hundred-mile message. But I came home disappointed. It didn't work that way."[9]

It was not difficult to see the deep concern in Elder Bowers's demeanor. He was anguished by what he perceived as something akin to abandonment, rejection, or worse. He seemed to be harboring thoughts of personal failure, a loss of "call." However, only a few moments after he made the last statement quoted, Bowers captured what he and the congregation obviously perceived as being "carried out." His rhetoric lost the low, soft-spoken, conversational quality with which he had begun; his words rose to a higher level of passion and joy; his vocal rhythm quickened and approached chant, with certain expressions ascending into song; his volume and rate of speech increased; his general confidence soared, accompanied by a heightened relish for this moment in the stand. His fervor generated reciprocal responses in his audience, as several women began to shout. Indeed, every aspect of this situation suggested that Elder Bowers and the Stoney Creek congregation perceived a "quickening" to have occurred, an elder and a fellowship to have been made "alive" to the Spirit. The shouting of the women showed their own freedom to extemporize, to plunge into a "carried out" moment with whatever explosive contribution they desired to make, including occasionally some spoken messages.

Distinctive Delivery Modes

This description of Elder Bowers's being "carried out" should provide some understanding of PBU delivery style, at least during more impassioned ("quickened") moments. This, however, is not the way a PBU sermon begins. In fact, were a preacher to develop a delivery mode that thrust him precipitously into the style described above, congregations would become suspicious of his spiritual status, suspecting that contrived dramatics, more than "blessed" inspiration, were involved. Therefore, it is understood that the preacher needs some unrushed settling-in time—time during which he is relatively soft-spoken, slow, and even lethargic; time for humility, for halting mannerisms, and for the postures of apprehension and reservation; time perhaps for acknowledging inadequacies and uncertainties; time to yield to higher controls. During these moments, the speaker's voice may be inaudible beyond the stand area, and he even may turn his back on much of the congregation, focusing primarily on the other elders, from whom he seeks support.

The proverbial "starting off with a bang" will violate all these requisite attitudes of humility and reserve, communicating a sense of improper hurry and suggesting a projection of self into the process. God will or will not opt to use the speaker on this day; therefore, any unseemly rush will suggest an unwillingness to wait for God's will to materialize. If an unquickened state becomes the reality of the moment, the preacher may occupy the stand for only five or ten minutes, speaking earnestly and perhaps even movingly to the congregation, but never losing an awareness of self, never ceasing to struggle for something to say, never rising to that level of transcendence that causes words to flow without effort, never soaring into the "carried out" message that he devoutly hopes will emerge.

During this period he may confess that he feels nothing, that he is "cold," "dead." He may even suggest to the other elders in the stand that one of them ought to get ready, because he does not believe that God is going to "bless" him. At such a time, several voices in the stand might encourage him, saying something like "Take your time, Brother. We can't rush the Lord."

Still, if this preacher does not begin to soar soon, he will yield the stand to another elder, perhaps with no sense of shame or remorse, recognizing that on another day the deity might choose to use him. Furthermore, it is the ideal that all elders accept this understanding—that the higher power is doing the choosing—and keep their own attitudes free of criticism, condescension, and jealousy. It was in recognition of this ethic that Elder Landon Colley, after a period in the stand that appeared uninspired, told a congregation, "I enjoy hearing these other brothers get carried out even when I'm not."[10]

If, however, an elder experiences his "blessing," he quickly will move into his particular version of the delivery mode described in connection with Elder Bowers. His tempo will quicken; his rhythm will become enhanced; his more impassioned statements will be accentuated by a rising inflection, an outcry of exhilaration, an explosion of passion; his physical behavior will take on more dynamism; and his every emotion will mount, especially when met by a mirroring congregational response.

One delivery characteristic which PBU preachers share with Old Regular Baptist exhorters is the habit of constantly making physical contact with other elders in the stand, most frequently through handshakes or embraces.[11] The traditional pattern is for the handshakes to begin during the preliminary, more sedate stage of the sermon, with the preaching elder moving slowly to each of the other elders in the stand area, shaking hands as they are outstretched to him. The cycle may be repeated a number of times, causing the preacher to pace back and forth behind the pulpit.

These handshaking contacts establish an important support system during those moments when the preacher is trying to find his "quickened" message, and they translate into expressions of understanding and encouragement. Then, when a "carried out" status is established, a role reversal seems to occur, as the other elders now are moved to make physical contact with the "blessed" preacher, initiating the handshake or embrace.

During such moments, regular members too may rise from their pews and approach the stand, there warmly to embrace the speaker. Here is another example of the congregation's freedom to make individual responses, without being tied to any "in unison" mandate. Generally speaking, the stand area is the domain of the elders; but lay PBU worshipers—females or males—feel no qualms about moving into that space to make contact with a "quickened" preacher.

There is one Old Regular preaching characteristic that PBU elders do not adopt: the practice of placing either the right or left hand against the corresponding ear or upper jaw before rocking sharply forward, often with eyes tightly closed, all of this usually occurring on a phrase that receives an elongated and dramatically wailed delivery.[12] PBU elders are more likely to keep their bodies erect and their hands free, employing the latter in dramatic chopping or slicing motions, moving them high in the air for vigorous crisscrossing waves, or slapping them together for sharp punctuating sounds. A favorite, very physical delivery style is that of Elder Jennings Shortt of Pound, Virginia, moderator of the Three Forks Association, whose chopping arm movements are the hallmark of his style.

Emotionality

It is difficult to write about the emotionality of PBU preaching without also treating the emotionality of congregational responses. The two are mutually reinforcing and merge into one unified effect. Once an elder reaches a "quickened" state, his words usually will be met by one or more bursts of congregational shouting, predominantly from women but occasionally from a man;[13] and these shouts will intensify the fervor of the preacher. Two events that occurred during the 1995 union meeting season will illustrate this process.

Elder Aaron Williams was "called" to Salem Church's 1995 union meeting. That is, the membership specifically requested that four preachers make themselves available for preaching at that service, and he was one of these.[14] As noted earlier, the Salem meetinghouse lies in Tazewell County, Virginia. It is situated roughly midway between Cedar Bluff and Brandy, near a particularly rugged section of the Laurel Fork region known as "The Jumps." This church produced the initial controversy that in 1924 split Washington Association.

Elder Williams, a schoolteacher who lives in Portland, Indiana, is one of the youngest elders within the PBU movement. He seems also to be—within the three PBU associations—one of the favorite preachers, having been called for nine union meetings in 1995. Each summer, Williams—as is true of several of these PBU preachers—drives literally thousands of

miles to meet his "call" obligations, to attend the three association meetings, and to make himself available as a preacher at certain special services,
most particularly the numerous home services and family memorials.[15]
Church moderators understand the hardships of such travel, however, and
collect contributions to pay the out-of-pocket expenses of these modern-
day circuit riders. In addition, during any spring-summer-fall period, a
PBU preacher may spend several nights—or entire weekends—in private
homes, attentively cared for by host families.

When Elder Williams spoke to the Salem congregation that June
morning, he was "carried out," and he generated several episodes of shouting from at least a dozen women in the audience. Nevertheless, toward
what initially looked like it might be the close of Williams's sermon, Sister Peggy Johnson, a member of Macedonia Church, began to shout, cry,
and move about, making her contributions to this dramatic moment
especially noticeable.

Johnson commenced her exertions in the right down-front area of the
church, where several women already had been vigorously active in
spirited responses to Williams's preaching. Embracing each of the women
near her—which in many instances started new episodes of shouting—
Johnson began to work her way up the right side of the meetinghouse, now
hugging everyone in attendance and still joyfully crying. Her emotions
were genuine and moving, and the scene should not be imagined as a
ludicrous one.

Sister Johnson's maneuvers continued, eventually reaching the back of
the church and then starting up the left side of the sanctuary, ending in
the stand area while Williams was still preaching. Not only did she excite
fervent responses almost everywhere she went, but also she seemed to help
extend the "carried out" performance of Elder Williams, whose preaching appeared to catch that proverbial "second wind"—in this case, a second "quickening." What developed was an impassioned "high" that took
this congregation about as far as any could go in terms of emotionality.
The mood built to peaks, subsided, and then built again, until a certain
degree of exhaustion set in. The important point here is that Williams and
Johnson were working in tandem, each making a significant contribution
to the moment. "Carried out" contributions of both preacher and respon-
dent lifted these PBU worshipers to a level of ardent expression that would
have been difficult to exceed.

Elder Williams was the second preacher of the morning, following
Elder Denton Brown, from the Pennsylvania church, Mount Grove. More

often than not, it is the closing episode of preaching (the third or fourth sermon in a typical service) that generates a scene like the one just described. Expectations seem to favor these terminating moments as the time when the highest plane of emotionality will be reached, and moderators occasionally decree that a particular preacher will "close," seemingly in response of this expectation.

On that Sunday, Elder Landon Colley, moderator of the PBU Washington Association, was to close; more often than not, Colley's preaching is "quickened." That day, however, there did not seem to be any more these people could give, at least at that moment; and Brother Landon was unable to generate a "carried out" passion in himself or in the congregation. Both appeared spent, having already experienced the climactic moments of the morning.

Elder Landon doubtless would argue that God already had executed his plan for the preaching part of that Salem service. This Sunday was the church's union and communion meeting, so a footwashing service still lay ahead, during which emotions again might run high; but perhaps Elder Colley would say that, as far as the preaching was concerned, all divine expectations had been met.

A second example was observed at Bee Branch Church, an affiliate of the Elkhorn Association. This church is located beside Highway 83 in Paynesville, West Virginia, an unincorporated community that occupies a lofty perch just inside the West Virginia line on the crest of State Line Ridge. Paynesville is approximately five miles from Wimmer Gap "as the crow flies," or perhaps four times that distance by the most direct hard-surface route. When standing in front of Bee Branch Church, one can view, to the south, what I think of as the "back" side of Compton Mountain, the north face from which the waters of Slate Creek originate, before that stream runs its southwestward route toward Grundy.

There actually are two Bee Branch churches in close proximity to each other, the one currently under discussion, and an Old Regular church that also sits beside Highway 83, but on the Virginia slope of State Line Ridge. Like the two Hale Creek fellowships, the Bee Branch churches once were one and the same congregation, founded in 1887. That was about three splits ago, however.[16] Now approximately three miles of twisting road separate the two, and neither church actually rests beside Bee Branch, a community lying to the northeast of Paynesville in the Tug Fork drainage area.

On August 6, 1995, I made my first visit to the PBU Bee Branch meetinghouse. I already was acquainted with all of the members of this fellowship, having met them at other churches. In particular, I knew the family of Elder Unice Davis, moderator of Bee Branch and of the Elkhorn Association. Also I had met Sister Adeleah Davis and her two daughters and two sons. Three of these siblings are vital participants in the activities not only of the Elkhorn Association but also of Washington District and Three Forks. This family has been especially supportive of my PBU fieldwork. It is also a family that yields itself completely to the intense emotions of PBU worship. At no time has that fact been demonstrated more clearly than during the August service at Bee Branch.

As moderator of this fellowship, Elder Unice Davis took the stand after the opening session of singing. Ordinarily he would not preach at this point. Instead he would simply start the service, turning after a moment or two of commentary to the available elders and instructing them to "make their own arrangements," meaning that these elders—some "called" for the service, some perhaps not—then would discuss among themselves who would "introduce," who would follow (one or two of them), and who would "close." This typical PBU procedure for scheduling the morning's preaching is different from that generally seen among the Old Regulars. There, the tradition is for the moderator to control that scheduling, sequencing the preachers in accord with some strategy for the morning's emotional development.[17] The PBU system creates some slightly awkward moments of deliberation, since no elder wants to propose himself for any particular position, especially not the closing one.

That morning, however, Elder Davis continued to talk for a few moments, most pointedly about the death of a member of the Elkhorn Association family. The consequence was that he began to be "carried out." Still, he stopped himself, saying that he did not mean to preach, that one of the other elders should take over. By this time, however, the other preachers had sensed some special emotion on the rise and urged him to keep his place. Almost immediately, Sister Adeleah, his wife, began to shout and cry, and she soon was joined by her two daughters and several other women in the congregation. The outcome was a female participation that was perhaps less mobile than the one at Salem Church, but certainly not less intense. Once again there was clear evidence of a partnership at work, the contribution of the preacher coalescing with the reciprocal spirit of the women, one seeming to be no less powerful than the other in creating a total outcome.

Elder Aaron Williams also had been called for this service, but on this morning, he followed a "carried out" event. The effect was that he appeared to be in much the same situation as Elder Colley's at Salem Church only a few weeks earlier. I have witnessed two and even three episodes of "carried out" preaching in a row, but when the response to the first or second exhorter is exceptionally energetic, it is difficult for the preacher who follows to generate the same degree of congregational passion.

Physicality

No single physical behavior typifies PBU preaching quite as decisively as the hand-to-side-of-face behavior does Old Regular preaching. True, the handshaking practice is almost universal among PBU preachers, but that conduct is encountered also among Regulars, Old Regulars, Uniteds, and other Primitives. Indeed, it would be useful to discover the origin of this widespread Old-Time Baptist practice. It is certainly a typing characteristic of the broader genre.

There is, nevertheless, a high degree of general physicality in the platform behavior of these PBU elders, and no PBU preacher I know of has adopted a staid and stoical stand demeanor, except perhaps during those beginning moments of settling in. In the throes of being "carried out," dynamic movement becomes essential to fervor and tantamount to "quickening." Movement that surges and swells, that plunges and pulses, that drives a body across space, that thrusts a body upward or downward—such behavior suggests to these congregations that the material man has been lifted and transformed into something other than his corporeal self. This is the movement of "carried out" preaching.

I do not want to create an image of bizarre frenzy; that would be not only unfair but untruthful. I do want to project a picture of delivery without the fetters of undue decorum, delivery that is free of both pretentiousness and unwarranted protocol or propriety. These are not "dignified" people; they are impassioned people, insisting that their religion is a joy and that, as such, it demands full expression.

With that demand in mind, again we must add women to the formula, simply because they are vital parts of the picture being drawn. Sister Peggy Johnson is not the only PBU female who enjoys translating her joyous emotions into dynamic physical expression. Women wave their arms, clap their hands, jump up and down in exaltation, even occasionally make quick twirls. They do not, however, as the Pentecostal or Holiness church members are prone to do, "perish in the spirit," collapsing to the floor in a swoon.[18] Instead, they stay on their feet and move, sometimes throughout the church, including the raised stand platform, as Sister Johnson did, and sometimes simply within those spaces that inevitably exist between the regular front pews and the stand area.

In addition to preaching, footwashings occasionally give rise to the emotions prerequisite to such episodes of female physical expression. At the July 23, 1995, union and communion meeting of Pilgrim's Rest Church, a footwashing scene served to illustrate this point. As is traditional in most Old-Time Baptist subdenominations, a gender separation does occur during footwashing, with women washing only the feet of women. Furthermore, females seem to become more emotionally stimulated during these moments than do males, but this is not to suggest that the latter never cry or exult.

In the case of the Pilgrim's Rest service, a group of six women was washing feet in the lower front on the left side of the church, in that space between the regular pews and the raised stand area. Prominent in that cluster was Sister Dorothy Horne, a member of Bee Branch Church; when it came her turn to wash and be washed, Sister Horne exploded into what may have been the most vigorous display of spiritual joy that I have ever witnessed in PBU environments. Before and after both the act of administering ablution and the act of receiving it, Sister Horne cried, shouted, and jumped up and down in complete exhilaration, exciting some of the same behaviors in the women around her. For a short time, she became the provider of the "carried out" inspiration upon which the rest of the congregation fed. Women such as Sister Johnson, Sister Davis, and Sister Horne make important contributions to the "quickened" status of PBU worship. From one perspective, PBU worship may appear to be dominated by men, since the preachers are all male. From another perspective, however, the balance seems to shift toward women: they generally outnumber the males, and audience responsiveness is controlled by them. Without the female element, PBU worship dynamics simply could not materialize as they do.

Transcendence

Old Regular Baptist Elder Raymond Smith, of Canada, Pike County, Kentucky, employs an invented term, *revealed,* when he speaks of his version of what PBU elders call *carried out.* He argues that at these times something is being revealed.[19] The PBU terms for this phenomenon suggest a similar idea, the contention again being that God has exerted control over the preaching and the precise message. In support of this claim, Old-Time Baptist preachers, including PBU elders, occasionally state that they have little or no recollection of what they say during these moments. PBU preachers are expressing a similar thought when, at the beginning of a sermon, they frequently volunteer the comment, "I don't know why this is on my mind."

Since the delivery aspects of transcendence already have been addressed, this section merely calls attention to a basic problem with the concept. The claim for this idea of transcendence compels all Old-Time Baptists who come to its defense to face a significant question: How can one be certain of when it has occurred? Obviously, the state cannot be identified solely by the accompanying delivery techniques, because those can be manufactured; nor can it be associated with emotion alone, for that can be misjudged or feigned. One is left, then, with what appears to be the crux of the question: Does the state of having been "blessed" depend completely upon the judgments of receivers, divergent as they may be in their perceptions; or are there universals that the elect can, with general agreement, recognize?

In a jesting way, some members of the congregation at Pilgrim's Rest Church, on July 23, 1995, acknowledged this entire issue when, after a service, they were joking with Elder Unice Davis, who himself was completely engaged in the jocular spirit of the conversation. Davis had just asserted laughingly that he had given the final answer to some question, when a Pilgrim's Rest member, Brother Bill Davis, retorted, "Yes, but you weren't blessed when you said that."

The laughter on both sides of this verbal sparring clearly indicated acceptance of the lightheartedness of the latter statement, but the words still communicated the problem mentioned above. Given the two options— acknowledging and accepting the vagaries of individual interpretation, and asserting that there are universals that the elect can detect—it seems obvious that the latter would be far more comforting to the faithful. I have not obtained a consensus on this matter, however, other than in the straightforward statement that "spirit tells." My impression, nevertheless, is that the movement seems willing to assign to all preaching the benefit of the doubt, unless specific doctrine is being defended or attacked. In that instance, all assertions are scrutinized closely.

ARRANGEMENT OF PBU WORSHIP

My early experiences of Old-Time Baptist worship led me to think that nothing therein had form or structure.[20] An uninitiated visitor to a PBU service might draw the same conclusion. The beginning and the arrangements that follow appear low-key, casual, and devoid of any precise schedule. Indeed, churchgoers accustomed to a fixed and published liturgy, presided over by a priest, minister, or layperson who announces and directs events, would experience a kind of culture shock, not knowing how to behave in an environment in which so few signals are given as to what is coming next.

Of course, the Old-Time Baptist churchgoer knows what is coming next, at least in general terms, and is content merely to wait for those arrangements he or she cannot with any degree of certainty predict—such things as the number of sermons, which preachers will perform, and which hymns will be sung. Indeed, the same rationale that decrees extemporaneous preaching seems to prevail concerning worship structure: that which man rigidly controls precludes God's control. PBU worship procedures, however, do differ in some ways from Old Regular protocol. This discussion focuses on the similarities and contrasts between these two Old-Time Baptist traditions, simply because they are the two I know best.

There is no significant difference between these two conventions in the way services begin. Both de-emphasize precise starting times, treating beginnings with a casualness that seems to eradicate the entire notion of tardiness. The resulting freedom of behavior can be quite enjoyable. There is absolutely no assumption that everyone should engage in the worship process—or any part of it—at exactly the same time. Thus, in a service that begins *around* 10:00 A.M., no code prohibits the individual who arrives at 10:20 from making her or his handshaking rounds of the congregation, even if the preaching has already begun; or from walking directly into the stand to embrace an elder not seen for a year, before finding a place in the regular worship area of the meetinghouse.

Nor is there any substantial difference between the ways the two traditions handle hymn singing. Both start the singing part of the service without announcement. A seated elder, perhaps unseen by much of the congregation, simply begins the first hymn by singing the initial verse. He starts his "lining" with the second verse or the second couplet. During the first half of this initial hymn, only four or five voices, primarily those of the other elders, may be heard. The congregation joins the process by degrees, as each individual worshiper starts singing at a time of her or his own choosing. By the close of that first hymn, most of the congregation will be engaged, but not all; a number of people still may be entering the church and making their round of handshaking.

Lined Old-Time Baptist singing is slow and stretched out, lacking any of those fast-paced, hand-clapping rhythms one might expect to hear in a southern gospel church.[21] Thus the visitor who has grown up accustomed to the latter may find herself or himself wanting to surge ahead of the lining, even with a traditionally slow hymn like "Amazing Grace." The interval between hymns will be stretched out, too, as the moderator and other elders pause and discuss among themselves a possible next selection. After a moment, someone in the congregation may suggest a hymn, and then there will be an additional delay, as everyone finds the song and a decision is made among the elders about who will line it. In fact, one elder may try to start the singing but then give up when he has trouble getting the pitch he wants, leaving it for a second elder to try his skills with the song.

The main contrast being drawn here is between the snappy, energized process that is directed by a song leader and is pleasing to a small-town Southern Baptist congregation, and this more relaxed, unhurried, leaderless, and sometimes uncertain and stumbling process which is more comfortable to a PBU fellowship. In terms of an end result, the PBU congregation might defend the virtues of its system on the basis that hymn singing alone frequently produces a "carried out" church.

Old Regular and PBU fellowships do differ in hymnal usage. The Old Regulars prefer to compile their own songbooks, and a number of individual churches market them at association sessions. The PBU churches primarily employ the old Goble publication, *Primitive Baptist Hymn Book.*[22] In addition, PBU fellowships more frequently will introduce into a service—especially in closing moments or after a footwashing—an unlined hymn. When this happens, the song in question will be a well-known old gospel hymn, such as "Give Me That Old-Time Religion," rendered, however, at a pace much slower than generally is expected. Moderators, however, are careful not to allow too many of these "modern" hymns to be sung; in all cases, the traditional mode is preferred over the contemporary mode.

Another distinction between the two conventions is this: there appears to be no PBU custom comparable to the Old Regular "sing down," a standard feature of that Old-Time Baptist tradition. At the turn of the century and even much later, the "sing down" was used to help the extemporizing preacher close out a sermon that had grown too long. Today, however, Old Regulars use the procedure at the end of the introductory sermon, creating a sound dynamic (hymn against preaching) that can become very rousing.[23] A PBU custom closely related to the Old Regular "sing down" deals with the way in which closing preaching and closing singing often are handled. What occasionally happens is that the closing sermon will have been preached, a final hymn will be begun, and the last preacher will start preaching again. The result is the same dueling sound dynamic that Old Regulars like at the conclusion of the introductory sermon. One sound competes with the other; the competition drives both to a higher level of emotion.

In yet another way, the typical PBU preaching service differs from the typical Old Regular service. As already noted, the PBU elders, more often than not, are asked "to make their own arrangements." These moments of "arrangement making" can become awkward, as there is at least a tendency to think of the "close" as being the most coveted of the speaking spots in a standard service. It is, of course, a clear violation of PBU preaching ethics to covet any honor in the stand. Like most Old-Time Baptist preachers, PBU elders practice a carefully crafted art of self-effacement, assiduously avoiding any semblance of ego, ambition, or pride, in line with that argument that, if any pulpit success is achieved, it is solely to God's credit. Therefore, the deliberations engaged in while "making arrangements" must never appear self-serving and indeed should give every indication of being just the opposite. As a result, respected elders in high positions may be heard to whisper something like the following: "Why don't you brothers let me introduce? I won't take long, and then I'll be out of the way. I'd prefer to hear you other brothers."

The number of preachers used in a PBU service will vary, but the usual quantity for a regular monthly service is three—one to open, one to follow, and one to close. A variety of circumstances, however, may alter the picture. First, the first couple of preachers may go "unblessed" and hence produce brief sermons. Second, several popular elders may appear on a given day, creating some pressure for the moderator to use all of them. Third, a union and communion meeting always necessitates one additional sermon.

Congregations traditionally call four elders for union and communion services—three for the regular meeting and one extra for the preaching just before communion, an added event that extends the church's Sunday meeting by an hour and a half or two hours. Preaching for the Saturday session of meeting weekends varies, depending on both availability of elders and the amount of important business before the church that day.

PBU congregations are prone to be more conservative in their number of sermons than are Old Regulars. In the latter, as many as eight preachers may speak on a Sunday, especially on a union meeting, memorial meeting, or communion meeting Sunday (the union and communion services often are held on separate Sundays within the Old Regular tradition). For purposes of comparison, this study averaged the number of elders called to 1995 union meetings within the Union Association of Old Regular Baptists and the number called to that same year's union meetings within the Regular Primitive Baptist Washington District Association (PBU). The PBU average was 4.1, while the Old Regular average was 6.5.[24]

Once the preaching is over, usually only four things remain in a regular PBU service: a closing hymn, coinciding with an "opening of the church door"; announcements of other services; and the closing prayer (benediction). The "opening of the church door," of course, is the invitation to any nonmember to come forward, make a profession of "call," and ask for baptism. This "living water" immersion may take place later that afternoon, or it may be scheduled for some future date, giving time for all relatives and friends to be notified.

Announcements—made by those elders who may be involved in the respective events—frequently are for regular monthly meetings, but they also may be for "fifth Sunday" activities or for other special happenings—family memorials, funerals, baptisms, and the like. Since standard meeting weekends are set in accord with first, second, third, and fourth calendar Saturdays, occasionally a fifth Sunday of the month occurs, on which no regular meetings are scheduled. Those days become favorite times for home services, graveside memorials, and other preaching events for which no set timetable exists.

The reader should note that in a PBU service there is no formal time for "taking up the collection." As is true in most Old-Time Baptist groups, PBU Sunday services seldom mention money. In fact, during the last three years, the only times when I have heard the subject broached have been at the close of union meetings, when a moderator said something about helping out with the traveling expenses of the called elders. Individuals wishing to make any regular contributions to the church must do so at business meetings or by dropping currency on the stand at the close of the Sunday service, usually during the announcements. In the latter situation, no appeal is made, and the contributor must go out of her or his way to move forward to make the donation. However, many PBU members visiting from other churches do just that, feeling a responsibility to support financially not only her or his home fellowship, but also other churches attended frequently. In truth, PBU constituents tend to feel that, although membership places an individual in one church, true belonging places that individual in all PBU fellowships. Therefore there is movement back and forth between meetinghouses, especially within a given association, with a certain sense of being "at home" in each facility.

A Final Thought on the "Carried Out" State

A clear distinction should be made between "carried out," as understood in the PBU movement, and "anointment" or "Holy Ghost possession," as featured in the Pentecostal tradition. Nowhere in the PBU convention does one find such Pentecostal "under anointment" acts as glossolalia (speaking in tongues), revival exercises (perishing in the Spirit, running in the Spirit, laughing in the Spirit, and the like), the handling of deadly things (snakes, fire, and so forth), or spontaneous spiritual healing.

In the first place, PBU rhetoric applies the term *carried out* only to preaching. I have broadened the phrase, making it representative of certain levels of congregational behavior—a usage with which PBU elders, in particular, might not be comfortable. In addition, PBU discussions of the "carried out" state suggest heightened sensitivity, greater spiritual awareness, more perfect alignment with God's will, and being so in tune with the deity that supernatural meaning is allowed to emerge from natural man. Those discussions do not suggest, however, an ability to nullify natural law or to become one and the same with the Spirit. Furthermore, "carried out" appears not to imply charismatic powers of healing or prophecy.

The PBU faith does practice "laying on of hands," usually at the close of a service, when a physically infirm individual approaches the stand to have all of the elders present place their hands on her or his head or shoulders. Such acts, though, are dissociated from the "quickened" state of spiritual expression and become quiet but intense moments of focused prayer. Little about these episodes duplicates either the images of death or the claims to special powers inherent in those high-drama moments of "immediate healing" associated with charismatic evangelical movements.

7

"KEEPING THEM NEAR"

Thompson Valley, in Tazewell County, Virginia, runs a northeast-to-southwest course between the Clinch Mountain range on the southern side of the depression and two disconnected mountains on the northern side: Rich Mountain at the valley's head, and Knob Mountain at the valley's feet. Virginia's Route 604 travels the lower half of this elongated glen, roughly paralleling Maiden Spring Creek. Part of the creek is called Dry Run, because, at the mouth of the valley, the stream temporarily drops into an underground limestone channel.

Near the middle of this fifteen-mile depression, at a spot where the valley floor is wedged between "The Knobs" and a section of Clinch Mountain named "Big Doubles" and "Little Doubles" (twin peak formations, side by side), lies the old Harrison-Beavers family farm. The farm was established in 1904 by Thomas Harrison (1855–1942), who, sometime prior to that year, had married Martha Beavers (1856–1929). Each summer for at least the past half-century—the beginning date apparently has been lost to family memory—this old homestead has been the site of the Harrison-Beavers Family Reunion and Memorial, an event that today regularly attracts approximately one hundred Harrisons and Beavers. The reunion belongs to a PBU religious tradition that meshes well with the Old-Time Baptist custom of keeping progenitors alive in words, actions, and memories.[1]

When the Harrison-Beavers Family Reunion and Memorial was in its heyday, it was a three-day event that attracted as many as three hundred persons to a celebration that had familial, religious, social, and even political aspects. The gathering afforded opportunities for preaching, general socializing, courting, feasting, respectable merrymaking, and whatever other wholesome types of human interaction such a clustering of people might facilitate. It was held on a prosperous farm that grazed animals (horses, cattle, and sheep), cultivated orchards (cherries and apples), yielded a variety of produce (for animal and human consumption), and provided the nurturing ground for a large family. Heirs have preserved the memorial, even after the farm itself has largely fallen into disuse and decay.

Although the Harrison-Beavers Family Reunion and Memorial is today only a shadow of its former self, it still symbolizes the key values that underlie the Old-Time Baptist commitment to memorialize the dead: reunion, remembrance, relations, respect, reverence, religiosity. Perhaps no other tradition is more consistently woven into the fabric of Appalachian Old-Time Baptist subdenominations than that of memorializing the dead.

MEMORIALS WITHIN PBU TRADITION

Home, graveside, and church memorials are as much parts of Primitive Baptist Universalist customs as they are of the customs of other Old-Time Baptists. "Passed on" friends and family are not forgotten, but instead remain indelibly present both within the church and within the ancestral household, to the fourth, fifth, and perhaps sixth generation. The main factor determining whether ancestors remain alive in the memories of relatives is whether these progenitors lived in approximately the same geographical area and thus are buried near the homes of descendants. Graves establish a fixed and permanent point for memory.

At least three causal factors appear to be operative in this tradition of reverence for the dead. First is a theological one: PBU doctrine maintains that the deceased are only sleeping, caught in an endless, peaceful, insensate time warp, until Resurrection restores them to a union in heaven with God, Christ, and the total human family. The doctrine maintains that this will be a resurrection of bodies, returning families to each other in a recognizable condition. Individuals will be reunited with mothers, fathers, grandmothers, grandfathers, and so on in a state of being that allows awareness of, and joy in, that longed-for "unbroken circle."[2]

Indeed, so strong has been the faith's commitment to this principle of resurrection of the body that preaching in opposition to this doctrine—suggesting the resurrection only of an unembodied spirit—has caused two painful splits—the one already reported, concerning the now-defunct Stony Creek Association, and a smaller one covered in the last chapter of this book. A related controversy arose in the late 1940s and continued through much of the 1950s, temporarily splitting the Three Forks Association and also causing both Three Forks and Washington to cease correspondence with Elkhorn. In that dispute, a collection of Washington and Three Forks elders alleged that Elkhorn elders—along with elders representing Colly Creek Church and Sulphur Springs Church (Three Forks fellowships)—were preaching a doctrine that denied the physical form of God himself, except as represented in Christ.[3] This line of argument also threatened the physical-body nature of heaven.

While insisting upon a physical, as opposed to merely a spiritual, afterlife, the PBU stance concerning the precise nature of the resurrected body—its age and its exact corporeal condition—remains unexplicated. The prevalent presumption is that this state will be a perfected one, a beautiful one, and—again—a recognizable one. This belief concerning bodily resurrection seems to intensify many of the strong feelings inherent in the memorialization process.

A second factor contributing to the PBU tradition of reverence for the dead arises from the movement's deep respect for patriarchs and matriarchs, again both within the church and within the home. The voices of age and ancestry carry weight with these people—far more, it seems, than is the norm in contemporary American society. All other things being equal, the beliefs and values of age remain dominant over the beliefs and values of youth, especially within the church hierarchy.

Furthermore, this respect seems to increase once an individual has died, this being most pointedly so in the case of "passed on" elders. One need not spend an inordinate amount of time among these churches before gaining a sense of the eminence of such past leaders as Noah Adair, S. F. (Sammy) Adair, T. F. (Tommy) Adair, E. M. Evans, Morgan T. Lipps, Stuart Owens, William Robinette, and others. That these men are still mentioned so frequently and that their likenesses still hang on stand walls suggest their ongoing presence and their continuing influence.

Similar traditions are at least partially operative for the women of these churches. Oral histories recall women who were known for their exuberant worship styles—their crying, shouting, praising, jumping. Unfortunately, these oral histories concerning women do not as often work their way into stand rhetoric as stories about the elders mentioned above. Still, this strain of matriarchal reverence continues strong within at least the female world of these fellowships.

A third factor giving rise to the PBU tradition of reverence for the dead is the fact that the typical PBU congregation is aging. It would be difficult to overlook the graying of these fellowships. In these churches there is a moderately strong element of people in their early thirties to late fifties but, numerically, the group aged sixty and older predominates. People under thirty, except for grandchildren who are not church members, are largely absent, except at family memorials or association meetings.

Of course, one reason why the age distributions of these congregation are skewed toward the elderly is that, like the members of several other Old-Time Baptist groups, Primitive Baptist Universalists tend to be baptized and join the church at a much later age than is true for Freewill Baptists, Missionary Baptists, Southern Baptists, and other Arminian divisions of the faith.[4] While these latter groups usually baptize individual in their teens or even earlier, PBU fellowships are more Anabaptist in leaning, frequently baptizing individuals who are in their forties or older. During my three years of traveling among Primitive Baptist Universalists, have only witnessed three baptisms, largely because there usually are so few of these events in any given year (there was, for example, a total of ten within the three associations during the 1993–94 session year). The three such events I did observe—all in Dismal River—involved one young mother who probably was in her mid-twenties, a man who appeared to be in his mid- to late forties, and a woman who probably was in her sixties. Unfortunately, I was unable to witness the baptism of McGennis Adair's granddaughter, an event mentioned in chapter 8.

In considering the absence of young people, another point to remember is that there are no Sunday schools in the PBU churches. Like many Old-Time Baptist subdenominations, Primitive Baptist Universalists believe that Sunday schools are unnecessary and unwarranted, since, according to their faith, God will call whom he has elected to call, regardless of any human attempts to nurture that individual into belief and goodness. In any case, aging congregations appear more naturally disposed to focus on death and dying than are younger congregations. Furthermore, as age increases, so too does the propensity toward reminiscing, as each individual seeks that connection of past, present, and future that seems so essential

Baptism by Elder Unice Davis (right), moderator of the Elkhorn Association, in Dismal River, near Hale Creek Church, Buchanan County, Virginia, summer 1995.

to an expectation of immortality. Finally, the desire to remember seldom is disconnected from the desire to be remembered, with the obligation of the former motivated in part by the hope of the latter.

The PBU reverence for ancestry generates the three types of memorials most frequently found in Old-Time Baptist circles: home memorials, graveside memorials, and church memorials. In the first of these, family, church members, and friends gather in a private home for what will develop much as a regular PBU service does. The service begins with singing, progresses to the preaching of several elders, and closes with a round of emotional "fellowshiping." The final portion of the service may even include the opening of a church door (if these are primarily members of one church), the announcement of future church meetings, and a prayer or benediction. If the event memorializes one family member, such as a prominent past elder from that household, then mention probably will be made, at the introduction, of this person's accomplishments. Nevertheless, the evening's rhetoric will not focus exclusively on that individual, centering instead on traditional themes present in any PBU preaching.

Graveside memorials, too, follow the regular format of a PBU worship service, varied only according to the precise nature of the burial site in question. Central Appalachia is replete with hundreds, perhaps even thousands, of small family cemeteries, which may contain from three or four graves to two score or more, and these private burial spots frequently provide the sites for these graveside memorials, again celebrating the heritage of one family. However, church cemeteries also exist, containing the resting places of deceased members of a number of families, and such a sacred spot often has a stand built as an open arbor and intended especially for memorial services.

During the summer of 1995, I attended the Owens Family Memorial, which annually is held on a picturesque ridge just northwest of Highway 83 in a segment of Buchanan County, Virginia, known as Little Prater, after the name of the creek that runs through the area. Currently organized by Elder Willard Owens of the Washington Association, this event celebrates the lives of four generations of Owenses who are buried there on the ridge, including Willard's father, Claude; his grandfather, Patton; and his great-grandfather, Floyd, all of whom in their times were prominent within PBU circles. Indeed, the various branches of the Owens family have produced one of the larger collections of PBU elders and clerks, this last name figuring prominently throughout the seven decades of PBU association minutes.

Finally, memorials are held inside PBU churches, sometimes as an annually scheduled event and sometimes as a fifth-Sunday event. When a month's calendar includes one of those fifth Sundays, there will be no regularly scheduled church meetings, allowing that day to be used for a special event such as a memorial for all the deceased members of the particular church.

PBU church memorials occasionally follow the tradition practiced in Old Regular Baptist churches—calling out the names of all deceased members of the congregation, for as far back as the church records go. This can become a very poignant event, as families wait for their loved ones to be mentioned. With the right dynamics, this service can become as emotional as any to be witnessed within Old-Time Baptist circles. Furthermore, this annual calling out of names symbolizes more pointedly than perhaps any other practice that desire to keep even deceased members within the church family.

Harrison-Beavers Family Reunion and Memorial

The old Harrison home sits approximately fifty yards from the southeast bank of Maiden Spring Creek, and most of the acreage of the farm that once was tilled or grazed stretches up a gentle slope at the base of Clinch Mountain. Today it is not easy to reach this spot in Thompson Valley, simply because the old private road that runs down from Route 604 is, after a point, no more than a narrow, deeply rutted single lane of dirt and rock that is traveled regularly only by a tractor or a four-wheel-drive pickup truck. Brush and tree limbs, evidently left unpruned for a number of years, scrape the sides of any vehicle that labors down this road. When such a vehicle reaches the bottom of the valley, it has to ford Maiden Spring Creek, which contains large rocks that seem eager to snare the underside of any low-hung vehicle. Before each memorial, one of the family members strings rope markers across the creek, showing drivers the best place to ford the stream.

At the time of this writing in 1995, no one lives on the Harrison farm. The old two-story home has fallen into irreparable decay, abandoned to the unrestricted trespasses of animals (wild and domesticated) and the occasional human wanderer who has hiked out to enjoy the quiet beauties of Maiden Spring Creek. Except for a large open field climbing up the base of Clinch Mountain, the farm is returning to wilderness. The one field in question is maintained by someone for haying purposes.

Approximately five hundred yards above the creek and the old home, on the Clinch Mountain side of the valley, is the small Harrison-Beavers family cemetery, with only fifteen marked burial spots. The earliest of the interments is the 1929 grave of Martha Beavers Harrison, and the most recent are three 1982 graves. These latter contain the remains of Wanda Beavers, Candace Beavers, and Peggy Beavers. Wanda, the first wife of Elder Farley Beavers, and their two young daughters were killed on August 31, 1982, in an automobile accident. Brother Farley already has placed his own marker beside the other three, in preparation for his demise, whenever it may come.

A low chain-link fence surrounds the cemetery, and on the Clinch Mountain side of this fence stands a roofed, open preaching arbor that provides roughly five hundred square feet of sheltered space to be used when the Harrison-Beavers Family Reunion and Memorial is staged at this spot each year. On those days, the sheltered area is augmented by two large camping canopies, one stretched out from the Clinch Mountain side of the arbor and the other extending from the southwestern end of the structure. These canopies ward off the early afternoon sun that otherwise would pour down into the seating area. Additional shade is provided, on the creek side of the shelter, by a young maple tree.

For these memorial services, the arbor is arranged much as a small PBU meetinghouse would be. The southwestern end of the structure becomes

the stand area, equipped with a pulpit and a long bench where elders sit;
the remainder of the covered space becomes the congregational area, filled
with metal folding chairs brought from Salem Church and with a number of plastic chairs moved temporarily from Elder Farley Beavers's barber shop in Tazewell, Virginia. This seating is augmented by a wide variety of outdoor chairs and lounges transported to this event by individual
family members and set up in one of the canopied areas. Occasionally a
family will park a recreational vehicle near the southeastern side of the arbor and provide its own shaded area for sitting. In two recent years, the
crowd numbered approximately one hundred each time, including children and young people who wandered all around the old farm while the
memorial service was being conducted.

According to contemporary Harrison-Beavers family members, this
attendance of approximately one hundred is much smaller than the number attracted in the early years of the event. Kelly and Anna Ruth McGuire,
family members on the wife's side, report that at one time the old farm
annually hosted between two and three hundred persons, who slept in every
shelter available on the homestead.[5] That sleep-over tradition continues
at nearby homes of family members, but the total number of visitors has

*Under the preaching arbor, Harrison-Beavers Family Reunion and Memorial, Thompson
Valley, Virginia, summer 1995.*

decreased sharply, perhaps in response to changing values and new family exigencies. The religious character of this event is still strong, however, in part because emphasis has tended to shift over time from the reunion aspects to the memorial aspects.

To get to the old farm, family members initially gather at the home of Kelly and Anna Ruth McGuire, which sits near the upper end of the old private road and is accessible by two-wheel-drive vehicles. Then people climb into the backs of pickups and other higher-built trucks or vans—usually also loaded with folding chairs, foods for dinner-on-the-grounds, picnic blankets, and various sunscreen devices—and head down toward the creek.

In July 1995, during my second experience with this memorial, I accompanied a family member on the half-mile trek down to the farm. As I pulled off my shoes, rolled up my trousers, and waded through the calf-deep, chillingly fresh water of Maiden Spring Creek, I wished that I could have been present when, in a supposedly simpler time, perhaps in the 1920s or 1930s, the Harrisons and Beavers gathered for this annual day of celebration and renewal. Then I could have seen the large home sturdy and well maintained, the apple and cherry orchards tended and productive, sheep grazing the upper Clinch Mountain pasture, acres of corn growing to use as fodder for cattle, and a large family living on this land. No doubt the image in my mind was romanticized, but it was pleasurable.

Earlier, the Harrison-Beavers Family Reunion and Memorial was an all-day affair, but the present celebration does not last that long. People start arriving at the old farm between 9:30 and 10:00 A.M., bringing chairs, coolers of food and drink, perhaps a picnic blanket, and possibly a video camera. Teenagers and children, if large enough to run free, immediately start ranging across the vacated farm. Occasionally parents must tell youngsters to stay out of the old house, since decay has rendered it dangerous. Adults, however, quickly gather in the vicinity of the cemetery, the older women being first to stake their claims on favorite seats under the arbor.

Sometime around eleven o'clock, the singing and preaching service begins, with between three and six elders being heard and responded to by numerous "carried out" female family members. By 1:00 or 1:30 P.M., the preaching service is over; and a traditional dinner-on-the-grounds is served, followed by a relaxing time of group socializing or individual pilgrimages to the creek or the old homestead.

During the preaching, stand rhetoric focuses on tradition, family, and loved ones who have "passed on"—all in an effort, as one preacher put it, to "keep them near." Thomas Harrison and his wife Martha Beavers Harrison, as the patriarch and matriarch of the family, receive particular attention; and much emphasis is placed upon the notion of sanctifying struggles—those ordinary hardships that all endure if they are to persevere in building a family heritage.

Place is emphasized—this spot of ground, the old farm, the house, the creek, the mountains. Recollections are related that champion the virtues of persistence and endurance, the sense of being anchored, the long-range perspective, a covenantal faith. The graves are referred to as metaphorical sleeping places, where—according to PBU doctrine—the dead await, without awareness of time, the Resurrection that will lift *all* and reunite *all*. As Elder Farley R. Beavers proclaimed in his 1995 memorial sermon, "The great ages will be as the twinkling of an eye."[6]

"Family," "parents," "grandparents," and "kin" are potent themes in these sermons, and occasionally shouting will erupt at the mere mention of one individual in this pantheon of relatives. At the 1995 Harrison-Beavers memorial, one woman began to shout, "That's my grandfather! That's my grandfather!" There appeared to be little need for any message other than "There are kin asleep here, waiting." That understanding alone triggers joyful expectations.

Elder Farley R. (Ronnie) Beavers, the moderator of Salem Church, also assumes leadership of this family memorial, since he is the reigning religious figure among the Harrisons and Beavers. Two earlier family members—Columbus Harrison (1892–1959) and Farley A. Beavers (1902–1979), the latter being Farley R. Beavers's father—were elders in the Primitive Baptist Universalist movement. Indeed, for a number of years, Elder Farley A. Beavers served as the moderator of Washington Association (the PBU side). Suffice it to say that the Harrisons and Beavers have made major contributions to the larger PBU heritage.[7]

Elder Farley R. Beavers, mentioned in the preface to this volume as one of the collaborators crucial to this study, is the proprietor of the Zion's Clippers Barber Shop in Tazewell, Virginia. He passes out a business card which contains on its back the following message: "A saint is a sinner saved by grace that knows they're a sinner saved by grace." Elder Beavers was ordained at Salem Church in 1975 while he was still in the Air Force, from which he retired in 1980. After a couple of years of attempting to rejuvenate some farm property, Beavers enrolled in a West Virginia barber's school in 1982, and that is where he was in August 1982, when his wife and two daughters, one eight years old and the other eleven, were killed in the

Members of the Harrison-Beavers family, at the Harrison-Beavers Family Reunion and Memorial, Thompson Valley, Virginia, 1994.

automobile accident mentioned above. Today Brother Farley, or "Brother Ronnie," as most PBU members call him, has remarried, and his second wife, Sister Sandra, works closely with him in all his church-related duties. Elder Beavers definitely is one of the more popular PBU preachers, frequently called to union meetings and other special services; and he keeps busy moderating two fellowships and assistant-moderating three.

During the Harrison-Beavers Family Reunion and Memorial in 1994 and 1995, family members shared their personal memories of the event and their own judgments of the event's meaning. They told tales of parents and grandparents, of well-remembered elders and their preaching, of a baptism in Maiden Spring Creek, and of numerous celebratory scenes of singing and shouting. They gave accounts of heavy rains that made crossing the creek particularly treacherous; of people sleeping in the old house and barn; of cherry picking in the old orchard; of sheep on the lower rise of Clinch Mountain; of marriage proposals made and accepted (one such story is related in chapter 8); of horse-drawn wagons around the graves of the original matriarch and patriarch; and of special emotions felt during the World War II years, when many of the younger family members were in the Armed Forces. The web of memories was thick and various, capturing in its threads all the elements of family folk history. The collective family narrative assumed an epistemological role, as a chronicle carefully crafted for integration with Primitive Baptist Universalist covenantal theology, especially the contention that the elect have been chosen to witness and preserve.

Indeed, for PBU folk, there seems to be no clear separation between religion and legacy, as the one supports or extends the other. God's plan and man's history are essentially the same, especially for "the elect." Therefore, this ongoing celebration of family becomes a rejoicing in faith, an annual affirmation of that central theological premise of Universalism: that we all shall be together "by and by," as an "unbroken circle" far more inclusive than that envisioned in other religious thought. A PBU family memorial proclaims that belief at every annual meeting, "keeping them near" until Resurrection makes that nearness more tangible.

8 MIGRATION OF THE FAITH

Centerburg, Ohio, received its name because it lies at the geographical center of the state, a spot northeast of Columbus and approximately two-thirds of the way between Columbus and Mount Vernon, in a panhandle segment of Knox County. About three miles northwest of Centerburg, on a small rise overlooking miles and miles of cornfields, lies the unincorporated community of Rich Hill.

Today, during the mid-1990s, Rich Hill, Centerburg, Sunbury, Mount Liberty, Mount Vernon, and nearby small towns are experiencing considerable residential growth, as families move out from Columbus to escape that city's problems. Villages in Knox County, Ohio, preserve the tranquillity of small-town America, an ambiance that is equally attractive to retirees and to working heads of households who, in order to secure a provincial lifestyle, are willing to endure a one-hour commute to the segments of Columbus located north of Interstate Highway 70.

This middle region of Ohio experienced an earlier immigration, one important to the subject of this work. The years during and after World War II saw an influx of people from Central Appalachia—Virginians, West Virginians, Kentuckians, and others, many of whom were recruited to labor in the state's various wartime industries. Because these migrants brought their culture with them when they left Grundy, Tazewell, Pikeville, or Welch, there are pockets of Appalachian Old-Time Baptist religious practices in Ohio and other states of the Midwest. Thus, Rich Hill, Ohio, is the home of Rich Hill Church, an outmigrant member of the Elkhorn Primitive Baptist Association. In this chapter, Rich Hill, Ohio, and Rich Hill Church represent not only themselves, but also three other locales outside Central Appalachia and three other Primitive Baptist Universalist fellowships that have been established far from the PBU heartland.

I visited Rich Hill Church twice, on May 21–22, 1994, for a regular Saturday and Sunday monthly meeting of the fellowship; and on September 1–3, 1995, for the 134th Annual Session of the Elkhorn Primitive Baptist Association. During both these trips, I was struck by the paradoxes of place and culture that this PBU meetinghouse represents—the oddity of this small slice of Appalachian life having been lifted from its native base and settled among these midwestern cornfields, and the tenacity of Appalachian religious culture that resulted in this transplantation.

This was not the first time I had encountered such oddity of cultural persistence in a new place, however. In 1990, in Ypsilanti, Michigan, I had examined the results of such a transplantation of the Old Regular Baptist tradition.[1] The only significant differences between these two experiences have to do with in the contrasting natures of the two faiths and the dissimilarities of the two locales—one urban, one rural.

Rich Hill Church and the Appalachian Sense of Place

Two features of Appalachian character are relevant to the central topic of this chapter, the maintenance of PBU faith when its adherents move outside the Appalachian region: (1) the "sense of place" that is so strong in Appalachia and its people, a love not only of setting but of all the cultural references embedded in that setting; and (2) a strong desire on the part of Appalachian outmigrants either to return to that place or to take to the new locale essential characteristics of the former home.[2] Both these features have received considerable attention from scholars. The outmigrant sense of both place and culture seldom is expressed more powerfully than it is in regard to religious practices, in large part because of the distinctive nature of Appalachian worship styles and religious doctrines.[3]

It often is extremely difficult, if not impossible, for the Appalachian outmigrant—finding herself or himself in Ohio, Pennsylvania, Indiana, Michigan, Florida, eastern North Carolina, or wherever—to locate outlets for the type of religious expression experienced back in the Southern

Highlands. Therefore, the Rich Hill meetinghouse symbolizes a phenomenon that emerges wherever Appalachians go in numbers sufficient to establish a religious community.

On my first visit to Rich Hill church, I met a man originally from Pike County, Kentucky, whose family had been affiliated with the Original Mates Creek Primitive Baptist Association. That Primitive Baptist group ordinarily has no relationship with PBU churches at all. Still, this man attended the Rich Hill service that Sunday, because, he said, this church provided his only access to the type of preaching and singing he had been accustomed to in Kentucky. He understood the doctrinal differences involved, but he could overlook those differences in favor of the general atmosphere and worship style of the church. He was interested primarily in what amounted to the "tonal" qualities of this fellowship.

Elder Tommy (T. F.) Adair and the Founding of Rich Hill Church

Rich Hill Church (the membership, not the meetinghouse) was established in 1951 by Elder Tommy Adair, identified in the minutes of the Elkhorn Association throughout the 1950s, 1960s, and 1970s as "T. F. Adair." This man was the brother of Noah Adair and the first cousin of Sammy (S. F.) Adair, both individuals mentioned in chapter 4 as leaders in the 1924–25 split between the "Hellers" and "No-Hellers." Tommy Adair moderated the Elkhorn Association immediately after Sammy Adair's tenure. Indeed, for a number of years, the Elkhorn Association operated under a kind of Adair family leadership package, with Sammy as moderator and Tommy as assistant moderator. Therefore, it would be difficult to ignore the Adairs of West Virginia when discussing PBU history.

The members of the Adair, Davis, Horne, Looney, McGlothlin, Smith, and Webb families, who constituted much of the membership of Rich Hill Church in the 1950s, came to central Ohio primarily from Buchanan and Tazewell counties, Virginia, and from McDowell County, West Virginia. Their homes had been on both sides of Bradshaw Mountain, in mining communities such as Beartown, Grundy, Jolo, Paynesville, and Stacey; and initially they had belonged to churches affiliated with either the Elkhorn or the Washington Association. Indeed, there may have been some Three Forks of Powell's River people within this group.

Rich Hill Church did not "arm off" from an already established fellowship, as is often the practice in Old-Time Baptist subdenominations.

Although the leadership of this new PBU congregation came out of Mount Zion Church in Beartown, West Virginia, the dozen or so initial fellowship members were a diverse lot, having previously belonged to five or six different churches on both sides of State Line Ridge. Elder Tommy Adair simply gathered them together for what, in 1951, became an independent Primitive Baptist Universalist church. Then, in 1952, Rich Hill Church joined the Elkhorn Association.

Prior to all this, Elder Tommy Adair had moved to Knox County, Ohio, from his native McDowell County, West Virginia, purchasing a small farm near Centerburg. His move followed the earlier outmigration of a son, McGennis Adair, Sr., who, at the time Rich Hill Church was established, was employed by the Continental Can Company in Mount Vernon, Ohio. McGennis Adair currently is Rich Hill's one and only deacon. He and his wife are the subjects of a case study, presented below, in Appalachian migration to central Ohio.

In addition to organizing and moderating the Rich Hill fellowship, Elder Tommy Adair served for over two decades as either assistant moderator or moderator of the Elkhorn Association. In relatively short order, after organizing the Ohio church, he was instrumental in bringing the centennial meeting of the Elkhorn Association to Rich Hill in 1960 and, five years later, in returning Elkhorn's annual association to this small Ohio community.[4] Elder Adair remained as moderator of Rich Hill Church until his death in 1979, by which time he had moved back to his native West Virginia.

THE RICH HILL MEETINGHOUSE

When the church fellowship was organized in 1951, there was no physical structure within which the small assembly regularly gathered. Meetings were held in homes until the fellowship acquired temporary use of an old worship facility that sits on the south side of the hill, adjacent to the Rich Hill Cemetery. This wood-framed building, locally called Rich Hill Church, is owned by the local township and over the years has been used by various religious groups. It is not, however, the present Rich Hill meetinghouse that Tommy Adair ultimately acquired for use by this PBU fellowship. This latter structure once had been a one-room schoolhouse in Bloomfield, Ohio, but it had been relocated in the Rich Hill community and initially put into service as a garage. Much of the left side of the building had been removed, allowing cars to be driven onto the old hardwood flooring.

*Rich Hill Primitive Baptist Church meetinghouse, Rich Hill,
Ohio, summer 1995.*

When the small PBU congregation purchased the structure, it was returned to more dignified use. The building again was moved, this time to
its present location on the northwestern side of Rich Hill. It was placed
on a concrete block foundation, furnished with a new left wall, cleaned
inside and out, and equipped with approximately one hundred used school
or theater auditorium seats.[5] In addition, asbestos siding of a type common in the 1950s was applied to the front and two long sides of the building, while a sublevel furnace room was added at the rear.

The old Bloomfield schoolhouse had been equipped with the custom-
ary school bell, situated in an open-sided turret affixed at the front point
of the roof line. Today that turret, similar to the one that rests on the old
Oak Grove church, looks like a boxy steeple. This suggestion of a steeple
and the large lettering on the front of the structure, announcing the
facility's connection with the Elkhorn Primitive Baptist Association, com-
bine to identify this building as a place of worship.

The old meetinghouse exterior has seen better days. Rain gutters and downspouts gradually are pulling away from the remainder of the structure; the building appears to need a new roof; all the eaves and window trims need fresh paint. The rear wall, which seems never to have received paint or siding, reveals the deterioration of the schoolhouse's original outer planking; and the once-white coverings of the other three walls now are badly discolored, dislocated, and chipped. Parts of the concrete-block foundation have been broken through, perhaps to allow more recent plumbing and heating to be installed; the old furnace room has fallen in and been removed, leaving a gaping hole partially filled with broken concrete blocks. Grounds surrounding the church, however, are attractive and well shaded by maple, oak, and locust. In addition, the edges of the lot are trimmed of all encroaching underbrush, providing reclaimed space not only for outdoor meals but also for parking cars around the church. At meeting times, the grass is always neatly mowed.

The structure's interior is in good repair. Modern restroom facilities have been added, a kitchen cabinet with sink (needed for preparation of dinner-on-the-grounds) runs half the length of one wall, and all the worship areas are clean and well maintained. The church once was heated through vents running from the bottom of the stand platform back to that subfloor furnace room; but those openings have been covered, and heat now is supplied by a large, relatively new, freestanding oil stove. As in a number of the PBU meetinghouses, a rustic charm prevails within this interior, preserving an old-fashioned ambiance that pleases many elderly PBU worshipers. In fact, one receives the impression that, were these church interiors to become too modern and plush, there would be, for some of these worshipers, a substantial loss in comfort and identification.

Rich Hill's interior is not especially spacious, accommodating only 100 to 125 worshipers before extra chairs are needed. Normally, however, that is more than adequate seating. The peak years of growth for the fellowship apparently were the late 1960s, when the membership hovered around forty.[6] Most of those members were native Virginians or West Virginians who had come to central Ohio during World War II, when work was plentiful in area munitions plants and on the railroads.[7] Today that membership has shrunk to thirteen, but the small fellowship is still strongly supported by the Adair family, including Brother McGennis Adair, Sr. (the deacon); Sister Phyllis Adair, his wife; Brother McGennis Adair, Jr., their son; Sister Sherry Harley, their daughter; and finally, Sister Harley's daughter, who only joined the church during the 1995 association meeting.

The last three of these Adair family members are absentee fellowship members: Brother McGennis, Jr., owns and operates a farm in western Kentucky; Sister Sherry teaches school in Florida; and the Adairs' granddaughter is enrolled at West Virginia Wesleyan College. Nevertheless, both the son and the daughter frequently serve as Rich Hill Church messengers at Elkhorn Association sessions, and the granddaughter probably will do the same.

Sister Opel Mae Smith, Phyllis Adair's sister and a Rich Hill Church member, also is an absentee member, living in Fort Myers, Florida. Indeed, of the thirteen fellowship members, only Brother McGennis, Sr., and Sister Phyllis live anywhere near the small Rich Hill meetinghouse.

Rich Hill fellowship certainly is stronger in terms of membership than is Holston Church, with its one member, but this dependence on absentee support—not only from these members who live outside Ohio, but also from out-of-state elders in the Elkhorn, Washington, and Three Forks associations—makes regular monthly meetings very difficult. No PBU elder lives in the immediate vicinity of Rich Hill, and no current Elkhorn Association elder even lives in Ohio. Indeed, Elder Quinton Looney, of the Washington Association, by virtue of the fact that his home is in Mansfield, Ohio, is the PBU preacher closest to Rich Hill. Elder Howard Coleman, another Washington Association preacher who is helpful to the congregation, lives considerably west of Elder Looney, in Continental, Ohio. Three other Washington Association elders live in Ohio, too, but at the time of this writing in 1995, their service—to any of the outmigrant PBU fellowships—apparently is minimal.[8] All of these details suggest the difficulties of maintaining PBU outmigrant fellowships and the sacrifices involved in such maintenance.

THE VIRGINIA–WEST VIRGINIA–OHIO CONNECTION

On May 22, 1994, breakfast was in full swing at the In-Town Restaurant in Centerburg. The In-Town clearly constituted an early-morning meeting place for a lot of local people, especially older men, and the diner had one of those tables informally reserved for these gatherings. This particular morning, five or six men were occupying this eating space.

I did not approach this group, knowing full well how that would have been received, but when all but one of the men had left, I did join that straggler, a retiree, originally from Cincinnati, who had yielded to his wife's request that they relocate to the community of her roots, Centerburg. He was waiting for a fishing buddy who was to meet him at the In-Town.

When this man heard that I was in the region to visit a church with ties to West Virginia, he quickly responded, "Half the people around this place are from the Virginias. You meet more people who came here from Grundy, or Tazewell, or Welch than who came from just about anywhere else. They've been here a while, but they're still Virginians. And they still tell you where they came from, like they just moved here yesterday."[9]

Obviously this man's comments were exaggerated, but they helped to confirm, anecdotally, a strong Appalachian presence in central Ohio. Marvin F. Pruitt, a man living behind the Rich Hill meetinghouse, informed me that the two sides of his family had come to the region from Grundy and from Welch. In addition, he noted that the small farming community of Bloomfield, about three miles due north of Rich Hill, had been resettled, in the late 1940s, almost exclusively by migrants from Buchanan County, Virginia. "They took that town," he said, "without firing a shot."[10]

Although many of them later turned to farming, what brought many of these Virginians and West Virginians to this central Ohio area was a huge munitions manufacturing, assembling, and shipping complex in Westerville, Ohio, just north of Columbus. At the beginning of World War II, labor recruiters scoured the Appalachian region, among other places, seeking workers for this complex. In addition, wartime manufacturing and shipping activities along the southern shore of Lake Erie pulled thousands of Appalachians into the state.[11] This was the era during which Federal Highway 23 earned its pejorative title, "the Hillbilly Highway."

Undoubtedly, many of these outmigrant Virginians and West Virginians became absorbed into the culture—religious and otherwise—of central Ohio. A number who were not fully assimilated, however, became the small congregation of PBU faithful whom Elder Tommy Adair was able to gather at the old cemetery church. Two of those individuals, Tommy Adair's son McGennis and McGennis's wife Phyllis, had preceded Elder Adair in this migration to Ohio.

McGennis Adair and Phyllis Adair: A Case Study in Appalachian Outmigration

In 1941, McGennis Adair, a seventeen-year-old with only an eighth-grade education, was working around the coal mines of McDowell County, West Virginia, when he was approached by a labor recruiter who offered to transport him to Cleveland, Ohio, on the condition that the young West

Virginian sign a "wartime contract" under which he would serve as a railroad brakeman, traveling the lines between Cleveland and Cincinnati.

"I was actually offered my choice between being a brakeman or a fireman," McGennis said. "But I knew what a fireman did, and I'd already had enough of shoveling coal."

The wartime contract Adair had to sign stipulated that, once employed, he could not turn down any travel assignment given him. The Ohio lines were heavily responsible for both troop movements and transportation of military equipment and supplies, and they could tolerate no employee behaviors that might cause shipping delays. Furthermore, this work would constitute vital war-effort labor and as such would keep the West Virginian out of the military—not that the latter was of particular importance to this young man.

Apparently recognizing some quality of leadership in Adair, the recruiter placed this seventeen-year-old in charge of fourteen other men and boys who also would be taking this journey out of Appalachia. Only twelve of these charges made it all the way to Cleveland; two changed their minds during a several-hour stopover in Columbus. Furthermore, none of these fourteen was still in Cleveland at the beginning of what would have been their second six months with the railroad, all having returned to West Virginia or entered military service.[12]

McGennis Adair, however, still was in that Lake Erie city after the initial six months, and he was still there five years later. During that period, he made more money than he ever had thought possible, benefiting from wartime salaries and overtime work schedules. Nevertheless, Adair had been lonely in Cleveland—away from family, friends, and familiar settings—and he had managed several returns to West Virginia, traveling free on a railway pass available through his employer. On one of these trips, he met a fifteen-year-old girl at an event connected with the Elkhorn Primitive Baptist Association, the organization in which his father was a leader.

During the summer of 1947, another of these meetings took place at that year's Harrison-Beavers Reunion and Family Memorial in Thompson Valley, Virginia. At that time, this event attracted between two and three hundred persons and stretched over a two- or three-day period that became ideal for courting. McGennis Adair, then twenty-two, had decided that Cleveland, Ohio, was far too lonely a place for him and that he wanted to get married. Consequently he used the occasion to propose to Phyllis Keene, the fifteen-year-old girl whom, by this time, he had encountered at several Elkhorn Association activities.

Initially the proposal was neither accepted nor rejected, as young Sister Phyllis knew that she would need the permission of at least one of her parents to get married in West Virginia at age fifteen. By the time she decided that she wanted to ask for that permission, it was after one o'clock in the morning on the last day of the reunion, and her parents were bedded down in the large Harrison house, along with perhaps fifty other family members and guests.

Several times the young couple crept into the old house and walked past the room in which Phyllis's parents were sleeping—or were thought to be sleeping—trying to steel themselves for an encounter they did not know how to anticipate. Finally they entered the room, only to find the Keenes awake and anticipating the query.

The mother could not give her consent right away, choosing silence when the question was asked; but the father seemed more amenable to the idea. However, the question was not settled then and there, with the result that it was not until a month later that the young couple formally became engaged. In the end, only the father signed the permission form, but that one signature apparently was sufficient. Therefore, in December 1947, on McGennis Adair's next visit to West Virginia, the young couple was married, Sister Phyllis Keene Adair having by that time turned sixteen and having become convinced that she was prepared to live in Cleveland, Ohio.

During the winter of 1948, however, Adair and his teenaged wife experienced one major problem they had not anticipated. He was on the road much of the time, gone for three or four days each trip; and she was alone, terrified by the city, and homesick for every face and place in West Virginia. She spent weeks crying, and eventually he decided to return to the more comforting environment of McDowell County, West Virginia, despite the fact that he would be abandoning a job with good pay and some meaningful seniority.

Back in Bradshaw, West Virginia, McGennis Adair secured a job as a mechanic at the tipple of a coal mine. His salary was not what he had earned in Cleveland, but his young wife was not constantly in terror of what she viewed as the hostile environment of that large city. Unfortunately, an economic tide was turning, and this mining employment did not last very long. By the close of 1948, the wartime demand for coal had evaporated, and the black mineral was piling up at all Central Appalachian shipping points. Adair found himself laid off from his tipple job and unable to find other work. The only thing he knew to do was to return to railroading, but even that was not possible in West Virginia. So back to

Cleveland he and his young wife went. Apparently she was not at all happy with the turn of events but felt helpless to affect the flow of circumstances.

Once again Adair worked as an Ohio railroad brakeman, but now he had no seniority or wartime wages. In addition, shipping demand was low. It was clear that Adair had lost the state of affluence that had marked his World War II bachelor days. Nevertheless, he was not absent from home as frequently as he had been during his prior stay in Cleveland, simply because his low seniority won him only short local routes. That circumstance at least made Phyllis more comfortable in Cleveland, and all was well with her until she received another emotional blow. Back in West Virginia, her father and brother were involved in a serious automobile accident, coming out alive but badly injured. Her response again was to ask her husband to take her home. By this time, it was 1950.

Back in Appalachia, McGennis Adair could find no mining work, and he ended up taking a position as a vacuum cleaner salesman, knocking on doors in the area of Kingsport, Tennessee. He needed a dependable car for this work, so he purchased a 1951 Kaiser. "It didn't have much in it— no heater, no radio," Adair recalled. "The dealer wanted to get rid of it and gave me a good price. But I wish I had that car today. Restored, it would be worth a fortune."[13]

Although Adair managed to sell some vacuum cleaners, his efforts were not sufficiently rewarding to keep the couple out of debt, and their situation quickly became rather desperate. "We owed money to just about everybody we knew," remarked Adair after dinner on May 22, 1994, sitting in front of his now-comfortable home in Mount Liberty, Ohio, "including our parents, a grocery store, a gas station, and that car dealership—two payments behind and needing the car to work. We had to do something."

When the automobile dealership finally sent two men to repossess the vehicle, McGennis lied to them, telling them that he had loaned it to a friend without a clear understanding of when it would be returned. In truth, Adair had hidden the car, being at the time uncertain what action he would take. The two repossessing agents made it clear that they would be back the next morning for the vehicle and that Adair better have it.

McGennis waited until after midnight, spending the interim gathering enough gasoline money to get the couple to Ohio. Then he and Phyllis fled McDowell County, fearing at every moment that their flight might be stopped and heavy with guilt over what they were doing. Indeed, that guilt stayed with the couple until they had been able—much later—to liquidate each of those debts, including all that they owed on the car loan.

This retreat to Ohio in the dark of the night took the Adairs to Mount Liberty in Knox County, where they arrived with fifty cents of that gasoline money unspent. A painter friend took them in and promised to help them until Adair could secure another job. While that task still was not easy, this resourceful young man did find employment of sorts, this time driving a Mount Vernon taxicab, something that the West Virginian rather enjoyed doing. Indeed, operating automobiles always has been a pleasurable activity for Adair. Later in his Ohio experience, he tried stock-car racing for a while.

"I did pretty good at that taxi driving," remarked Adair. "I tried hard to get people to work on time, and once I picked up a rushed trip from Mount Vernon to Columbus, trying to get these people to a plane before it took off. They thought I wouldn't make it, and when I did they gave me a big tip. But my break came when I started picking up a man every morning and taking him to work at the Continental Can Company. I told him not to bother calling a cab; I would be there each morning at the necessary time. And I was."[14]

The man in question turned out to be the head of maintenance at the can company, and eventually he hired Adair as one of the company's janitors. That was late in 1951, and over the next four decades Adair steadily improved his status with the company, moving up through several levels of maintenance and eventually being trained as a refrigeration specialist. The company was air-conditioning the plant, and Adair was placed in charge of the entire system.

Once connected with Continental Can, McGennis Adair became steady and industrious, the type of worker everyone seemed anxious to advance. Therefore he prospered, and his returns to West Virginia consisted only of frequent family visits and Elkhorn Association annual sessions. Eventually he retired from this company, and now he and Phyllis live in relaxed style on several acres of rural property near Mount Liberty, devoting their time to the management of some rental property that they own and to McGennis's new interest, real-estate speculation. They also have children and grandchildren, and they travel back and forth to West Virginia, Florida, and Kentucky. In addition, there are the activities centered around a large garden, a spacious house and lawn, several hunting dogs, frequent fishing trips to Lake Erie, and the work of Rich Hill Church and the Elkhorn Primitive Baptist Association.

After his father organized Rich Hill Church, both McGennis and Phyllis were baptized and became faithful members of this congregation, transplanted West Virginians practicing a transplanted faith. Following retirement, Adair started buying and selling pieces of rural real estate, quickly demonstrating a knack for this business. Success in the latter has made him financially comfortable and seemingly very satisfied with his life—and with his stay in Ohio. Nevertheless, he and Phyllis still consider themselves West Virginians, and they have two burial plots waiting for them back in McDowell County. Apparently they have maintained that "sense of place" discussed earlier, perhaps because, as loyal members of the Elkhorn Primitive Baptist Association, they have a permanent tie to their heritage.

At the close of the 1995 session of the Elkhorn Association, the Adairs experienced the joy of seeing their granddaughter baptized into the Primitive Baptist Universalist faith, becoming the thirteenth member of the Rich Hill Church. As noted earlier, this granddaughter is enrolled at West

Brother McGennis Adair, Sr., and Sister Phyllis Adair, Rich Hill, Ohio, summer 1995.

Virginia Wesleyan College, in Buchanan, West Virginia, holding both an academic and an athletic scholarship (basketball).

PROBLEMS IN MAINTAINING OUTMIGRANT FELLOWSHIPS

Only four outmigrant PBU fellowships exist: the Rich Hill Church; the Little Flock Church in Greenfield, Highland County, Ohio; the Little Village Church, located near Continental, Putnam County, Ohio; and the Mount Grove Church, near Airville, York County, Pennsylvania. In terms of membership, Little Flock is the largest of the four (20), with Rich Hill second (12), and both Little Village and Mount Grove trailing (6 each). None of these churches has a membership sufficiently numerous to support the costs that even the smallest of congregations faces—meetinghouse maintenance, utility expenses, annual contributions to the association, and, if necessary, help with the expenses of "messengers" sent to annual association meetings.

In addition, because these churches are located far from the PBU heartland, they do not receive a large number of visits from other PBU fellowships. Thus the number of people who might move forward during announcements to place a few bills on the stand is small. In fact, the membership must stand ready to assist in the travel costs of elders called to union meetings. PBU elders are not mercenary in their dealings with host congregations. Indeed, the operative ethic demands that this financial assistance (for travel) be almost forced upon the recipient. Otherwise, the gesture violates the Old-Time Baptist principle that the ministry be unpaid.

The Little Flock meetinghouse, the only other of these four outmigrant PBU churches that I have seen, is a small concrete-block structure situated in a lower-middle-class residential area of Greenfield, Ohio. The sign above its front entrance reads "Primitive Baptist Church" and, printed below that, "Little Flock." There is no indication that, in fact, this facility is an Ohio home for twenty Primitive Baptist Universalists. Moderated by Elder Quinton Looney of Mansfield, Ohio, a town approximately one hundred miles north of Greenfield, Little Flock is an affiliate of the PBU Washington District Association. I first met Elder and Sister Looney at Hope Church during the 1991 Washington Association session. Although Little Flock and Rich Hill are in different associations, Elder Looney also helps with preaching duties at the latter, which actually is much closer to his home than is Little Flock. Elder Looney receives considerable assistance from Elder Howard Coleman of Continental, Ohio, but little help from the other three Washington Association elders resident in that state. At the 1995 meeting of the Washington Association, debate developed about whether the association should keep these three men on its list of elders. Ultimately it was decided that, since all three had been ordained by Little Flock, any punitive action against the elders should originate in that church. As is true in the broader Baptist tradition, PBU local churches control the ordination process, and usually they also control the process for withdrawing ordination.

Moderated by Elder Denton Brown of Dallastown, Pennsylvania, Mount Grove is also affiliated with Washington District. As noted above, the meetinghouse is situated near Airville, Pennsylvania, a small community approximately two miles from the Susquehanna River and roughly midway between Harrisburg and that river's juncture with Chesapeake Bay. I never was able to visit this church, but I frequently met Elder Brown during his travels back to churches in the PBU heartland.

Rich Hill, Little Flock, and Little Village are close enough to each other that their respective memberships support all three churches; but Mount Grove meetinghouse, lying several hundred miles east of the three Ohio fellowships, appears especially isolated. In 1995, Elder Keith Bowers—his preaching travels were mentioned in chapter 6—was called to both Mount Grove and Rich Hill for their union meetings, and he drove approximately five hundred miles each way to meet the Mount Grove call obligation. Aaron Williams, the young elder from Indiana, also was called to both of these services, two of the nine calls he was asked to meet in 1995. These examples suggest the sacrifices in time, energy, and money necessary to sustain these outmigrant churches. Nevertheless, both the Elkhorn and the Washington districts appear particularly protective of their congregations out of the heartland, as is illustrated by Elkhorn's willingness occasionally to hold its annual session at Rich Hill, a decision that always results in a lowered attendance.

THE 1995 ELKHORN ASSOCIATION MEETING AT RICH HILL CHURCH

Attendance at the 1995 session of the Elkhorn Association was smaller than it had been for either of the three previous years, at which times the three-day gatherings had been held at Pilgrim's Rest Church. This is only a four-church association; in the recent past, the three churches in the Virginia–

West Virginia area have agreed that, when the association meeting is hosted by one of those three fellowships, the event will be held at Pilgrim's Rest meetinghouse. Therefore, in most years the Elkhorn Association conducts its annual session there on State Line Ridge, near Wimmer Gap.

Two differences were notable between the 1995 event and three earlier ones I attended. First, a significant number of older people simply found the trip from Virginia or West Virginia to Rich Hill, Ohio, too arduous to make. Second, as a result, fewer visitors from the Three Forks and the Washington district elected to make the long journey. The Elkhorn Association knew that these factors would influence the 1995 attendance,[1] but the feeling was that the Ohio church deserved and needed an association meeting on its home turf. Because of the annual travel requirement, and the positive influence that an association meeting exerts on a host church, it seemed only fair that the session take place in Ohio.

Elkhorn follows a three-day agenda that varies only slightly from the session schedules followed by Old Regular Baptist associations. In fact these shared schedules and procedures are among the factors clearly demonstrating Old-Time Baptist kinship, particularly among all the Appalachian Baptist subdenominations that developed from the Regular Baptist tradition. On Friday morning, usually at 10:30, the association session is called to order by that elder who served as moderator the previous year. In the case of the death of the previous year's moderator, then the assistant moderator will convene the session. As in any regular PBU service, the session begins with singing, followed by preaching and a prayer; but on these opening mornings, the initial sermon and prayer usually are delivered by the moderator of one of the other two associations, Washington or Three Forks.

That first sermon, however, is not labeled the "introduction." Instead it is the second preacher, chosen a full year in advance, who "introduces" the service, in the hope that his efforts will be "carried out" and thus lead into the opening session of emotional handshaking and embracing. That is the ideal, since this round of warm tactile contact will unify the association as it moves into its annual business deliberations, some of which could produce tensions.

Following the "introduction," last year's moderator calls for the church letters, those documents that provide not only an annual report on each fellowship but also designate the three "messengers" and one "alternate messenger" whom each individual church has sent to the association meeting as its representatives. Each letter is read aloud by the clerk, and then the temporary moderator asks for a "move and second" to accept the letters. Unless there is some major problem that has been brewing among the four churches, these letters will be accepted routinely, allowing the "messengers" to be seated as the session delegates.

Most Old-Time Baptists (including the three PBU associations) do not follow *Robert's Rules of Order.* In fact, the procedural rules they follow predate the post–Civil War efforts of Col. Henry Robert to institute a commonly accepted code of parliamentary procedure. Therefore, in PBU proceedings—at both the local church and the association levels—a motion will pass if it is moved and seconded and no objection is heard. This has the effect of placing "presumption" on the side of the motion, since, in order simply to move the issue into a discussion mode, an individual opposed to the motion must "object." In sharp contrast with the procedure mandated in *Robert's Rules,* if no objection is heard, no discussion is conducted.

Only after the letters are read and the messengers are formally seated can the association "organize," electing officers for the current association session. As indicated earlier, PBU messengers usually elect the same slate of officers that was in place the year before, except in the case of one or more deaths or if some trouble has arisen within the alliance of fellowships. During these elections, the old Elkhorn moderator turns the stand over to an elder from one of the other two associations, usually one of the two moderators.

Once the officers (moderator, assistant moderator, clerk and treasurer, and assistant clerk and treasurer) have been elected, the association moves to its first item of business, the "call for newly constituted churches." There have been none of the latter since Rich Hill joined in 1952. This item takes precedence over all other items, simply because, if a new church is seeking to ally itself with the association, that church will be admitted—if at all—before other critical business comes before the association.

Traditionally, the next procedure is for the clerk to read the "Rules of Decorum." Here the document's original grammar, punctuation, and spelling are preserved:

1. The Association shall be opened and closed by prayer and the prayer for the Introductory be for opening of Association. [This will be the second prayer of the morning, again the prayer following the introductory sermon.]

Elder Jennings Shortt moderates the Three Forks of Powell's River Regular Primitive Baptist Association's Annual Session, Oak Grove Church, Keokee, Virginia, 1994.

2. The Moderator, Asst. Moderator, Clerk, Asst. Clerk and Treasurer shall be chosen by the suffrage of the Messengers present.
3. Only one Messenger shall speak at a time, the Messenger shall arise and address the Moderator, as permission to speak. Give his or her name and the name of the Church they represent. [It should be noted that Elkhorn, like the other two PBU associations, accepts female messengers and female clerks, a practice that many Old-Time Baptist associations do not allow.]
4. The Messenger thus speaking shall not be interrupted by any one except the moderator; the Moderator shall interrupt only if the Messenger is in disorder. Then, if the Messenger fails to set their self in order they shall be silenced by the Association.

5. The Messenger shall strictly adhere to the subject, and in no way reflect on the Messenger who spoke before. Such as to make remarks on his or her feelings or imperfections. But shall fairly state the case or problem as clearly as they can so as to convey their thoughts and ideas to the Association.

6. No Messenger shall speak more than three times on one subject without liberty obtained from the Association.

7. No Messenger shall abruptly break off or absent theirself from the Association, without liberty obtained from the Association.

8. No Messenger shall address another Messenger, or Correspondent from a sister Association in any other term or appellation other than a Brother or Sister.

9. No Messenger or visiting member shall have the liberty of laughing, talking, or whispering while a Messenger is speaking.

10. The names of the Messengers shall be enrolled and called over as often as the Association requires.

11. The Moderator shall be entitled to speak to the Association provided the chair be filled. But he shall not vote except the Association be equally divided, then he may cast the deciding vote.

12. Any Church troubles that may arise, must be settled by your home Church if possible. If it cannot be settled by the Church, then the offended party may bring it to the Association. You must present your case to the committee on arrangements. The committee shall take the case in consideration after a close study, then by a majority vote decide whether it should go before the Association.

13. Any Messenger who willingly or knowingly violates any of these rules shall be reproved by the Association as she may think proper.

14. The Association maintains the right to withdraw from any Church which may be in disorder or that deviate from the orthodox principles and doctrines of religion, either in faith or practice.[16]

The next item of business on the agenda is the "calling for Correspondents from Sister Associations." At this point, one representative from Three Forks Association and one representative from Washington Association each presents to Elkhorn a letter containing a declaration of desire to remain in "correspondence" with Elkhorn. Each letter also lists several elders who will "sit in council" with Elkhorn and represent the association from which they come. The one elder who presents the letter also hands to the clerk several copies of the *Minutes* of that association' most recent session. These published minutes will have been in circula tion for nine or so months, but the formal exchange of these documents— in addition to the exchange of letters—symbolizes the larger nature of "cor respondence." Again a "move and second" is required to finalize th continuation of these formal relationships.

At this point on the agenda, two important committees are established the Committee on Arrangements and the Committee on Preaching. It i the responsibility of the latter group to determine which elders are to oc cupy the stand during the Friday afternoon preaching service, the Satur day morning opening service, and the Saturday afternoon and Sunda morning periods of preaching. Customarily, four preachers are selected fo each of these periods. Including the contributions of the two elders hear on Friday morning, the association usually hears eighteen sermons dur ing the three-day session, not counting the unplanned preaching that fre quently breaks out at the close of the two afternoon services, in respons to the emotionality of these events. Members of the Committee on Preach ing also select the elder who will be delegated to "introduce" the next year' association session. Being selected for this task can be an honor, especiall for a young elder.

Once constituted, the Preaching Committee usually leaves the proceed ings to go outside and immediately make their selections. In the absenc of this group of four messengers (one from each of the churches), the worl of the association continues, moving next to the appointment of the Ar rangements Committee.

This second committee can become a powerful one, since it plays gatekeeping role in determining what matters may come before the large association, in what form, and with what recommendations. For example Article 12 of the Rules of Decorum places the Committee on Arrangement between the local church and the association, when problems within th local church are being presented to the association for advice or action. I addition, any queries concerning faith or practice go first to the Commit tee on Arrangements for placement on the session's Saturday mornin agenda. In most circumstances, however, the committee simply make scheduling decisions, determining in what order items for consideratio will be heard.

While the Committee on Preaching is deliberating, the moderator als calls for "visitors from Sister Associations," and at this point all forma members of churches in Washington or Three Forks districts move forward and present their names to the clerk to be recorded in the published minutes. Ten to fifteen minutes may transpire before this recording is finished; by that time, the Committee on Preaching usually is back in the church, prepared to report the Friday afternoon and Saturday morning preaching agendas. After the noon meal, the committee continues its deliberations, determining the preaching schedules for Saturday afternoon and Sunday morning, as well as the elder who will "introduce" at the next annual session.

After the report of the Committee on Preaching, the association usually adjourns until Saturday morning at ten o'clock. Dinner-on-the-grounds is then served, and the two committees discussed above find time to continue their deliberations. Finally, the Friday afternoon preaching service begins around one-thirty or two o'clock and continues until about four or five.

On Saturday morning, the session opens with hymn singing, preaching, and prayer, and then moves to a formal roll call of messengers and correspondents (representing the other two associations). Next the "Bill of Arrangements" is read and received, placing on the morning's agenda any controversial issues with which the association must contend. Following this, a string of routine actions must be undertaken: hearing and approving a second report from the Committee on Preaching, this time the names of the elders who are scheduled to preach on Saturday afternoon and Sunday morning; appointing "Correspondents to Sister Associations," the elders who are to formally represent Elkhorn at the next annual sessions of Washington and Three Forks; receiving a financial report from the clerk; hearing and accepting a report from each elder concerning his fulfillment of union meeting calls and other similar preaching obligations (at memorial meetings, family services, and the like) during the past year; hearing the clerk's reading of all union meeting calls for the coming association year; approving the number of copies of the minutes to be printed; approving instructions to the clerk and assistant clerk concerning letters of correspondence to be written to Washington and Three Forks associations for delivery at their next annual sessions; and approving the agreement to hold next year's session at a particular church, under the sponsorship of a particular church, to be convened "on Friday, before the first Sunday in September" of that year.

At this point, special items listed on the "Bill of Arrangements" come before the association. This is a moment that session moderators occasionally dread, simply because any church query has the potential to generate an association-splitting fight over doctrine or practice. Elkhorn Association has remained peaceful for over a decade; thus, in recent years, this agenda moment has come and gone without any significant issues being brought before the association. That was the case in 1995, and, following a formal expression of thanks to Rich Hill Church for hosting the session, Elkhorn adjourned the business portion of its 134th annual meeting. The Sunday service is devoted exclusively to singing, prayer, and preaching; and the session ends on a traditional celebratory note, filled with much shouting, praising, and crying.

At that point on Sunday, September 3, 1995, McGennis Adair's granddaughter came forward, seeking membership in Rich Hill Church. Thus the association was able to close with an event that, for these believers, perhaps represents the peak church moment, a baptism.

A Joyful Moment for Rich Hill Church

At this association gathering out of the PBU heartland, attendance was small, with perhaps only eighty or eighty-five persons present for one or more of the three days. Even so, enthusiasm was high at the Saturday afternoon service on September 2, 1995, at Rich Hill meetinghouse; on several occasions, episodes of joyful crying and shouting erupted. That was especially true on Saturday, when Elder Aaron Williams preached the third and final sermon of the afternoon. As noted earlier, Elder Williams frequently is very effective with PBU audiences, and that afternoon was no exception. He himself became "carried out," and in the process he "carried out" all, or nearly all, of the seventy or eighty members of his congregation.

When an emotional celebration such as this occurs, it usually begins with one woman—one woman who first starts crying and shouting, turns immediately to each of the women around her, embracing each of them, and usually elicits reciprocal crying and shouting from them. In little time at all, that first woman is likely to get to her feet, clapping her hands and perhaps jumping up and down.

The men about this time move forward to shake hands with the preaching elder or to embrace him. These movements toward the stand place more people on their feet, and they begin to move about, making tactile contact with each other as they do so. Thus, before long, most of the congregation is standing and moving, clustering closer to the stand, while the preacher is still engaged in his "carried out" work, generally climbing to his own peaks of emotional expression. Often his eyes are shut, as if he were unaware of the intense congregational response developing around him.

These are the times when I have heard, within the PBU tradition, the equivalent of the Old Regular "sing down," in the sense that another elder—usually the moderator—may begin to line a song, and the resultant singing builds—in cooperation with the preaching, the crying, the shouting, and the embracing—so that all together constitute an explosion of sound and action that follows no precise model. Each participant feels completely free in her or his expression, but the totality emerges as an exuberant declaration of collective joy.

If all this emotion occurs at the close of the preaching service, then eventually sound and action subside sufficiently to allow the moderator to take charge, probably "opening the door of the church" at this point and often himself beginning to preach. During all of these happenings, the congregation remains standing, having abandoned the orderliness of the pews lined up in rows and instead clustering in the aisles or in the open space immediately in front of the stand.

Dominating all this behavior is the image of oneness—a coming together, a movement toward core, forging the cohesiveness so essential to PBU fellowship. If, out of all this passion, an individual's decision for membership emerges, then the collective joy is complete. That did not happen on Saturday afternoon at Rich Hill Church, but an emotional groundwork was established that, on the next day—at the close of the 1995 Elkhorn Association session—someone did come forward. The result was that day's baptism of the Adair granddaughter.

"Her decision will forever make that association meeting a high point in my life," said Sister Phyllis Adair when we met the following weekend at the Washington Association gathering. "You've got to imagine how a grandmother feels at such times."[17]

9 PILGRIMS IN THE HANDS OF A HAPPY GOD

Theologies obviously have ramifications that go far beyond the establish‑ ment of mere doctrinal beliefs; they also influence heavily the tone an‑ temperament of a people. Thus, in accord with Hosea Ballou's "happifie God" principle, Primitive Baptist Universalists themselves are a happ group of humans, reveling in their certainty of a heaven for everyone, a eternity under the reign of a happy and truly loving God-Father figure In addition, to a much greater degree than most Old-Time Baptists, the are open to outsiders, at least when those outsiders manage actually to fin a PBU church. Believing as they do in that universal and egalitarian popu‑ lating of heaven, the PBU congregations never are hostile to the nonmem‑ ber visitor, although they make little or no effort to invite that visitc through their doors. Finally, PBU fellowships are composed largely c nonjudgmental people who live and let live, understanding that their deity plan is a multifaceted one that extends far beyond their understanding c its exact details.

Such PBU traits—joy in religious expression, inclusiveness, refrainin from judgment, belief in an egalitarian afterlife—color the world outloo of these people. Their views are based solidly on a belief that God's atone ment strategy ultimately calls for reuniting the human family. Still, the accept the thesis that, in accord with some design unknown to tempor man, God chose to create a world diverse not only in language and colors but also in mind and spiritual understanding, with some of the elect scattered everywhere and some of them unknown even to the PBU members. Perhaps, as is partially explained in Gen. 11:1–9, that diversity was designed to thwart the haughty ambitions of God's children; or perhaps it had some other divine motive yet to be revealed. Remember that PBU thinkers are not biblical literalists; thus the Tower of Babel story can hold some truth for them that is greater than the precise claim within the narrative.

Regardless of their recognition of the vast diversity in spiritual thinking that exists, these impassioned believers still accept their own theology as being the "true vine" of religious correctness and themselves as being the main body of the elect—those who were chosen to the divine purposes of witnessing and preserving. They are not necessarily "better" or the "best," but they are, they believe, set aside, given a role to play as long as the temporal condition exists. In turn, they say, that role provides them with great joy, allowing them to be a part of the wonderful temporal fellowship of God, which is the Church. At the same time, that role burdens them, delegated as they are to preserve righteousness within a world in which the unrighteous seem to have both the advantage in number and the advantage in freedom of behavior. Nevertheless, they accept Ballou's thesis that sin is not pleasurable, but righteousness is. There, they contend, is their temporal-world reward, the elation constantly generated by their alignment with God's will. Only those who live that alignment, they argue, are capable of knowing the bliss that ensues from that righteousness. This intimacy with God's will, they argue, is all the discipline they need to keep them on a virtuous course, since the loss of that intimacy plunges them into a temporal-world hell that is the punishment for temporal-world sin.

Yet these people are very few. First, within the totality of religious thinking, Christianity is a minority viewpoint. Second, within the totality of Christian thinking, Primitive Baptist Universalism is infinitesimally underrepresented. Indeed, it is so small that the movement's existence is totally unknown to most of the larger world of Christianity. At the time of this writing in 1995, the PBU official membership total for the three associations treated in this study is just 571.[1] Do not such minuscule numbers imply a challenge to the PBU claim of importance in God's plan? When Primitive Baptist Universalists think of themselves as chosen, do these tallies bother them? Were these individuals the only elect of the moment—which they do not claim to be—then God would have been highly selective indeed when he made his choices "before the beginning of time." Even so, the PBU movement is not particularly troubled by its small count. The faithful find solace in one very special Paulinian pronouncement: "But ye are a chosen generation, a royal priesthood, an holy nation, a peculiar people; that ye should shew forth the praises of him who hath called you out of darkness and into his marvelous light" (1 Pet. 2:9; see also Titus 2:11–14).

PBU doctrine, then, advances the same claim that all Old-Time Baptist groups (among others) make—that such small numbers have no negative meaning, that the chosen are, by design, a "peculiar people," "called . . . out of darkness" to serve God's larger purpose.[2] Exact totals are irrelevant; if God had needed to do so, he would have created a larger elect by his initial call.[3]

Nevertheless, for Primitive Baptist Universalists (in contrast to more traditional Primitives), that call provides no advantage in atonement and in the afterlife; it merely appoints the temporal-world cadre needed to witness and preserve. Access is given to a life of spiritual joy not fully available to the nonelect, but also there is an obligation to stay within the righteousness camp.

If Chosen, Why So Reclusive?

Primitive Baptist Universalist congregations do not advertise their existence. Their small churches seem almost deliberately hidden. The small sign typically tacked to such a meetinghouse suggests only that it belongs to some Primitive Baptist subdivision. Nor does such a church have one of those welcoming roadside marquees that announce meeting Sundays and times of worship. Information of this type occasionally is found on the small sign, but that does not help much when the placard in question is almost invisible. As a result, the visitor must arrange some kind of connection with the faith in order to learn how and when to attend services. To do otherwise is to risk bumbling into the worship of some other of the much larger selection of Old-Time Baptist faiths.

A question frequently asked when I lecture on Old-Time Baptist topics is: "How do you find those places?" My answer usually is that the churches themselves are not difficult to locate. One can drive almost any secondary road in Central Appalachia and discover some type of traditional Baptist meetinghouse. What the questioner usually is asking is: "How do you identify a particular structure with a particular subdivision of theological thought?" That is not always easy to do, without the initial connection mentioned above. Why do PBU congregations not recognize that difficulty and find ways to assert themselves in the external world?

The answer to that question must take at least two directions, one theological and one psychological or sociological. Theologically, the answer is simple. This faith preserves that element of Calvinistic thought which says that God chooses you, rather than you choosing God. The basic tenet of this "God calls, not man" principle is that if you belong within the faith, God will find a way to make the introduction. If a church were to go out of its way to entice people to its doors, then that church would be meddling in a divine process, violating God's prerogative to "call."

The psychological-sociological argument is a bit more complicated and has arisen, it seems, from two aspects of Central Appalachian religious history. First, these Baptist subdenominations developed at a time when their meetinghouses needed no advertising. They were community churches drawing their memberships primarily from the particular ridge, hollow, or river basin, upon or in which the worship structure sat. Therefore, it made no particular sense to generate any messages proclaiming presence; word-of-mouth advertising was sufficient for local communication, and the "outside world" was not anywhere nearby.

Moreover, when the outside world finally did visit some of these churches, it frequently came in the form of an uninvited intruder who was there to condemn and to change. The eastern missionary was convinced of the utter backwardness of mountain faith and practice; and the social scientist was determined to indict Appalachian religious traditions as the causes of all sorts of presumed deficiencies in mountain character and sociopolitical structures.[4] One result of those harsh judgments by outsiders was that many strains of Appalachian religion did become reclusive, being understandably unwilling to subject themselves to the probing of investigators presumed to be hostile.

More recently, similar reactions developed concerning the operations of outside media representatives. All too frequently, Appalachians saw themselves depicted on national television in a highly biased and unflattering light. To resentment over such characterizations must be added the fact that television production crews occasionally demonstrated complete disrespect for religious worship services. Once I was told of a camera crew barging into an Old Regular church in Dunham, Kentucky, without any prior arrangement or request.[5]

In proposing video documentaries with both the Old Regular Baptists and the Primitive Baptist Universalists, I have met frustration after frustration. Both subdenominations trusted me but could not extend that trust to the larger television world—either the producers or the audience of television viewers. The members of these churches had seen too many examples in which the media mistreated the region, unabashedly focusing on the deviant and the sensational.[6]

I myself always have been welcomed within Old-Time Baptist fellowships, especially PBU congregations. These religious communities may never relax their concerns, however, about the larger world of outside investigators representing academia and the popular media. It should be noted, of course, that the field of Appalachian studies is replete with scholars who carefully avoid violating Appalachian sensitivities.

Primitive Baptist Universalism and the Issue of Inclusiveness

PBU theology does not escape completely the unfortunate dichotomizing—the polarization of ins or outs, "we" or "they," believers or unbelievers, chosen or rejected, elected or nonelected—that plagues most religion of the world. The elect/nonelect pair obviously figures in PBU doctrine. Still, in the PBU concept of the elect, the latter's inherent exclusiveness terminates with the close of the temporal world, making the PBU heaven the ultimate in inclusiveness. In this age when "inclusiveness" has become a value term connoting warm acceptance and appreciation, a multitude of humanistic unbelievers may be ready to praise the merits of this one PBU tenet. My own respect for any religious doctrine increases with the degree to which that doctrine manages to apply equally to all humankind. In contrast, I grow increasingly concerned about a theology that becomes divisive, whether through its basic tenets or through the practices derived from those tenets. Recognizing that sectarianism and denominationalism axiomatically are divisive, I am encouraged by those theologies which encompass all humankind, even when the encompassing pertains only to the afterlife. At least, positive thoughts concerning others are present, certainly more so than in a faith that envisions—perhaps even takes delight in envisioning—those "others" spending eternity in the most unimaginable of agonies: burning, burning, burning, without reprieve, without end.

I do not want to suggest that PBU fellowships never are exclusive. That image would not be an accurate one. These people certainly exclude individuals from their churches, and churches and associations have excluded each other, sometimes bitterly. Indeed, the birth of Primitive Baptist

Universalism as an identifiable faith arose out of an act of exclusion, and each side of that 1924–25 split still bears at least some animosity toward the other. If inclusiveness existed at some absolute level of perfection within the faith, then such divisions never would take place. Nevertheless, they do, primarily because Primitive Baptist Universalists show a particular sensitivity with regard to certain key doctrines, usually ones that have given them trouble in the past. "You can love your brother," Elder Farley Beavers said to me, "but if he errs in doctrine, you must separate yourself from him."[7]

Elder Beavers was making reference to the latest doctrinal dispute that has erupted within PBU ranks, a dispute that generated considerable pain during the 1995 annual session of the Three Forks Association. As mentioned in chapter 2, Three Forks of Powell's River Regular Primitive Baptist Association convenes its three-day yearly meeting on Friday before the fourth Saturday in August, one week before Elkhorn meets. In 1995, that session was hosted by Point Truth Church. Because the particular controversy described below is, at the time of this writing, in a delicate period of evolution, and because I have made certain promises to Elder Jennings Shortt, moderator of Three Forks, this is one time when, to protect individuals and churches, I shall employ anonymity in my narrative. I hope, by not printing unnecessary details, to avoid "carving in stone" a reality that may have a chance of changing. Here I readily admit an unscholarly bias: I want peace and unity restored to Three Forks. The controversy involves—on both sides—people for whom I have considerable affection, and I hope to see the pain ended.

DISHARMONY AND EXCLUSIVENESS IN THREE FORKS, 1995

The issue that severely disrupted the peace and harmony of Three Forks is an old one, being essentially the same question that destroyed the Stony Creek Association. Such old issues of dispute are the ones that continue to be most sensitive. Certainly that has been the case with Three Forks Association.

On the fourth Saturday in July 1995, during the regular monthly business meeting of one of the Three Forks churches, charges were brought against an elder, accusing him (as I have been given to understand) of having promoted a Resurrection doctrine that is contrary to PBU theology— resurrection of the spirit rather than resurrection of the body. As noted in chapter 7, mainline PBU doctrine insists upon resurrection of the body, with afterlife recognizability seeming to be an essential component of the dogma. Both stand rhetoric and lay discussions impart the idea that, following Resurrection, loved ones will be reunited in a heavenly state that permits identification of, and interaction with, loved ones who have "gone on before." Although considerable variation in thought exists within the movement concerning the precise nature of the resurrected physical self, the general consensus appears to be that what is resurrected and thus emerges in heaven will be some type of perfected physical self—lacking, for example, the infirmities of old age and illness.[8]

When PBU preachers have strayed from this accepted premise—the resurrection of a physical body—and embraced any doctrine of a less tangible self, the response has been predictable, especially in Three Forks. As noted earlier, that association contains two fellowships that came out of the old, destroyed Stony Creek Association, where in the mid-1950s controversy developed over even the physicality of God. Allegedly, what happened in the case of this particular Three Forks elder is that he began to preach a spirit-only resurrection doctrine (debate continues concerning this part of the case narrative, however).

During the 1995 church business meeting in question, the elder supposedly first was asked to explain his theology, but during the proceedings, tension apparently escalated quickly, resulting in the charged elder walking out of the meeting. Article 8 of Three Forks' Rules of Decorum is essentially the same as Article 5 of Washington District's rules and Article 7 of Elkhorn's rules: "No person shall abruptly break off or absent himself from the Association without leave having been obtained from the Association."[9] Since the individual churches also accept these rules as governing their own deliberations, the elder's walking out placed him in disorder with his church, and the congregation so ruled. Apparently, however, the elder was excluded only after requesting that particular termination of his case.

Nevertheless, a month later—when Three Forks met for its annual session—the controversy had spread, touching one additional church and two additional elders, who were supporting the preacher who had been charged with promoting heresy. The additional church, which I shall call fellowship X, was questioning the "work" of the first church, which I will call fellowship Y; and the two additional elders were proclaiming that the first elder had not preached precisely what he had been charged with preaching. One of those men, however, did argue before the association that the

Bible gave no clear guidance as to precisely what would be resurrected: if the physical self, then at what age and in what condition?

After considerable debate—which, although impassioned, was remarkably civil and controlled—the association supported the "work" of church Y, leaving the affected elder in a "disordered" state—meaning, among other things, that he could not occupy the stand of any church in the association or the two corresponding associations. That move resulted in two other actions: the two supporting elders' walking out, and the withdrawal of its letter by fellowship X.

The single most poignant instant in this Three Forks event was that moment when the clerk of church X asked for that fellowship's letter and, after receiving it, walked out of Point Truth meetinghouse. I make no judgment of this event, but I want the reader to understand the emotional intensity of that moment. These people feel deeply about doctrine, and occasionally they sacrifice their own treasured friendships for the sanctity and purity of religious belief. They do not do so without personal pain, however, and at that moment of "splitting," muffled sobs were heard and tears welled in the eyes of both women and men. Women cried at the thought of being separated from acquaintances of many years, while men who had been authentic friends realized that they had just "gone to the wire" against each other over a doctrinal division that seemed not to have existed a month before. Such, however, is the nature of these splits in Old-Time Baptist churches and associations; they sometimes redefine reality with lightning speed, leaving bitter disunity where a deep sense of community existed only a short time before. Occasionally the people who seem most injured by such events are those who had least influence upon the events' course—the laity in general, and especially the women, who feel compelled to align themselves with their husbands' causes even when the consequences are quite painful.

One irony in all this is that the very brother from whom a PBU elder may separate over doctrine also is viewed as a future fellow heir of eternity. Therefore, the deeply serious and sorrowful doctrinal confrontation that supposedly separates the "true vine" from the "untrue vine" itself is only temporal in consequence; the battling forces are destined to join each other in heaven, presumably never to battle again. This thought has interesting implications for all the historic disputes of Old-Time Baptist heritage, not to mention the horrific struggles that have spattered the history of nations.

A People of Joy

I do not want to end this work on a negative tone. Therefore I have held back for this final moment a topic relating to the most dominant characteristic of the PBU fellowships—their absolutely joyful and celebratory worship style. This behavioral mode frequently moves celebrants into a crescendo of actions and sounds that convey increasing exaltation, a "carried-out" state most frequently occurring near the close of a powerful service.

During more than two decades of fieldwork among Appalachian churches, I have witnessed a wide variety of highly emotional religious expressions. Some examples include:

—The "Flower Service" at Mount Paran Missionary Baptist Church in Deep Gap, North Carolina. This blossom-exchange ritual is designed to motivate reconciliation in any intrachurch relations that have turned heavy with guilt or hostility.

—A seventeen-convert baptism, in the North Fork of New River, that grew so joyful that it inspired an eighteenth immersion. This last convert rushed into the water to meet the preacher before he could return to the bank.

—A name-calling-out memorial service at Bull Creek Old Regular Baptist Church near Grundy, Virginia, with almost every name of a deceased member generating an emotional burst from family and friends.

—Scores of tearful and emotionally draining footwashing services, at least one of which, in Lansing, North Carolina, precipitated the mending of an old friendship destroyed long ago by bitter discord.

—At a tent revival, a coming-to-the-pit "rejection of sin" left a woman in McDowell County, West Virginia, collapsed, for at least twenty minutes, in the hardest crying I have ever witnessed.

—A runaway daughter from Burke County, North Carolina, sought the altar as an act of reunion with her parents.

—A Letcher County, Kentucky, man "running in the Spirit," who brought a Thornton Creek Freewill Baptist congregation to an arm-waving climax of crying and shouting.

In some of these scenes, the emotional display was dark with guil shame, remorse, and pain, illustrating that the processes of tearing awa sometimes are necessary to purge the human spirit. In others, the domina mood was grief, that anguish arising from deprivation and loss, perhaps of loved ones, perhaps of spiritual self-worth. Finally, in some instances, the emotional texture was that of exaltation and joy, an ultimate euphoria, the exuberant pouring forth of a happiness perhaps captured best by the traditional word *jubilation*. It is to this third category of expression that the "carried-out" episodes in PBU worship belong, and it seems almost unnecessary to say that such displays are motivated by the firm belief that heaven unconditionally awaits all.

The doctrine pronounces that uncertainties concerning that afterlife are gone, and all that is left to worry about is the trouble-plagued temporal world, a phase of existence that is transitory and of only minute importance when compared to the scope of eternity. In addition, given the assurance that this temporal world experience is so much better than it would be were they not of "the Church," these believers hold that they have much in which to glory and little about which to grieve. A wayward son, daughter, husband, wife, or any other loved one lost to God's focus and care— such a concern occasions pain, but never in comparison to the elation experienced through faith in Christ's complete atonement, an atonement that ultimately will redeem that wayward son, daughter, husband, wife, or other loved one. Thus the causes of the Primitive Baptist Universalists' joy seem clear and rational, given the context of their faith.

A Closing Statement

In the early 1970s, when I first began my field investigations of Appalachian religious traditions, I did so with a firm commitment to "scholarly objectivity." For me, that phrase entailed scholar-subject distance; there would be no crossing the line between observer and participant. The more years I spent in the field, the more illusory that original goal became. Pressed so forcefully against the realities of human passion and faith, the empathic part of my nature frequently came to the forefront in my feelings. That was especially true during my three years of work among PBU fellowships, when celebrants seemed so determined to pull me into their world of joy. Therefore, I want to thank the Primitive Baptist Universalists of Central Appalachia for reaching out to me with such warmth and acceptance. I hope that I have been able to return at least some of that positive spirit.

NOTES

CHAPTER 1. PRIMITIVES, PRIMITIVES, AND MORE PRIMITIVES

1. U.S. Tennessee Valley Authority, "Holston Baptist Cemetery: Graves Reinterred by TVA," in Maps and Surveys Department, Tennessee Valley Authority, Chattanooga, Tenn.

2. U.S. Tennessee Valley Authority, Southeast Region, East Point, Ga. "Holston Church: CK-731," National Archives.

3. Ibid.

4. Three Forks of Powell's River Regular Primitive Baptist Association, *Minutes*, 1991, p. 6.

5. The two denominations merged in 1961.

6. Spelled "Colley Creek" in all Three Forks minutes, but spelled "Colly Creek" on the front of the church.

7. Farley Beavers, interviewed by the author, Dante, Va., Aug. 22, 1992.

8. Unice Davis, interviewed by the author, Wimmer Gap, Va., Sept. 3, 1994.

9. Regular Primitive Baptist Washington District Association, *Minutes*, 1994, p. 14; Three Forks of Powell's River Regular Primitive Baptist Association, *Minutes*, 1994, p. 10; Elkhorn Primitive Baptist Association, *Minutes*, 1994, p. 13.

10. Ernest Cassara, *Universalism in America: A Documentary History of a Liberal Faith* (Boston: Skinner House, 1971), 7.

11. Farley Beavers, interviewed by the author, Trout, W.Va., June 19, 1994.

12. Howard Dorgan, *Giving Glory to God in Appalachia: Worship Practices of Six Baptist Subdenominations* (Knoxville: Univ. of Tennessee Press, 1987), 36–41; H. L.

McBeth, "Free Will Baptists," in *Dictionary of Baptists in America*, ed. Bill J. Leonard (Downers Grove, Ill.: InterVarsity Press, 1994), 122.

13. Carolyn Blevins, "Dunkers," in *Dictionary of Baptists in America*, ed. Bill J. Leonard (Downers Grove, Ill.: InterVarsity Press, 1994), 107.

14. Martin B. Bradley et al., *Churches and Church Membership in the United States, 1990* (Atlanta, Ga.: Glenmary Research Center, 1992).

15. In Appalachia, there are many wholly independent churches, particularly of the Baptist, Holiness, and Pentecostal faiths, that are not affiliated with any larger organizational unit. Indeed, it is not unusual for some of these churches to maintain no membership roll. Therefore, it is extremely difficult to canvass the memberships of these churches.

16. Clifford A. Grammich, Jr., supplied hard copy of his computerized working notes, including 1989 or 1990 data, from research on a large number of Old-Time Baptist associations. This hard copy, housed in the author's private collection, hereafter is cited as Grammich Notes.

17. Clifford A. Grammich, Jr., *Appalachian Atlas: Maps of the Churches and People of the Appalachian Region* (Knoxville, Tenn.: Commission on Religion in Appalachia, 1994).

18. Charles Chauncy, *Seasonable Thoughts on the Sate of Religion in New England* (1743; reprint, Hicksville, N.Y.: Regina Press, 1975); C. C. Goen, ed., *The Great Awakening* (New Haven, Conn.: Yale Univ. Press, 1972); Nathan O. Hatch and Harry S. Stout, eds., *Jonathan Edwards and the American Experience* (New York: Oxford Univ. Press, 1988); Maloy Alton Huggins, *A History of North Carolina Baptists 1727–1932* (Raleigh, N.C.: State Baptist Convention of North Carolina, 1967); Morgan Scott, *Separate Baptist Church* (Indianapolis, Ind.: Hollenbeck Press, 1901); William Warren Sweet, *Religion on the American Frontier: The Baptists* (New York: Cooper Square Publishers, 1964); Joseph Tracy, *The Great Awakening: A History of the Revival of Religion in the Time of Edwards and Whitefield* (1845; reprint, New York: Arno Press, 1969).

19. Huggins, *History of North Carolina Baptists*, 50–51; Robert Baylor Semple, *History of the Rise and Progress of the Baptists in Virginia* (1810; reprint, Cottonport, La.: Polyanthos, 1972), 11–13.

20. Huggins, *History of North Carolina Baptists*, 23–24; Glenn A. Toomey, *The Centennial History of the Holston Valley Baptist Association and Its Affiliated Churches 1884–1983* (Rogersville, Tenn.: Holston Valley Baptist Association, 1983), 4–7; George Washington Paschal, *History of North Carolina Baptists* (Raleigh: North Carolina Baptist State Convention, 1930), 44–45.

21. Huggins, *History of North Carolina Baptists*, 51–52; Semple, *History of the Rise*, 12–14; Scott, *Separate Baptist Church*, 108–35, 158–229; Sweet, *Religion on the American Frontier*, 8–9.

22. Dorgan, "Separate Baptists of Central Appalachia: Followers of Shubal Stearns," *Journal of the Appalachian Studies Association* 5 (1993): 110–16.

23. Semple, *History of the Rise*, 12–14; Sweet, *Religion on the American Frontier*, 8–9.

24. Semple, *History of the Rise*, 375–87.

25. Deborah Vansau McCauley, *Appalachian Mountain Religion* (Urbana: Univ. of Illinois Press, 1995), 203; Scott, *Separate Baptist Church*, 111; Sweet, *Religion on the American Frontier*, 10–11.

26. Dorgan, "Separate Baptists of Central Appalachia," 110–16; McCauley, *Appalachian Mountain Religion*, 92; J. H. Spencer, *A History of Kentucky Baptists* (1886; reprint, Lafayette, Tenn.: Church History Research and Archives, 1976), 1:482–83.
27. J. T. Spivey, "Separate Baptists," in *Dictionary of Baptists in America*, ed. Bill J. Leonard (Downers Grove, Ill.: InterVarsity Press, 1994), 111.
28. General Association of Separate Baptists in Christ, *Minutes*, 1990, pp. 19–38.
29. Spencer, *History of Kentucky Baptists*, 1:483–84; 2:93; 2:138–40.
30. Cassara, *Universalism in America*, 114–17; G. T. Miller, "Elhanan Winchester," in *Dictionary of Baptists in America*, ed. Bill J. Leonard (Downers Grove, Ill.: InterVarsity Press, 1994), 291.
31. Semple, *History of the Rise*, 375–85.
32. Spencer, *History of Kentucky Baptists*, 2:1.
33. Toomey, *Centennial History*, 4–5.
34. Dorgan, *Giving Glory to God*, 28–31; Grammich Notes.
35. Dorgan, *Giving Glory to God*, 31–36; J. F. Fletcher, *A History of the Ashe County, North Carolina, and New River, Virginia, Baptist Association* (Raleigh, N.C.: Commercial Printing, 1935), 31–38.
36. Grammich Notes.
37. Dorgan, *Giving Glory to God*, 69.
38. Ibid., 34.
39. John G. Boles, *The Great Revival* (Lexington: Univ. Press of Kentucky, 1972); Catharine C. Cleveland, *The Great Revival in the West, 1797–1805* (1916; reprint, Gloucester, Mass.: Peter Smith, 1959); Fredrick Morgan Davenport, *Primitive Traits in Religious Revivals* (New York: Macmillan, 1917), 73–86; Sweet, *Religion on the American Frontier*, 615–16.
40. Sweet, *Religion on the American Frontier*, 23–25.
41. Howard Dorgan, *The Old Regular Baptists of Central Appalachia: Brothers and Sisters in Hope* (Knoxville: Univ. of Tennessee Press, 1989), 29–31; Dorgan, "Separate Baptists of Central Appalachia," 113–14.
42. Sweet, *Religion on the American Frontier*, 23–24.
43. Spencer, *History of Kentucky Baptists*, 1:16.
44. Mount Zion Association of United Baptists, *Minutes*, 1991, p. 13
45. Grammich Notes; Grammich, *Appalachian Atlas*, 38–39.
46. Dorgan, *Old Regular Baptists*, 43; Thornton Union Association of Old Regular Baptists, *Minutes*, 1992, p. 7.
47. Little Dove Association of Old Regular Baptists, *Minutes*, 1989.
48. Union Association of Old Regular Baptists, *Minutes*, 1994, pp. 4, 6.
49. Sweet, *Religion on the American Frontier*, 58–62.
50. Ibid., 61–76. On attitudes toward Appalachian religion, as expressed in the home mission movement, see the thorough discussion in McCauley, *Appalachian Mountain Religion*, 392–464.
51. Grammich Notes; Grammich, *Appalachian Atlas*, 30.
52. Grammich Notes.
53. Dorgan, *Giving Glory to God*. Mt. Paran Missionary Baptist Church, at the time of this writing in 1995, is changing quickly, losing much of the traditionalism it exhibited in the 1970s and early 1980s.

54. W. P. Throgmorton and Lemuel Potter, *Who Are the Primitive Baptists? The Throgmorton-Potter Debate*, stenographically reported by Joseph Losier and Laura Potter (St. Louis, Mo.: Nixon-Jones Printing, 1888).

55. Ibid., 2–3.

56. Ibid., 19–20.

57. Sweet, *Religion on the American Frontier*, 70–72.

58. Dorgan, *Old Regular Baptists*, 31–36.

59. In Sand-Lick Association documents both the association and the church are spelled three different ways: "Sand Lick," "Sandlick," and "Sand-Lick." I am using the latter spelling since that is the way the contemporary association spells it name.

60. Dorgan, "Fulton Confession," in *Dictionary of Baptists in America*, ed. Bill J. Leonard (Downers Grove, Ill.: InterVarsity Press, 1994), 123–24.

61. Grammich Notes; Robert Webb, interviewed by the author, Carthage, Ill., Aug. 9, 1994.

62. Grammich Notes.

63. Ibid.

64. Dorgan, *Old Regular Baptists*, 43.

Chapter 2. "They Call Us the No-Hellers"

1. Wallace Cooper, interviewed by the author, Pilgrim's Rest Church, State Line Ridge, near Whitewood, Va., and Jolo, W. Va., Sept. 3, 1994.

2. Dorgan, *Old Regular Baptists*, 77–102.

3. Union meetings are traditional among most of the Old-Time Baptist subdenominations, as explained in Dorgan, *Old Regular Baptists*, 112–14.

4. U.S. Geological Survey maps identify this stream as "Dismal Creek," but the "locals" call it a river; therefore, it is called that here.

5. Farley Beavers, interviewed by the author, Trout, W. Va., June 19, 1994.

6. Reece Maggard, interviewed by the author, Colly Creek, Ky., May 29, 1994.

7. Charles F. Nickels, *Salvation of All Mankind; and Treatise on Predestination, the Resurrection of the Dead, and a Bequest* (Nickelsville, Va.: Published by the author, [1937?]). No publication date appears on the title page of this document, but internal dating (p. 72) suggests that it was published in 1937.

8. E. M. Evans, "Circular Letter," in Washington Regular Primitive Baptist Association, *Minutes*, 1931, pp. 1–8; E. M. Evans, "Circular Letter," in Washington Regular Primitive Baptist Association, *Minutes*, 1939, pp. 9–16.

9. G. H. Coleman, "Circular Letter," in Washington Regular Primitive Baptist Association, *Minutes*, 1941, pp. 8–10.

Chapter 3. The Split between "Hellers" and "No-Hellers"

1. Washington District Primitive Baptist Association, *Minutes*, 1907, p. 5.

2. Farley Beavers, interviewed by the author, New Garden, Va., July 10, 1995.

3. Union Association of Old Regular Baptists, *Minutes,* 1994, p. 33.

4. Regular Primitive Baptist Washington District Association, *Minutes,* 1994, p. 14.

5. Dorgan, *Giving Glory to God,* 44; Howard Dorgan, *Airwaves of Zion: Radio and Religion in Appalachia* (Knoxville: Univ. of Tennessee Press, 1993), 186.

6. Washington District Association of Primitive Baptists, *Minutes,* 1921, pp. 3–4.

7. Ibid., 7.

8. Regular Primitive Baptist Washington District Association, *Minutes,* 1994, p. 12. After 1924, there is considerable confusion about the precise names of the two sides of the Washington Association.

9. Elkhorn Primitive Baptist Association, *Minutes,* 1994, p. 9.

10. Three Forks of Powell's River Regular Primitive Baptist Association, *Minutes,* 1994, p. 15.

11. Old Constitutional Washington District Association, *Minutes,* 1924, pp. 5–10.

12. Ibid., 6.

13. Washington District Association, *Minutes,* 1924, p. 4.

14. Elkhorn Association, *Minutes,* 1925, p. 1.

15. Washington District Regular Primitive Baptist Association, *Minutes,* 1993, p. 23.

16. Washington District Association, *Minutes,* 1925, p. 3.

17. Elihu Jasper Sutherland, *Sand Lick Primitive Baptist Church: The First Hundred Years, 1837–1937* (Clintwood, Va.: Sand Lick Church, 1938?), 36. Although this work contains no publication date, internal evidence suggests that the material was published in 1938. Today Sand-Lick is spelled with a hyphen.

18. Sutherland, *Sand Lick Primitive,* 36; Elihu Jasper Sutherland, *Regular Primitive Baptist Washington District Association: Short History, Abstract of Principles, Preamble and Constitution, Rules of Decorum, Other Data* (Clintwood, Va.: Regular Primitive Baptist Washington District Association, 1952), 20–22.

19. Washington District Association, *Minutes,* 1923 and 1924; Old Constitutional Washington District Association, *Minutes,* 1924.

20. Washington District Association, *Minutes,* 1932, p. 5; Sutherland, *Regular Primitive Baptist,* 21.

21. Sutherland, *Regular Primitive Baptist,* 21.

22. Ibid., 60.

23. Washington District Association, *Minutes,* 1921, p. 1.

24. Dorgan, *Old Regular Baptists,* 206–14.

25. Rufus Perrigan, comp., *History of Regular Baptists and Their Ancestors and Accessors* (Haysi, Va.: Published by the author, 1961), 195.

26. Washington District Association, *Minutes,* 1924, pp. 2, 4; Old Constitutional Washington District Association, *Minutes,* 1924, pp. 1–2.

27. Old Constitutional Washington District Association, *Minutes,* 1924, p. 3.

28. Washington District Association, *Minutes,* 1924, p. 5.

29. Washington District Regular Primitive Baptist Association, *Minutes,* 1993, p. 12.

30. Old Indian Bottom Association of Old Regular Baptists, *Minutes,,* 1989, p. 40.

31. Regular Primitive Baptist Sand-Lick District Association, *Minutes,* 1990, p. 10.

32. Washington District Association, *Minutes,* 1932, pp. 4–5.

33. Ibid., 5–6.

34. Ibid., 1925, 3–4.

35. Ibid., 1921, 9.
36. Ibid., 1926, 3.
37. Ibid., 1927, 3.
38. Ibid., 1932, 5–6.
39. Ibid., 1931, 1–8.
40. Ibid., 1924, 4.
41. Ibid., 1925, 4.
42. Sutherland, *Regular Primitive Baptists*, 22.
43. Farley Beavers, interviewed by the author, New Garden, Va., July 10, 1995.

CHAPTER 4. "SALVATION FOR ALL"

1. Frank Merritt, *Early History of Carter County* (Knoxville: East Tennessee Historical Society, 1975), 87–89.
2. Ibid., 76–77.
3. O. W. Taylor, *Early Tennessee Baptists, 1769–1832* (Nashville: Tennessee Baptist Convention, 1957), 12–14.
4. Merritt, *Early History of Carter County*, 71–87; Herman A. Norton, *Religion in Tennessee, 1777–1945* (Knoxville: Univ. of Tennessee Press, 1981), 10; Taylor, *Early Tennessee Baptists*, 143–443; Samuel Cole Williams and Samuel W. Tindell, *The Baptists of Tennessee* (Kingsport, Tenn.: Southern Publishers, 1930), 1:5, 1:19–30.
5. Merritt, *Early History of Carter County*, 72–77; Taylor, *Early Tennessee Baptists*, 143–44.
6. Taylor, *Early Tennessee Baptists*, 22.
7. Merritt, *Early History of Carter County*, 76–77; Norton, *Religion in Tennessee*, 10; Sweet, *Religion on the American Frontier*, 26–27.
8. Taylor, *Early Tennessee Baptists*, 105.
9. Ibid., 109.
10. Ibid., 28–31.
11. Semple, *History of the Rise*, 56–61.
12. Sweet, *Religion on the American Frontier*, 24–25.
13. Sutherland, *Regular Primitive Baptists*, 13.
14. Ibid., 18.
15. Spencer, *History of Kentucky Baptists*, 16
16. Sutherland, *Regular Primitive Baptists*, 15; Washington District Association, *Minutes*, 1816, p. 3; Washington District Association, *Minutes*, 1821, pp. 3–4.
17. Sutherland, *Regular Primitive Baptists*, 16–17.
18. Charles F. Nickels to churches of the Stony Creek Association, letter printed in Point Truth Church, *Minutes*, Aug. 16, 1946, in vol. 3, pp. 98–100, of typescript kindly prepared by Ganell Marshall, now in Appalachian Collection, Belk Library, Appalachian State Univ.; Point Truth Church, *Minutes*, May 28, 1949, in vol. 3 of Marshall typescript.
19. Three Forks of Powell's River Primitive Baptist Association, *Minutes*, 1946, p. 5.
20. Nickels, *Salvation of All Mankind*, 66–72.
21. Scott County Historical Society, comp., *Scott County, Virginia, and Its People* (Wayneville, N.C.: Walsworth Publishing, 1991), 260–61.

22. Charles F. Nickels to churches of the Stony Creek Association, letter printed in Point Truth Church, *Minutes,* Aug. 16, 1946.

23. Nickels, *Salvation of All Mankind,* 31–42.

24. Walter Cash, *Autobiography and Sermons* (St. Joseph, Mo.: Messenger of Peace, 1925), 75–76.

25. This tenet has been supported by the interview comments of a wide range of PBU elders, including but not limited to the following: Farley Beavers, Landon Colley, Lewis Allen Hill, Jack Horne, Roy McGlothlin, Reece Maggard, Willard Owens, Jennings Shortt, and Aaron Williams.

26. Evans, "Circular Letter," in Washington Regular Primitive Baptist Association, *Minutes,* 1931, p. 2.

27. Nickels, *Salvation of All Mankind,* 23–24.

28. Cassara, *Universalism in America,* 17–24.

29. Farley Beavers, interviewed by the author, Trout, W. Va., June 19, 1994.

30. Farley Beavers, Conference on Religious Heritage in Southwestern Virginia, May 20, 1995, Southwest Virginia Community College, Richlands, Va.

31. Landon Colley, interviewed by the author at Harrison-Beavers Family Reunion and Memorial, Thompson Valley, Va., July 30, 1995.

32. Lewis Hill, interviewed by the author, Hale Creek Church, Buchanan County, Va., Sept. 10, 1994.

33. Nickels, *Salvation of All Mankind,* 18.

34. Ibid., 8.

35. Farley Beavers, interviewed by the author, Trout, W. Va., June 19, 1994.

36. Elkhorn Primitive Baptist Association, *Minutes,* 1994, p. 8.

37. Three Forks of Powell's River Regular Primitive Baptist Association, *Minutes,* 1994, p. 15.

38. Regular Primitive Baptist Washington District Association, *Minutes,* 1994, p. 12.

39. Regular Primitive Baptist Sand-Lick District Association, *Minutes,* 1990, pp. 12–13.

40. Cassara, *Universalism in America,* 24–25.

41. Nickels, *Salvation of All Mankind,* 8.

42. Ibid., 9.

43. Ibid., 9–10.

44. Reece Maggard, interviewed by the author, Colly Creek, Va., May 29, 1994.

45. Elkhorn Primitive Baptist Association, *Minutes,,* 1994, p. 8.

46. Three Forks of Powell's River Regular Primitive Baptist Association, *Minutes,* 1994, p. 15.

47. Regular Primitive Baptist Washington District Association, *Minutes,* 1994, p. 12.

48. Nickels, *Salvation of All Mankind,* 21–22.

49. Evans, "Circular Letter," in Washington Regular Primitive Baptist Association, *Minutes,* 1939, p. 10.

50. Elkhorn Primitive Baptist Association, *Minutes,* 1994, p. 9.

51. Three Forks of Powell's River Regular Primitive Baptist Association, *Minutes,* 1994, p. 15.

52. Regular Primitive Baptist Washington District Association, *Minutes,* 1994, p. 12.

53. Farley Beavers to the author, after reading a draft of this chapter.

54. Farley Beavers, sermon, Salem Church, Tazewell County, Va., June 25, 1995.
55. Roy McGlothlin, interviewed by the author, Point Truth Church, near Nickelsville, Va., Aug. 15, 1992.
56. Nickels, *Salvation of All Mankind*, 21.
57. Farley Beavers, interviewed by the author, Jerusalem Church, Buchanan County, Va., July 9, 1995.
58. "Circular Letter," Washington District Regular Primitive Baptist Association, *Minutes*, 1931, pp. 5–6.
59. Nickels, *Salvation of All Mankind*, 26.

CHAPTER 5. THE "HAPPIFYING" OF GOD

1. Raus McDill Hanson, *Virginia Place Names: Derivations, Historical Uses* (Verona, Va.: McClure Press, 1969), 122–23.
2. Sutherland, *Regular Primitive Baptists*, 21.
3. Luther F. Addington, *History of Wise County* (Wise, Va.: Bicentennial Committee of Wise County, 1956), 70–71, 291.
4. Sutherland, *Regular Primitive Baptists*, 21.
5. Dorgan, *Old Regular Baptists*, 130–33.
6. Regular Primitive Baptist Washington District Association, *Minutes*, 1994; Three Forks of Powell's River Regular Primitive Baptist Association, *Minutes*, 1994; Elkhorn Primitive Baptist Association, *Minutes*, 1994.
7. Hosea Ballou, *An Examination of the Doctrine of Future Retribution, On the Principles of Morals, Analogy and the Scriptures* (Boston: Trumpet Office, 1834), 36.
8. Samuel Hopkins, "The Life and Character of the Late Reverend Mr. Jonathan Edwards," in *Jonathan Edwards: A Profile*, ed. David Levin (New York, N.Y.: Hill and Wang, 1969), 79–81.
9. Joseph Tracy, *The Great Awakening* (1845; reprint, New York: Arno Press, 1996), 21.
10. Dorus Paul Rudisill, *The Doctrine of the Atonement in Jonathan Edwards and His Successors* (New York: Poseidon Books, 1971), 22–23.
11. Jonathan Edwards, "Sinners in the Hands of an Angry God," in *American Public Address*, ed. A. Craig Baird (New York: McGraw-Hill, 1956), 20–23.
12. Cassara, *Universalism in America*, 21. "Happifying" was Ballou's term.
13. Hosea Ballou, *A Treatise on Atonement; in which, The Finite Nature of Sin is Argued, Its Causes and Consequences as Such; The Necessity and Nature of Atonement; and Its Glorious Consequences, in the Final Reconciliation of All Men to Holiness and Happiness* (Randolph, Vt.: Sereno Wright, 1805), iv.
14. Cassara, *Universalism in America*, 6.
15. James Relly, *Union, or, A Treatise of the Consanguinity and Affinity between Christ and his Church* (Boston: White and Adams, 1779).
16. Cassara, *Universalism in America*, 10–14.
17. Ibid., 16.
18. Edwin Martin Stone, *Reverend Elhanan Winchester: Biography and Letters* (New York: Arno Press, 1972), 22–29.
19. Ibid., 29–31.

20. Ibid., 41–57.
21. Cassara, *Universalism in America*, 15.
22. Spencer, *History of the Kentucky Baptists*, 1:483–84; 2:138–40.
23. John Corrigan, *The Hidden Balance: Religion and The Social Theories of Charles Chauncy and Jonathan Mayhew* (New York: Cambridge Univ. Press, 1987), 23.
24. Charles Chauncy, *Seasonable Thoughts on the Sate of Religion in New England* (1743; reprint, Hicksville, N.Y.: 1975), 35–332.
25. Corrigan, *Hidden Balance*, 24,
26. Cassara, *Universalism in America*, 9.
27. Charles Chauncy, *The Mystery Hid from Ages and Generations, Made Manifest by the Gospel-Revelation: or, The Salvation of All Men* (1784; reprint, New York: Arno Press, 1969), 10.
28. Cassara, *Universalism in America*, 9; Chauncy, *Mystery Hid*, 12.
29. Cassara, *Universalism in America*, 25.
30. Ibid., 22.
31. Ibid., 26.
32. Ballou, *Treatise on Atonement*, quoted in Cassara, *Universalism in America*, 100–101.
33. Cassara, *Universalism in America*, 23.
34. Russell E. Miller, *The Larger Hope: The First Century of the Universalist Church in America* (Boston: Unitarian Universalist Association, 1979), 734.
35. Ibid.
36. *Kentucky New Era* (Hopkinsville, Ky.), Oct. 17, 1992. In addition to the activity in Christian County, there were a number of other Universalist stirrings in Kentucky during the first half of the eighteenth century: Russell E. Miller, *Larger Hope*, 734–36.
37. Gwendolyn Wilkins, interviewed by the author, Hopkinsville, Ky., Aug. 5, 1994.
38. *Kentucky New Era* (Hopkinsville, Ky.), Oct. 17, 1992; Wilkins, interviewed by the author, Hopkinsville, Ky., Aug. 5, 1994.
39. Howard Box, "Unitarian Universalism in Appalachia," unpub. manuscript, n.d., 1, collection of Ida Metz Hyland, Johnson City, Tenn. At the time he wrote this brief essay, Box was pastor of the Oak Ridge Unitarian Church, Oak Ridge, Tenn.; Ida Metz Hyland kindly provided this document. Also see Russell E. Miller, *Larger Hope*, 731–33.
40. Russell E. Miller to Robert R. Walsh, Jan. 14 1974, collection of Ida Metz Hyland, Johnson City, Tenn. Ida Metz Hyland kindly supplied this letter. For additional information about Clayton, see: D. B. Clayton, *Forty-Seven Years in the Universalist Ministry* (Columbia, S.C.: Published by the author, 1889). The Glimpsville debate is summarized in an appendix to this work.
41. Russell E. Miller, *The Larger Hope: The Second Century of the Universalist Church in America, 1870–1970* (Boston: Unitarian Universalist Association, 1985), 193–96.
42. *Harriman (Tenn.) Daily Progress*, Apr. 6, 1896.
43. Miller, *The Larger Hope* (1985), 199.
44. Ibid., 196.
45. Ida Metz Hyland, *Unitarian-Universalism in East Tennessee* (Johnson City, Tenn.: Holston Valley Unitarian Universalist Church, 1979), 9. Hyland is a fifth-

generation Universalist. Her father and her maternal grandfather were Universalist ministers; both graduated from St. Lawrence University Theological School, Canton, N.Y., where Ida Hyland also received a degree in religious education in 1933. She has been responsible for most of the research on Dr. William Hale.

46. Russell E. Miller to Walsh, Jan. 14, 1972; Miller, *The Larger Hope* (1985), 193.
47. Ida Metz Hyland, interviewed by the author, Johnson City, Tenn., June 13, 1994.
48. "History of Universalism in East Tennessee," *Notasulga (Ala.), Universalist Herald,* July 15, 1879.
49. Hyland, interviewed by the author, Johnson City, Tenn., June 13, 1994.
50. Hyland, *Unitarian-Universalism,* 6.
51. Russell E. Miller to Walsh, Jan. 14, 1972.
52. Hyland, *Unitarian-Universalism,* 9.
53. Russell E. Miller to Walsh, Jan. 14, 1972.
54. Ibid.
55. Hyland, interviewed by the author, Johnson City, Tenn., June 13, 1994.

Chapter 6. "Carried Out"

1. O. L. Pruett, interviewed by the author, Honaker, Va., Sept. 10, 1994. This story of the church serving as a field hospital during the Civil War is widely reported by members of the congregation, but I have been able neither to prove nor to disprove the account.
2. Elizabeth Brown Pryor, *Clara Barton: Professional Angel* (Philadelphia: Univ. of Pennsylvania Press, 1987), 102–4.
3. Ethel Evans Albert, "From Thence We Came," *Historical Sketches of Southwest Virginia,* no. 27 (Coeburn, Va.: Crescent Printery, 1993), 64.
4. Washington District Association, *Minutes,* 1923, p. 1; Old Constitutional Washington District Association, *Minutes,,* 1924, p. 15.
5. Washington District Association, *Minutes,* 1926, p. 3.
6. Dorgan, *Giving Glory to God,* 55–85.
7. Ibid., 56–57; Dorgan, "'Ol' Time Way' Exhortation: Preaching in the Old Regular Baptist Church," *Journal of Communication and Religion* 10, no. 2 (Sept. 1987), 24–30; Dorgan, *Old Regular Baptists,* 7, 54, 57, 241; Dorgan, *Airwaves of Zion,* 13.
8. Willard Owens, sermon, Harrison-Beavers Family Reunion and Memorial, Thompson Valley, Va., July 30, 1995.
9. Keith Bowers, sermon, Stoney Creek Church, Carter County, Tenn., May 28, 1995.
10. Landon Colley, sermon, Harrison-Beavers Family Reunion and Memorial, Thompson Valley, Va., July 30, 1995.
11. Dorgan, *Old Regular Baptists,* 57.
12. Dorgan, *Giving Glory to God,* 60–61.
13. As previously noted, Elder Wallace Cooper of the Elkhorn Association has been known to shout, but he is by no means the only PBU male to practice this form of response.
14. Regular Primitive Baptist Washington Association, *Minutes,* 1994, p. 3.

15. On July 2, 1995, Elder Aaron Williams preached at the Owens Family Memorial, Prater Creek, Va.
16. Millard Cooper, interviewed by the author, Paynesville, W. Va., Aug. 6, 1995.
17. Dorgan, *Old Regular Baptists*, 58–59.
18. Dorgan, "Separate Baptists of Central Appalachia," 190–92.
19. Raymond Smith, interviewed by the author, Canada, Ky., Aug. 9, 1987.
20. Dorgan, *Old Regular Baptists*, 48–49.
21. Ibid., 6–7.
22. D. H. Goble, comp., *Primitive Baptist Hymn Book* (Greenfield, Ind.: Goble Printing Co., 1887).
23. Dorgan, *Old Regular Baptists*, 60–61.
24. Union Association of Old Regular Baptists, *Minutes*, 1994, pp. 14–16; Regular Primitive Baptist Washington District Association, *Minutes*, 1995, pp. 3–4.

Chapter 7. "Keeping Them Near"

1. Dorgan, "Memorial Meetings," in *Old Regular Baptists*, by Dorgan, pp. 77–100 (Knoxville: Univ. of Tennessee Press, 1989).
2. Mainline PBU theology does insist that a physical resurrection will be the reality, as opposed to a purely spiritual resurrection; however, this mainline theology seems somewhat undecided as to the exact nature of that physical body in which one will be resurrected. What appears critical is recognizability.
3. Regular Primitive Baptist Washington Association, *Minutes*, 1954, pp. 9–13; Regular Primitive Baptist Three Forks of Powell's River Association, *Minutes*, 1954, pp. 9–13.
4. Dorgan, *Old Regular Baptists*, 23–24.
5. Kelly and Anna Ruth McGuire, Point Truth Church, near Nickelsville, Va., Aug. 27, 1995.
6. Farley R. Beavers, sermon delivered at Harrison-Beavers Family Reunion and Memorial, Thompson Valley, Va., July 30, 1995.
7. Farley R. Beavers, interviewed by the author at Harrison-Beavers Family Reunion and Memorial, Thompson Valley, Va., July 30, 1995.

Chapter 8. Migration of the Faith

1. Howard Dorgan, "Trip to Ypsilanti: Traveling for Unity Among the Old Regular Baptists," *Appalachian Journal* 18, no. 3 (Spring 1991): 284–95.
2. For papers of the Conference on Sense of Place in Appalachia, Morehead State Univ., Morehead, Ky., Oct. 8–9, 1987, see S. Mont Whitson, ed., *Sense of Place in Appalachia* (Morehead, Ky.: Office of Regional Development Services, Morehead State Univ., 1988).
3. For the story of Sister Rena Caudill in Winnabow, N.C., see Dorgan, *Old Regular Baptists*, 152–59.
4. Old Elkhorn Primitive Baptist Association, *Minutes*, 1960, p. 1; Elkhorn Regular Primitive Baptist Association, *Minutes*, 1968, p. 14. Note the name change that occurred sometime between 1960 and 1968.

5. Marvin F. Pruitt, interviewed by the author, Rich Hill, Ohio, May 21, 1994; Phylli Adair, telephone interview by the author, Aug. 16, 1995; Phyllis Adair, interviewed by the author, Rich Hill Church, Rich Hill, Ohio, Sept. 2, 1995.
6. Elkhorn Regular Primitive Baptist Association, *Minutes*, 1968, p. 14.
7. McGennis Adair, Sr., interviewed by the author, Mt. Liberty, Ohio, May 22, 1994
8. During its Sept. 9, 1995, meeting, the Washington Association discussed all three of these men, questioning whether or not their ordained status should be with drawn by their local fellowship, Little Flock of Greenfield, Ohio.
9. Nathan Moore, interviewed by the author, Centerburg, Ohio, May 22, 1994.
10. Marvin F. Pruitt, interviewed by the author, Rich Hill, Ohio, May 21, 1994.
11. McGennis Adair, Sr., interviewed by the author, Mt. Liberty, Ohio, May 22, 1994
12. Unless otherwise noted, all biographical information concerning McGennis Adair Sr., is from ibid.
13. McGennis Adair, Sr., interviewed by the author, Hale Creek Church, Buchanan County, Va., Sept. 8, 1995.
14. McGennis Adair, Sr., interviewed by the author, Mt. Liberty, Ohio, May 22, 1994 and retold, Mt. Liberty, Ohio, Sept. 2, 1995.
15. Millard Cooper, interviewed by the author, Rich Hill, Ohio, Sept. 2, 1995.
16. Elkhorn Primitive Baptist Association, *Minutes*, 1994, p. 10–11.
17. Phyllis Adair, interviewed by the author, Hale Creek Church, Buchanan County Va., Sept. 9, 1995.

CHAPTER 9. PILGRIMS IN THE HANDS OF A HAPPY GOD

1. 1994 statistics, taken from the three associations' minutes of that year.
2. Dorgan, *Old Regular Baptists*, 4–5.
3. Jack Horne, interviewed by the author, Rich Hill, Ohio, Sept. 2, 1995.
4. See McCauley, *Appalachian Mountain Religion*, esp. 442–64.
5. Dorgan, *Old Regular Baptists*, 150.
6. I made preliminary arrangements for an Appalshop Films documentary on the 184th annual session of the Regular Primitive Baptist Washington District Association, held at Hale Creek Church, Buchanan County, Va. The project was aborted when a number of churches grew very concerned about the possibility that the documentary would be aired over PBS affiliates in Virginia, West Virginia, Kentucky, Tennessee, and North Carolina. A similar proposal, made to the Union Association of Old Regular Baptists in 1987, didn't make it as far as the proposal to the Washington Association. In addition, PBU congregations in southern West Virginia are embarrassed by, and angry about, intense media attention given to the snake-handling church in Jolo. They feel that the outside world views such practices as normative in Central Appalachian religious practice.
7. Farley Beavers, interviewed by the author, Hale Creek Church, Buchanan County, Va., Sept. 9, 1995.
8. Opal Smith, interviewed by the author, Rich Hill, Ohio, Sept. 2, 1995.
9. Three Forks of Powell's River Regular Primitive Baptist Association, *Minutes*, 1994, p. 16.

INDEX

Adair, Elder Noah, 62, 101, 147
Adair, Elder Samuel F., 62, 101, 147
Adair, Elder Tommy, 147; founding Rich
   Hill Church, 159–60, 164
Adair, McGennis, Jr., 162–63
Adair, McGennis, Sr., xii, 160, 163, 169
   (photograph); PBU migrant, 164–70
Adair, Phyllis, xii, 162–63, 169 (photograph),
   179; PBU migrant, 164–70
American Baptists, 8, 19
Arminianism, 7, 19, 94, 109, 112
Asbury, Gail, xii
Ashworth Memorial Regular Baptist Church,
   16 (photograph)
association meetings, PBU, 41–43; at Hale
   Creek Church, 52, 55–56; at New Garden
   Church, 124–27, 125 (photograph), 126
   (photograph), 127 (photograph); at Oak
   Grove Church, 174 (photograph); at
   Pilgrim's Rest Church, 34–35, 36
   (photograph), 37 (photograph); at Rich
   Hill Church, 158, 161 (photograph), 171–
   79; female involvements, 174; procedural
   rules, 173–75

atonement, 18, 25, 107; in Old Regular Baptist
   theology, 19; in PBU theology, 5, 90–92,
   180, 189

backsliding, 22, 28
Ballou, Hosea, 81, 121; "happifying" God,
   106–7, 180; on eternal punishment, 105; on
   the pleasure of righteousness, 181;
   universalist doctrine of, 111–12
baptism, 7, 8, 169; in the Old Regular
   tradition, 20; in the PBU tradition, 148,
   149 (photograph); "living water," 74
Baptist diversity, 8–9
Beavers, Elder Farley A., 154
Beavers, Elder Farley R., xii, 44, 46, 47, 48,
   71, 94, 151–52, 154–55, 185; on death, 96; on
   heaven, 97; on election of "the Church,"
   94; on Satan, 89
Beavers, Sandra, xii, 155
Bee Branch (PBU) Church, 6, 37, 138;
   "carried out" scene at, 135–37
Bland County, Va., 6
Bowers, Elder Keith, xii, 103 (photograph),
   171; "carried out," 129–31

Brown, Elder Denton, 134, 171
Buchanan County, Va., 6, 37, 70, 97, 150
Buffalo Ridge Church: founding of, 78
Burning Spring Primitive Baptist Association, 26, 29

"carried out": in preaching, 129–31
Carter County, Tenn., 6, 73, 76, 78
Cassara, Ernest, 91, 107, 111, 112
Chattanooga, Tenn.: Universalist church at, 115–17
Chauncy, Charles, 109; universalist doctrine of, 110–11
Childress, Elder J. J., 62, 64, 68, 101
Christian Unity Association of Separate Baptists, 13
Coleman, Elder G. H., 45
Coleman, Elder Howard, 163, 171
Colley, Elder Landon, xii, 132, 135, 137; on hell in the temporal world, 95; on Satan, 89
Colly Creek (PBU) Church, 92, 147
Compton, Elder M. L., 51, 56, 58, 64, 121
Consolation Universalist Church, 112, 115; historical marker for, 113 (photograph)
Cooper, Elder Wallace, 32–33, 33 (photograph)
Cooper, Millard, xii,
Croften, Ky.: Universalist church at, 112, 114 (photograph)

Davenport, James, 11, 110
Davis, Adeleah, xii, 136, 138
Davis, Bill, xii, 139
Davis, Elder Danny, xii, 44
Davis, Elder Ezra, Jr., xii,
Davis, Elder Unice, vii, 35, 139; baptizing, 149 (photograph); "carried out," 136–37
De Benneville, 108–9
Deism, 107–8
Delphia (PBU) Church, 42, 44, 95
Dickenson County, Va., 6, 80
dinner on the ground, 34, 74–75, 177
"double marriage," 9
Duck River Baptists, 9

Eastern District Primitive Baptist Association, 29–30, 41
Edwards, Jonathan, 11, 12; "Sinners in the Hands of an Angry God," 105–6

election, 13, 25, 27–28, 108; PBU doctrine, 87, 92–95, 156, 181, 184
Elkhorn Association, the original, 26; consolidation with South Kentucky Association of Separate Baptists, 17–18; founding of, 15
Elkhorn (PBU) Primitive Baptist Association, xi–xii, 7, 41, 42, 54, 57, 58, 60, 62, 71, 126, 135, 136, 147, 158, 159, 163, 165, 175, 177; association meeting, 34–35, 171–78; Rich Hill Church, 158–63
Enon Missionary Baptist Association, 23
Enterprise Association of Regular Baptists, 16
Evans, Elder E. M, 45, 58–59, 62, 65, 68, 70, 72, 86, 101, 123, 124, 147; on Adam's fall, 87; on Christ's church, 93–94; on free will, 94; on Scripture and hell, 97

family memorials, 150–56
Fields, Elder Bob, 43, 44, 45, 46, 47
Flanary, Cathy, xii,
Flanary, Elder Roy, xii, 44, 102–4, 103 (photograph)
Flanary, Pat, vii,
Flanary, Phil, xii
footwashing, 9, 19, 188; at Oak Grove Church, 103 (photograph); at Pilgrim's Rest Church, 138
Free Hill, Tenn. Universalist Society, 117, 118
Free Will Baptists, 7, 9, 10
Frelinghuysen, Theodorus, 11
Fulton Confession, 27

Gann, Arminda, 3, 4
gender separation, 124
General Association of Regular Baptist Churches, 8
General Association of Separate Baptists, 13
German Baptist Brethren, 9, 10; universalism in, 8
Glenmary Research Center, 10
Glimpville, Tenn.: Universalist church at, 115–16
Goode, Elder Ewell, 62, 101
Grainger County, Tenn., 1, 80
Grammich, Clifford A., Jr., 10–11, 18–19, 23, 29, 30
graveside memorials, 149–50
Great Awakening, 11–12, 105–6, 110

Great Western Revival, 17–18, 79
Grimsley, Elder Thomas, 62, 63, 64, 68, 72, 101

Hale, Aman, 117
Hale, Hiram Decatur, 117–18
Hale, William: headstone for, 120 (photo-graph); his Free Hill, Tenn. Home, 119 (photograph); introduced to Universalism, 117; licensed to preach Universalism, 117, 118
Hale Creek Old Regular Baptist Church, 53
Hale Creek (PBU) Church, 37, 51, 56, 58, 60, 61, 64, 126; meetinghouse, 51–53, 52 (photograph), 58; original log structure, 52, 53 (photograph)
handshaking: congregational, 140, 179; while preaching, 132, 137
Hankins, Elder John, 57
Harlen County, Ky., 6, 100
Harley, Sherry, 162, 163
Harriman, Tenn.: Universalist church at, 115–17
Harrison, Elder Columbus, 154
Harrison-Beavers Family Reunion and Memorial, 145–46, 150–56, 152 and 155 (photographs), 165–66
healing, 144–45
"hell redemption" doctrine, 13–14, 110
Hill, Elder Lewis, xii, 44, 47, 48; on Satan, 89
"Hillbilly Highway," 164
Holston Old Regular Baptist Church, 43
Holston (PBU) Church, 1–3, 2 (photograph), 43–44, 80, 84, 163
Holston Primitive Baptist Cemetery, 1
Holston Valley Association: founding of, 15, 78
Holston Valley Unitarian Universalist Church, 120–21
Hope (PBU) Church, 6, 42, 120–21
Hopkinsville, Ky.: Universalist church at, 113–15, 115 (photograph)
Horne, Dorothy, 138
Horne, Elder Jack, xii, 35, 44
Hyland, Ida Metz, 119

impromptu preaching, 19, 128–31
Indian Bottom Association of Old Regular Baptists, 21, 63
introductory sermon, 172

Jerusalem (PBU) Church, 60, 61, 97
Johnson, Peggy: "carried out," 134–35, 137, 138

Keokee, Va., 6, 100–101, 104
Ketocton Association, 12, 15, 77
Knoxville, Tenn.: Universalist church at, 115, 116

laying on of hands, 144–45
Lazarus, 97–98
Lee County, Va., 6, 80, 100
Leonard, Bill, xiii
Letcher County, Ky., 6, 92, 188
lined singing, 17, 19, 141
Lipps, Elder Morgan T., 1, 101, 104, 147; headstone, 3 (photograph)
Lipps, Elizabeth, 1
Little Dove Association of Old Regular Baptists, 20
Little Flock (PBU) Church, 130, 170, 171
Little River Association of Regular Baptists, 15
Little Stone Gap (PBU) Church, 96
Little Village (PBU) Church, 130, 170, 171
London Confession, 27
Looney, Elder Quinton, 163, 170

Macedonia (PBU) Church, 37, 60, 61, 65, 123, 126, 134
Maggard, Elder Reece, xii, 44, 46, 47; on universal atonement, 92
Marshall, Daniel, 11; involvement with the Separate Baptist movement, 12
Marshall, Darvin, xii, 41, 42, 47–48
Marshall, Gannell, xii
Mates Creek Primitive Baptist Association, 29
Mayhew, Jonathan, 109
McCauley, Deborah, xiii
McDowell County, W.Va., 6, 37, 159, 166, 167, 169, 188
McGlauflin, W. H. 116
McGlothlin, Elder Roy, 41, 42 (photograph), 44, 47; on natural body resurrection, 96
McGuire, Anna Ruth, xii, 152, 153
McGuire, Kelly, xii, 152, 153
Mickler, Peggy, xii
migration; of Old Regular Baptists, 20; of PBUs, 157–79
missionary/antimissionary split, 21–23; Holston Valley Association and the, 80; Washington Association and the, 79–80

Missionary Baptists, 7, 9, 10; beginnings of, 21–23; divisions of, 22–23
Mount Grove (PBU) Church, 130, 134, 170, 171
Mount Olive Association of Separate Baptists, 13
Mount Olive (PBU) Church, 37, 60, 61, 65, 67
Mount Pleasant Church, xii, 6
Mount Zion (PBU) Church, 160
Mount Zion Primitive Baptist Association, 29, 41
Mountain District Association of Primitive Baptists, 41
Mountain Union Association of Regular Baptists, 15
Mud River Association of Regular Baptists, 16
Murray, John, 108

National Baptists, 8
New Garden (PBU) Church, 56, 58, 60, 61, 62, 69; association meeting at, 124, 126 (photograph), 127 (photograph); meetinghouse, 124–27, 125 (photograph); use as a Civil War hospital, 122–23
New River Primitive Baptist Association, 29
New Salem Association of Old Regular Baptists: association building of, 20; organization of, 19
Nickels, Charles F., xii, 45, 47, 80, 96, 121, 123; biography of, 81–85; headstone, 82 (photograph); on election, 93; on hell in the afterlife, 88–89; on physical vs. spiritual resurrection, 83–84; on universal atonement, 91–92; "Salvation of All Mankind," 81, 85–86
"No-Heller Country": geographical location, 6–7
Nolynn Association of Separate Baptists, 13

Oak Grove (PBU) Church, 101, 104, 126; meetinghouse, 101–3
Old Indian Bottom Association Old Regular Baptists, 21, 63
Old Missionary Baptist Association, 23
Old Regular Baptists, xii, 9, 19–21, 26, 40, 135, 140, 141–43, 150, 172, 179, 183; gender separation, 124; location of, 20; preaching, 132, 133, 142

"Old-Time Baptists," 4, 15, 19, 22, 26, 31–32, 34–35, 43, 45, 52–53, 56, 63, 66, 68, 73–74, 97, 99, 120, 128–29, 142, 148, 180–81, 182; characteristics of, 8–10; female involvements in associations, 174; memorial services, 145–46, 150; splits, 187; unpaid ministers, 170
O'Quinn, Elder James, 104
Original Mates Creek Primitive Baptist Association, 29, 41, 159
Original Mountain Liberty Association of Old Regular Baptists, 20, 30, 43
Original Mountain Union Association of Regular Baptists, 15, 17
Osborne, Elder T. W., 57–59, 64, 68
Owens, Elder Columbus, 68
Owens, Elder Stuart, 147
Owens, Elder Willard, xii, 44, 46, 47, 130 (photograph), 150; "carried out," 129
Owens Family Memorial, 150

Paint Union United Baptist Association, 26
Pentecostals, 144
Philadelphia Association, 15, 77, 110
Philadelphia Confession, 13, 15, 79
Pilgrim's Rest (PBU) Church, 42, 48, 54, 60, 126, 139, 171; association meeting, 37 (photograph); "carried out" scene at, 138; geographical environment, 36–39; meetinghouse, 31–35, 58; preaching arbor, 35, 36 (photograph)
Point Truth (PBU) Church, xii, 40, 41, 47, 80–82, 95, 185
Potter/Throgmorton debate, 23–25, 44
Prater Creek (PBU) Church, 60, 61
preaching, PBU; delivery styles, 128, 131–33; emotionality, 128, 133–37; extemporization, 128–31; physicality, 128, 137–38; transcendence, 128, 138–39
predestination, 28–29, 49
Primitive Association of Regular Baptists, 15, 26
Primitive Baptist Library (Carthage, Ill.), 28, 47, 86
Primitive Baptist Library (Elon College, N.C.), 47
Primitive Baptist Universalism, 9; author's introduction to, 39–42; baptisms, 148, 149 (photograph); collecting money, 143–44; first mentioned in Washington

Association minutes, 51; gender separation, 124; hell, 88–89; hymn singing, 140–42; inclusiveness of, 184–85; late baptisms in, 7; memorials, 146–56; migrations of the faith, 157–79; numbers, 7–8, 181; on Christ's atonement, 91–92; on election, 92–95; on free will, 90–91; on hell in the temporal world, 40, 89–90, 181; on original sin, 87; on resurrection, 48, 91, 95–97, 146–47; on Satan, 45, 87–89; on sin, 95; people of joy, 188–89; preaching, 127–39; reclusive nature of, 182–84; rejection of biblical literalism, 86; sense of place, 158–59; theology, 4–5, 44–47, 57, 86–98; women's roles, 137–38, 179; worship service, 139–44

Primitive Baptists, 9, 23–30; subdivisions of, 28–30

Regular Baptists, 9, 10, 12, 26; Great Western Revival and the, 79; movement into Appalachia, 14–15, 77–78
"Restoration from Hell" theology, 13–14, 109–10
resurrection, 4; in PBU theology, 5, 57, 91, 95–97; spiritual vs. physical, 83–85, 146–47, 185–86
Rich Hill (PBU) Church, 130, 168, 170; and sense of place, 158–59; author's visits, 158; Elkhorn Association meeting at, 171–79; meetinghouse, 160–63, 161 (photograph); membership, 162–63
Robinette, Elder William M., 62, 101, 104, 147
rules of decorum, 67, 173–75, 176, 186
"running in the Spirit," 188
Russell County, Va., 6, 56, 80

Saint Clair's Bottom Primitive Baptist Association, 29, 41
Salem (PBU) Church, xii, 37, 56–58, 60, 61, 64, 66, 69, 72, 123, 133–34, 136, 137, 154; and the "Heller"/"No-Heller" split, 57–60; meetinghouse, 59 (photograph)
Sand-Lick Association of Regular Primitive Baptists, 27, 29, 41, 91
Sandy Creek Association, 77, 78
Sandy Creek Church, 12
Satan, 87–89
Scott County, Va., 40, 76, 80, 81

sense of place, 154, 158–59
Senter Primitive Baptist Association, 29, 41
Separate Baptists, 7, 9, 10, 26, 78; Great Western Revival and the, 79; in Appalachia, 13–14; movement into Tennessee, 77–78; origins of, 12–13; theology of, 12–13;
Seventh-Day Baptists, 9
Sexton, Elder Earl, 17
"short hell" doctrine, 110
Shortt, Elder Jennings, xii, 41, 96–97, 174 (photograph), 185; preaching style, 133
"sing down," 141–42, 179
Sinking Creek Church, 76; founding of, 78
"Sinners in the Hands of an Angry God," 11, 105–6
Six-Principle Baptists, 9
Slate Creek (PBU) Church, 37, 60, 63, 70
Smith, Elder John C., 62, 101
Smith, Elder Raymond, 138
Smith, Opel Mae, 163
Smith River Primitive Baptist Association, 29
South Kentucky Association of Separate Baptists, 13; consolidation with Elkhorn Association, 17–18
Southern Baptists, 8, 19
Southwest West Virginia Association of Separate Baptists, 13
Spencer, J. H., 13, 110
Sterns, Shubal, 11; founding the Sandy Creek Church, 12
Stoney Creek (PBU) Church, 6, 77, 129, 131; meetinghouse, 73–76, 74 (photograph); organized, 76
Stony Creek Association, 62, 76, 85, 147; founding of, 80–84; joins the PBU movement, 70–71; splitting of, 83–85, 185–86
Sullivan County, Tenn., 118
Sulphur Springs (PBU) Church, 98, 147
Sunday schools: in the Missionary Baptist tradition, 22; in the PBU tradition, 148; in the Regular Baptist tradition, 17; in the United Baptist tradition, 19
Sutherland, Elder William B., 63–64, 69, 70–72
Sutherland, Elihu Jasper, 61, 62, 63, 64, 71, 101
Swindall, Elder J. C., 63

Tazewell County, Va., 6, 58, 67, 133, 145, 159
Tennent, Gilbert, 11, 110

Tennent, John, 11
Tennent, William, Jr., 11
Tennent, William, Sr., 11
Thornton Union Association of Old Regular
    Baptists, 30
Three Forks of Powell's River (PBU) Regular
    Primitive Baptist Association, xii, 3, 6, 7,
    41, 57, 62, 81, 101, 127, 133, 147, 159, 163, 172,
    175, 177; disharmony in, 185–87; joins the
    PBU movement, 70–71
transcendence, while preaching, 138–39
Trout, W.Va., 6
Truevine Baptists, 9
Two-Seed-in-the-Spirit Predestinarian
    Baptists, 9

Union Association of Old Regular Baptists,
    53
Union Baptists, 9, 16; origin of, 17–18;
    presence of, 18–19
Unitarian Universalists, 4; merging of, 8, 113,
    117
Unitarianism, 107, 113, 114
United Baptists, 9, 10, 26; location of, 18–19;
    origin of, 17–18

Universalism, 5–6, 107–9; early American,
    105–12; in Tennessee, 115–21; west of the
    Allegheny Mountains, 14, 30, 62, 112–15

Wallis, Elder John, 63
Washington Association, the original, 26;
    antimissionary movement, 79–80;
    founding of, 79
Washington County, Tenn., 6, 51, 78, 117, 120–21
Washington District (PBU) Regular
    Primitive Baptist Association, xi, 7, 27, 41
    51, 54, 67, 68, 73, 127, 136, 147, 154, 159, 163
    170, 171, 172, 175, 177; association meetings
    124; formation of the PBU side, 67–68;
    impact of the 1924 split, 60–62; splitting
    from the "Heller" side, 56–60, 76, 123–24
Webb, Elder Robert, 28–30, 85, 86
Whitefield, George, 11, 12, 110
Whitt, Elder Robert, xii,
Williams, Arnie, xii
Williams, Elder Aaron, xii, 98, 171;
    preaching, 133–34, 136–37, 178
Winchester, Elhanan, 13–14; universalist
    doctrine of, 109–10
Wise County, Va., 6, 80, 98